The Ancients

ॐ · ॐ

The Ancients
Investigations into the Lost Civilizations of Lemuria and Atlantis

Fernando S. Gallegos

San Jose, California
2010

Book design and layout by Fernando S. Gallegos
Cover picture taken by Dr. Susan L. Ross, professor and author of
*The Hidden Half of Transformation: Nine phases to integrate life-changing
experience into daily life.*

ISBN 978-0-615-40966-5

"Believe nothing, no matter where you read it, or who said it,
no matter if I have said it, unless it agrees with your own
reason and your own common sense."
~ Gautama Buddha

Table of Contents

*This book is dedicated to the few people
who believed that I had a little more to offer the world.*

Special thanks to Jerad J. Yarborough for helping me edit this book and finally making it a reality.
Thanks to my friend Alfredo Nicodemus López for assisting me during the post-writing process.
And also many thanks to Denise Fernandez for her loving support during my long hours of research and writing.

Preface

IN the 1870's Heinrich Schliemann set off in search of the mysterious lost city of Troy. Troy was once thought to be a place of myth and legend, with a great Trojan War and amazing characters, Schliemann was ridiculed for his pursuit. His pursuit for the lost city was considered to be pseudo-archeology even by 1800's standards; Schliemann strongly believed that he would one day discover the city. And consequently, by accident, he did in fact stumble across the remains of Troy. The transition from myth into reality completely changed the consciousness of the mass public. With such dedication and enthusiasm in pursuit of the mysteries of the world anyone can uncover great things that would be towards the progress of human history. Now, if only modern day science would use these principles of imagination and pursue their dreams, what amazing achievements we can accomplish. Like the city of Troy, many enthusiasts believe that somewhere lost in the jungles may be the ruins that will ultimately settle the dispute over the existence of the lost civilizations of Lemuria and Atlantis, and there they rest waiting to one day be found by a sincere seeker.

The research for this book has taken place over the course of several years starting in 2003. Since I was a child I would always be reading books on lost civilizations, paranormal phenomena, and U.F.O's. While all the other children were reading age-appropriate books, I would be lost in the metaphysical section of the library. Through the years my curiosity persisted, until 2003, when I walked into the Rosicrucian Egyptian Museum gift shop in San Jose, California. Looking for esoteric books of interest to add to my very small collection, I came across a strange book entitled *Lemuria: the Lost Continent of the Pacific*, with a beautiful image on the cover. Because I was very low on cash I decided not to buy the book, but for the following week I could not get the image and word 'Lemuria' out of my mind. I managed to save up a little more, and went back to the gift shop and bought the book. Needless to say, my interest in ancient civilizations hit its maximum peak when I quickly read through the book, unable to set it down. My curiosity was intensified after discovering other books on the subject. In 2003, I started *Ghosts of Lemuria*, an Epic Folk Metal band, and I began writing and recording music based on Lemuria. We played various shows around Northern California and eventually the band fizzled out. However, my research did not end there. Slowly, what began as a small collection of books grew and grew. While attending university I worked seasonal low-paying jobs and spent what little money I made to fulfill my passion.

As I began to research more into the lost continent of Lemuria I became almost obsessed at times. I began accumulating articles ranging from peer-reviewed journals to stories of bizarre encounters with Lemurians. A drawer in my desk slowly began to fill with countless notes and articles on the subject. At certain times I felt that I was becoming too wrapped up in researching the elusive continent, and felt that the best way to stop was to literally burn all my notes. Many of my investigations led down fruitless ends. However, after continuously trying I would stumble across something completely beyond what I was anticipating. I can recall on several instances approaching professors one on one to discuss the possibility of such an event taking place (given the anomalous evidence). Most simply laughed, while others were rather open in hearing about what I had been researching. During my undergraduate studies I had the opportunity to travel quite a bit, collecting as much as I could regarding the subject.

At one point in time I had the opportunity to study abroad with several University students to Peru to become initiated into Andean Mysticism and learn from an indigenous people known as the Q'ero. I jumped on the opportunity and started reading on the South American connection with Lemuria and Atlantis. While in Peru we travelled to all the sacred sites, and underwent rituals constantly throughout the day. I took tedious notes and upon every opportunity questioned people who lived in Peru regarding several stories I had read. Upon returning back to the United States I simply stored my notes along with the others inside the drawer.

Once I finally graduated from University I figured I would either be able to continue on to graduate school or begin a career. After having found several interesting accounts and making some incredible correlations, I began to regret that other people would not be able to know what I had found. But likewise, I understood that a lot of people would not be able to understand and I would further be shunned. It was during this time that the economy took a turn for the worst and because of it, I was not allowed to continue on to graduate school. I figured with two degrees I should be able to get a stable career quickly within my field. I was wrong, and because of this new unforeseen circumstance, a new opportunity opened up that I never before planned. Having more than enough resources and materials to write a book, I quickly jumped on the opportunity.

During the writing of this book I purposefully chose to leave out some of the more interpretable accounts. There being plenty of highly imaginative narrations I felt that it would best be left out. I decided to focus more specifically on archaeological, ethnographical, and historical data. There being several metaphysical books on the subjects of Lemuria and Atlantis, I felt that somebody should present the information using a more 'middle of the road' approach. Using several scholarly journals I began to research the physical evidence, and began correlating it with indigenous accounts and their mythological perspective. Archaeologists sometimes uncover remains that lack explanation (called anomalies), and hopefully through the use of ethnographical or early historical writings, the stories may be able to fit in the gaps where science is at a loss to explain. Despite my best efforts, I still know a few researchers would deny such correlation and completely dismiss what I have presented.

I hope not to convince people regarding anything on Lemuria or Atlantis. Simply put, I would like other people to think critically about my findings and hopefully make their own conclusions on the subject matter. I hope somebody else can pick up where I left off and maybe one day find something even more incredible that I have missed. Or at the very least, I hope I have re-sparked some fascination or imaginative curiosity that has been lost. In an age where imagination is best left only for children, only those few who can regain a small sense of curiosity and awe can experience wonders beyond anything any amount of words can describe.

Chapter One
The Great Mystery of Being

MANKIND has always had a fascination with the mythical, from ancient tales of primordial creation to the emergence of the first humans. Such stories vary between different cultures and religions. Mythical tales of gods and goddesses creating man from the sands serve as metaphors that define unique cultural identities. Humanity can gain a deep understanding of cultural heritage and the mythological dramas that have been passed down through the ages. While variations of creation stories and lore exist throughout the world, humanity is bound together by a common thread of awe and wonder for their own existence. The same questions arise within the imagination, and though the answers vary, the similarities between themes remain the same. Without restraint one must uncover the seeds of passion and allow our imaginations to blossom. While staring into the eyes of our unconscious, we must discover what has been lost in order to gain back a forgotten piece of ourselves. Without knowing ourselves and our past, we will repeat the same mistakes. As one starts on his journey, he will first lose sight of his reality, for in this realm of learning there is but one true guide - our innate and unawaken unconsciousness. Truth can become blurred within the limitless bounds of the imagination, but the truth will always resonate from within.

Many creation stories around the world begin with an allegorical series of events which explain the origins of the world and humankind. Some stories begin with the universe being devoid of all space and time: an infinite darkness. From within the darkness, a cosmic force manifested by forming a physical reality - the universe as a conscious reflection of a divine essence. Other stories portray the world already being in existence; however, manifestation occurs with people crawling out of caves and underground caverns. Again, the allegorical beginning is concerned with the idea of coming into being from darkness. Within a reality devoid of time and space, as one seeks to know oneself, one can manifest into the world as a conscious being.

Science proposes many theories regarding the creation of the universe as it is understood today. Stephen Hawking and his peers hypothesized the *Big Bang Theory,* which speculates that a large explosion formed the galaxies over 13.7 billion years ago. The theory puts forth the idea that at one time there existed a concentrated mass of matter which maintained a high rate of density. Following a great explosion, mater expelled outwards, expanding into the universe. This naturally leads to questions as to what caused the Big Bang; in other words: which came first, the chicken or the egg? In a cosmological sense, the evolutionary model of the creation of the universe is one of the most scientifically accurate theories in modern times; however, the *Big Bang Theory* is a working description of how the universe came into being from that point in time, and is not meant to be taken as conclusive proof.

Others believe that tracing back the ultimate source of creation into a single concentration of matter is absurd. Proponents state that as humans, our limitations prevent us from grasping the philosophical concept of infinity. Humans cannot fully comprehend infinity and the true nature of all things, resorting to scientific inquiry in hopes of finding the physical reasoning behind the universe.

Many believe that in order to understand ourselves in relationship to the universe, we must first understand and acknowledge the presence of a higher force. The intangible concept of a Creator, or God, exists everywhere in the world. While there are many variations, there is always an underlying common representation. In an anthropological context, there are many conceptions of God because of interpretations on different levels of development. Additionally, the complexity behind the idea of God is tied to the progress of a cultural group's growth and achievements; however, this does not imply that one group is correct or superior to another: it offers insight relating to the social and cultural progressions of development.

One of the best examples to illustrate the culturally diverse concept of God would be the comparison between the Roman Catholic Church to that of an indigenous tribe of the Americas, such as the Navajo. The fundamental idea in Roman Catholicism is to understand that God exists as an independent entity, ruling mortal man from a throne in heaven. Regarding the motives and actions of God, I will simplify in basic terms. According to Catholicism, God has the ability to judge those who do wrongfully against others and to reward those who carry out good deeds. The Navajo view the concept of God as an entity who embodied the role of a creator bringing into existence all life in this world, looking upon humans as both independent and dependent beings. Humans maintain an interchangeable role between macrocosmic and microcosmic dualities. While the iconic bearded God in Catholicism sits on a throne overlooking the earth, the Navajo use the sun to represent the creator, making life possible through a delicate system of balance and harmony with that of the earth. The Navajo also possess separate entities that represent the creative or intelligent source. Specific spiritual manifestations are later attributed to those existing within the Roman Catholic Church upon conversion. It is simple to assimilate the original Navajo cultural traditions with the concepts perpetuated in Roman Catholicism. Throughout the Southwestern United States there is still evidence that remains of this assimilation between religions and spiritual practices, as indicated by various churches still standing. In several instances where a statue of a saint might once have been placed, there now stands a totem representing a given saint's equivalent within that tribe. In these observations, saints are seen as the embodiment of God, not as Gods themselves, but as a collective manifestation that God acts through. Elements in nature, as seen by many indigenous tribes, are either representations of the Creator or divine sources of intelligence.

Without dwelling on the alleged evidence of God that many claim, I will briefly mention notable conclusions that have inspired many. Albert Einstein coined the phrase "God does not play dice with the universe." Einstein's research, including the theory of relativity, revolutionized the scientific world. When asked by a Rabbi if he believed in God, Einstein replied "I believe in Spinoza's God, who reveals himself in the harmony of all being, not in a God who concerns himself with the fate or actions of men."[1] Einstein believed that religions around the world should focus more on ethics. In his essay "Science and Religion" he states that an "individual may place his powers freely and gladly in the service of all mankind."

> The fairest thing we can experience is the mysterious. It is the fundamental emotion which stands at the cradle of true art and true science. He who knows it not and can no longer wonder, no longer feel amazement, is as good as dead, a snuffed-out candle. It was the experience of mystery — even if mixed with fear — that engendered religion. A knowledge of the existence of

something we cannot penetrate, of the manifestations of the profoundest reason and the most radiant beauty, which are only accessible to our reason in their most elementary forms-it is this knowledge and this emotion that constitute the truly religious attitude; in this sense, and in this alone, I am a deeply religious man. I cannot conceive of a God who rewards and punishes his creatures, or has a will of the type of which we are conscious in ourselves. An individual who should survive his physical death is also beyond my comprehension, nor do I wish it otherwise; such notions are for the fears or absurd egoism of feeble souls. Enough for me the mystery of the eternity of life, and the inkling of the marvelous structure of reality, together with the single-hearted endeavor to comprehend a portion, be it never so tiny, of the reason that manifests itself in nature.[2]

Cambridge professor, physicist, and Nobel Prize recipient Brian David Josephson began realizing the parallels between mysticism - more specifically Eastern mysticism - to that of modern-day physics.[3] While many within the scientific community scoff at such claims, other people feel that it simply validates their own beliefs.

Mythological expert Joseph Campbell, known for his research on comparative mythology, has written several books on the subject of comparative cosmology and mythological parallels between cultures. His influence extends to the "Star Wars" films in their depiction of the parallel ideas of God, or gnosis, through the representation of a collective cosmic consciousness referred to in the film as 'the force.' As our society progresses with modern technology, principles related to cosmic and universal laws will always continue to exist. The following is taken from an interview which was later published into a book entitled *The Power of Myth*:

"God" is an ambiguous word in our language because it appears to refer to something that is known. But the transcendent is unknowable and unknown. God is transcendent, finally, of anything like the name of "God." God is beyond names and forms. Meister Eckhard said that the ultimate and highest leave-taking is leaving God for God, leaving your notion of God for an experience of that which transcends all notions.

The mystery of life is beyond all human conception. Everything we know is within the terminology of the concepts of being and not being, many and single, true and untrue. We always think in terms of opposites. But God, the ultimate, is beyond the pairs of opposites, that is all there is to it.

…The source of temporal life is eternity. Eternity pours itself into the world. It is a basic mythic idea of god who becomes many in us. In India, the god who lies in me is called the "inhabitant" of the body. To identify with that divine, immortal aspect of yourself is to identify yourself with divinity.

Now, eternity is beyond all categories of thought. This is an important point in all of the great Oriental religions. We want to think about God. God is a thought. God is a name. God is an idea. But its reference is to something that transcends all thinking. The ultimate mystery of being is beyond all categories of thought. As Kant said, the thing in itself is no thing. It transcends thingness, it goes past anything that could be thought. The best things can't be told because they transcend thought. The second best are misunderstood, because those are the thoughts that are supposed to refer to that which can't be thought about. The third best are what we talk about. And myth is that field of reference to what is absolutely transcendent.

…Everything in the field of time and space is dual. The

incarnation appears either as male or as female, and each of us is the incarnation of God. You're born in only one aspect of your actual metaphysical duality, you might say. This is represented in the mystery religions, where an individual goes through a series of initiations opening him out inside into a deeper and deeper depth of himself, and there comes a moment when he realizes that he is both mortal and immortal, both male and female.[4]

According to Campbell, God is represented in many cultures as a dualistic entity through which all life emanates, thus contradicting the mainstream view of God. If we, as human beings, are a living manifestation of a cosmic source, then we must exist on a metaphysical level as immortal beings, capable of transcending planes of existence. Because the concepts of divine entities differ among cultures, the representation of a single truth emerges.

Theory of Panspermia

The theory of panspermia hypothesizes that life on earth originated from elsewhere in the universe. Similarly, the idea of *exogenesis*, meaning 'outside origin,' carries with it significant ideas regarding the origin of microscopic organisms, which may have come from elsewhere. Theories regarding panspermia involve everything from asteroids hitting the earth billions of years ago, to extraterrestrial garbage being dumped on earth.[5] The panspermia that could have been deposited may have contained the simple building blocks to life. The complexity behind the scientific theories regarding panspermia is too intricate to mention, but there is a lot of scientific evidence being put forth by scientists.

Francis Crick, Nobel Prize recipient for his co-discovery of the DNA double helix, created controversy within the scientific community by proposing the theory of *Directed Panspermia*. According to Crick, over four billion years ago, while our solar system was being created, an advanced civilization existed elsewhere within our galaxy. This advanced civilization scouted out possible habitations for the production of life, and ultimately planted 'seeds of life.' Crick believes that probes were sent out to deposit bacteria during the cooling of earth's temperature. An ideal candidate for the creation of life, the bacterium could easily have thrived on extreme temperatures without the aid of oxygen. On the brink of extinction, Crick speculates that the civilization failed to establish successful colonies.[6]

The scientific community dismissed Crick and his theories of panspermia. Professor Robert Temple later examined the idea of panspermia through analysis of ancient texts in his article, *"The prehistory of panspermia: astrophysical or metaphysical."* Temple analyzes early texts from ancient Egyptian, Indian, Greek, and Gnostic sources. In many ancient Egyptian carvings, there stands a god with a large phallus ejaculating across the night sky, symbolizing a vagina; the image represents Egyptian gods spreading their divine seed throughout the Universe. The nature of the gods Ptah, Osiris, and Amum might have been disputed among priests and temples of ancient Egypt due to the interchangeable symbolism of Egyptian gods. Egyptologists have long identified the creator of Egypt to a little known god named Atum, the chief god of the priests of Heliopolis. The priests of Heliopolis were always quarrelling with the priests of Memphis, whose chief god was Ptah.[7] In the earliest Egyptian texts, called the Pyramid Texts (predating 2000 BCE), the Heliopolis supporters who wrote the text attribute "all the sperm" in creation as coming from Atum and not Ptah.

Ancient depictions show the phallus creating Horus and the celestial bodies in the night sky with sperm trails leading to various stars from the source - sometimes also being attributed to Osiris; the Egyptian god who is revered as the creator of all life as we know it. The symbolism contextualizes the correlation between the vast and dark chaos of the primordial waters and outer space. Ancient Egyptian texts state that "this world was thought to exist within an infinite ocean, called *Nu* ("*waters*"), which was kept from engulfing the atmosphere...The sky was seen as the surface of the cosmic ocean where it met the atmosphere...."[8] In the beginning, within the dark ocean of space (*Nu*), there was only one being, Atum (later translated to mean 'the universe'). The spreading of seeds across the cosmic universe by Atum represents the spreading of panspermia, with the seed of Atum depicted as being the star Sothis.

Ancient accounts of panspermia can also be found in the writings of the early Greek philosopher Anaxagoras, as well as early Jewish/Christian Gnostics. The symbolism in early Gnostic religion reveals the iconic depiction of the Madonna and Child - or Mary and Jesus - similarly to the goddess Isis nursing her son Horus. Traditions of Gnosticism can be traced back to the Egyptians through similar tales of resurrection and ritual. But what if ideas of panspermia were also borrowed? Second century Christian teacher Basilides said the following:

> Once upon a time there was nothing, nor was that nothing any kind of entity, but in plain, unequivocal, and unsophisticated language, there was nothing at all...Now when there was nothing, neither matter, nor substance, nor nonentity, nor simple nor compound, nor man nor angel no god, nor anything that can be named or perceived by sense of by thought,... (there) came into being afterwards...the germ of a world. And this seed of the world contained all things within itself, just as a grain of mustard-seed collects into the smallest body all things at once...(including) the seeds that are cast off as germs of innumerable other plants in an endless process. Thus not being God made a not being

world out of nothing. [9]

All things which we can enumerate and all the things of which we can say nothing because they have not yet been discovered, which were to belong to the future universe that has been developed progressively,...were heaped up within the original germ...a world in which everything was present in an undifferentiated state...For [this cosmic germ] contains piled up within it all the seeds...[10]

Before the Aryans conquered India around 1,500 BCE, the ancient Hindus wrote about the creation of life in a similar fashion. Ancient Veda manuscripts state the following:

As the Golden Germ he [*Hiranyagarbha*] arose in the beginning; when born he was the one Lord of the existent....When the great waters came, bearing all as the Germ, and generating fire (*agni*), then arose the one life-spirit of the Gods...who was the one God above the Gods....May he not injure us, who is the generator of the earth...who produced the heaven, who produced the shinning mighty waters. O Prajapati, none other than thou has encompassed all these created things.[11]

An older translation of the same texts says the following:

In the beginning rose Hiranyagarbha, born Only Lord of all created things...What time the mighty waters came, containing the universal germ...He in his might surveyed the floods containing productive force...who is earth's Begetter...the heavens' Creator Prajapati! Thou only comprehendest all these created things, and none beside thee.[12]

The heavenly waters mentioned in the ancient Vedic hymn are known as *Rasa*, which is a mythical river surrounding the earth and sky and was created by a god attributed to Sothis, or Sirius.

The star Sirius is the brightest star in the night sky, and is only 8.6 light years away making it the fifth closest star to Earth. Revered by the ancient Egyptians, Sirius was known as Sothis, represented by Anubis the jackal god. The Greek and Romans referred to Sirius as the Dog-Star that resides within the constellation Canis Major. Other similarities are found elsewhere around the world. In Chinese culture, Sirius is called *Tsien Lang*, which translates into *Heavenly Wolf*. The Alaskan Inuits call Sirius the "*Moon Dog*" and the Pawnee tribes in North America refer to it as the "*Wolf Star*" or "*Coyote Star*."[13] Ranging from great civilizations to rural tribes around the world, Sirius is often attributed to a canine entity. Perhaps the reason for this is due to some ancient association (or distant memory) dating back to our ancestral roots in Africa.

A Mystery Unfolds

The Dogon tribe is situated in the central regions of Mali, Africa. The population consists of approximately 800,000 people. They are recognized for their intricate wooden ceremonial masks and sculptures. Much of the Dogon territory contains large escarpments, and some of their villages are built alongside these cliffs, resembling ancient Anasazi Pueblo dwellings of the four corners region in the United States. As first recorded by Marcel Griaule, many Dogon villages are strategically arranged according to their cosmological beliefs, including the clothes they make containing symbolic images of themselves in relation to the greater universe.

As Anthropologist Marcel Griaule began observing the tribe, he was introduced to the Ogotemmeli, an elder possessing great wisdom. Continuing his observations, he discovered the Dogon to be a sophisticated society, comparable to other

advanced civilizations of the time. Griaule's journey into both
the exoteric and esoteric worlds of the Dogon furthered his studies of ancestral beings called *Nommo*, who were revered as
the greatest of spirits. The *Nommo* consisted of two homoge-
neous spirits: divine spirits and the products of God. The Ogotemmeli explained the following about the *Nommo*, (taken
from Marcel Griaule's book, *Conversations with Ogotemmeli*):

> This pair of twins, he explained, represented the per-
> fect, the ideal unit. The *Nommo*, looking down from
> Heaven, saw their mother, the earth, naked and speech-
> less, as a consequence no doubt of original incident in
> her relations with the Dog *Amma*. It was necessary to
> put and end to this state of disorder. The *Nommo* accor-
> dingly came down to earth, bringing with them fibers
> pulled from plants already created in the heavenly re-
> gions.[14]

Several aspects of human beings seem to have been created by
the *Nommo*. The Dogon beliefs of the *Nommo* are similar to
Sumerian myths, and the Egyptian myths of Osiris and Isis.
The Ogotemmeli also described a complex genealogy from
which the Dogon people were created by the *Nommo*.

The positions of the village huts and the beds in which
they slept were laid out in a manner that corresponded to esoteric knowledge regarding the *Nommo*. Through interpretations given by the Ogotemmeli, Griaule learned a great deal
about Dogon cosmology. Totemic shrines and alters laid
throughout the village correspond to the ancient *Nommo* and
the balance of male and female duality. Even the granary had
complex patterns, steps, and positions carefully aligned to different celestial bodies. Marcel Griaule explains that:

> The European, for himself, had no difficulty in accept-
> ing all these symbolical representations, these different

methods by which man sought to manipulate the invisible and was himself manipulated.[15]

The Ogotemmeli taught Griaule about the village cults, each with its own importance and significance towards the community. Though the Ogotemmeli left him with only a few things, he did not provide any details regarding the esoteric beliefs within them. It would not be until a few years after being initiated into the Dogon tribe that he and his student Germaine Dieterlen learned secrets that remain controversial today.

The Sirius Controversy

Published in 1954, a book entitled *African Worlds,* which contains a chapter written by Marcel Griaule and Germaine Dieterlen, provides a starting point for the Dogon controversy. The beginning chapter describes ideas related to modern day quantum physics. As stated in the chapter, "their conception of the universe is based, on one hand, on the principle of vibrations of matter, and on the other, on a general movement of the universe as a whole."[16] This energy, according to the Dogon, is small with unfolding matter revolving around a helix. These contain the first seven vibrations of the 'egg of the world.' The two fundamental notions along this helix are expressed much like a DNA strand which was not discovered until 1953 by James D. Watson and Francis Crick. This energy, according to the Dogon are the two opposite sides of a polarity, both male and female, which give rise to perfect equilibrium. Griaule and Dieterlen describe the following in their chapter:

> Two fundamental notions are thus expressed: on the one hand the perpetual helical movement signifies the conservation of matter... On the other hand, the infinite extension of the universe is expressed by the continual

progression of matter along this spiral path.[17]

> In fact, the order of the heavens, as it is observed and conceived by the Dogon, is no more than a projection, infinitely expanded, of events and phenomena which occur in the infinitely small.[18]

This is quite an amazing statement written by Griaule and Dieterlen, and if true, raises the question; how did this knowledge come about from such a remote tribe such as the Dogon?

Griaule and Dieterlen then made an outstanding claim which gave rise to the controversy surrounding their research regarding the Dogon knowledge of the stars:

> The staring-point of creation is the star which revolves around Sirius and is actually named the *Digitaria* star; it is regarded by the Dogon as the smallest and the heaviest of all the stars; it contains germs of all things. Its movement on its own axis and around Sirius upholds all creation in space. We shall see that its orbit determines the calendar.[19]

The word *Digitaria* itself is the botanical name for a seed, used by Griaule and Dieterlen to refer to the smallest seed known to the Dogon tribe, which in Dogon is spelled '*Po.*'[20] Sirius and its companion star revolve around each other forming an independent axis. '*Po Tolo*' (*Tolo* meaning Star)[21] refers to the companion star known as Sirius B (Sirius A's counterpart), which is one of most massive of white dwarfs in existence, making it the one of the smallest and dense stars known. When the Dogon drew out diagrams of these two stars, they proved to be astronomically correct. The Dogon organized their village according to these two stars; it is unknown how the Dogon would have known this, as Sirius B is invisible to the naked eye and was not photographed until 1970. [22]

The answer may be contained in what the Dogon said regarding the *Nommo*. Keeping in mind that Sirius is the brightest star in the sky and is only 8.5 light years away, it is the fifth-closest star to earth excluding the sun. The Dogon hold a ceremony to honor '*Po Tolo*' every 50 years, which is the average amount of time it takes for Sirius A and B to make a full rotational orbit. The *Nommo* maintain a cosmological role in the creation of man, but it is the description of their arrival that intrigues researchers:

> *Amma* decided to send to earth the *Nommo* of the other half of the egg, creators of the sky and the stars. They came down to earth on a gigantic ark, at the centre of which stood the two *Nommo* of the sky,...At the four cardinal points were the four other pairs of *Nommo*, avatars of the first and the ancestors of man,.. The ark constituted a new, undefiled earth; its descent coincided with the appearance of light in the universe, which till then had been in darkness. Water, in the form of rain, purified and fertilized the soil in which were sown the eight seeds which the mythical ancestors brought with them-each bearing a seed; human beings, animals, and pants forthwith came into existence,...with the aid of the skills taught by the *Nommo*, social life was organized. In this way everything which had been created in the egg was then made to manifest...Man is the 'seed' of the universe: that is to say, he was prefigured in the seed *Digitaria*, the vibrations and extensions of which produced the world.[23]

Several books published on the ethnographic work of Griaule and Dieterlen question the detailed precision of their knowledge. Parallels between String Theory and Quantum Physics to the Dogon's use of sacred symbols are analyzed.[24] In recent years, many pseudo-scientists, conspiracy theorists, and Ufologists learned of the research and started to manipulate Griaule and Dieterlen's findings in order to push their own agendas. Other Griaule books published after his death in 1956, such as *The Pale Fox*, have added more fuel to the fire; recent books shed light on the Dogon's knowledge of gravitational pull, elliptical movements, spherical alignments, solar system rotations, rings of Saturn, and the moons of Jupiter. Research later suggested that the Dogon obtained their information from the ancient Egyptians, indicating that the Dogon could be their descendants.

Robert Temple wrote extensively on these topics in his book *The Sirius Mystery*. Published in 1976, Temple's book covers Griaule and Dieterlen's work with the Dogon, as well as scientific comparisons of Dogon symbols. Temple's research also compares the Dogon's knowledge to that of other ancient civilizations. Following publication of the book, he was vilified to the point of losing his career with Royal Astronomical Society and as a broadcaster for the BBC, becoming blacklisted from any future advancement within the mainstream scientific community.

Dogon Hoax?

Walter E. A. van Beek, a professor in the Department of Cultural Anthropology at Utrecht University, in the Netherlands, explores ideas related to the Dogon. He traveled to Mali himself and traced Griaule and Dieterlen's tracks, reproducing their original fieldwork. He published his findings in an article in 1991 entitled "Dogon Restudied: A Field Evaluation of the Work of Marcel Griaule" for the journal *Current Anthropology*. According to van Beek, nobody within the Dogon tribe shared their ideas on the esoteric knowledge talked about by Griaule and Dieterlen; furthermore, no fellow anthropologists agreed with them either.

Walter E. A. van Beek, along with a team of anthropologists, found no evidence regarding Griaule's reports on Sirius. Van Beek spoke to the original people interviewed by Griaule, stating that "though they do speak about *sigu tolo* [interpreted by Griaule as their name for Sirius itself], they disagree completely with each other as to which star is meant; for some it was an invisible star that should rise to announce the *sigu* [festival] for others it was Venus that, through a different position, appears as *sigu tolo*. All agree, however, that they learned about the star from Griaule."[25] Griaule studied astronomy in Paris and brought with him maps of the stars. And van Beek claims that the Dogon do not use *Sigu Tolo* as a term for Sirius A, but rather *Dana Tolo*. Van Beek states also that the Dogon had no knowledge of Sirius B, and because Griaule visited during a colonialist period, the Dogon could have simply told him what he wanted to hear. He also details the myths that Griaule himself was creating throughout his field research, and how it could have been he who taught the Dogon a few things about astronomy and came back later with Germaine Dieterlen after tainting the Dogon's cosmological views.

In rebuttal to Walter van Beek's *Dogon Restudied,* Marcel Griaule's daughter Genevieve Calame-Griaule defends her father's work while attacking van Beek's research. She claims that van Beek was misguided and had preconceived notions of what he wanted to find, remaining ignorant of the esoteric traditions within the Dogon tribe.

There is no evidence defining who is right and who is wrong. In many cultures around the world, myth and reality coexist. Concluding the Dogon mystery, the following are quotes by Joseph Campbell in regards to the nature of myths:

> Essentially, mythologies are enormous poems that are renditions of insights, giving some sense of the marvel, the miracle and wonder of life.[26]

> The myth is the public dream and the dream is the pri-

vate myth. If your private myth, your dream, happens to coincide with that of the society, you are in good accord with your group. If it isn't, you've got an adventure in the dark forest ahead of you.[27]

Timeless stories pertaining to a mythical beginning can be found in many cultures around the world. The complexity of the stories depends on their level of subsistence. Civilizations with more substantial and plentiful resources spend less time hunting and gathering and more time contemplating abstract ideas; groups that spend more time hunting and gathering have less time to develop stories. Some will recall tales of man being created out of divine inspiration, while others are related to the understanding of their surroundings such as stories involving specific mountains and animals native to the region. Other tales deal with intricate melodramatic dramas involving many gods and goddesses. Pushing back through the chronicles of time, a common global legend emerges of a forgotten ancient culture and a mystical land. Known among the ancients as *Mu*, it is still referred to in legends today.

[1] Arieti, James A & Wilson, Patrick A. *The scientific & the divine: conflict and reconciliation from ancient Greece to the Present*, p. 243

[2] Einstein, Albert *The World as I See It*, p. 14-15

[3] *Merriam-Webster's Collegiate Encyclopedia: The Ultimate Desk Reference*, p. 855

[4] Campbell, Joseph & Moyers, Bill D. *The Power of Myth*, pp. 48-50

[5] Chaisson, Eric *Epic of evolution: seven ages of the cosmos*, pp. 225-6

[6] Lamb, David *The search for extraterrestrial intelligence: a philosophical inquiry*, pp. 83-6

[7] Temple, Robert *The prehistory of panspermia: astrophysical or metaphysical?* International Journal of Astrobiology (2007), 6:169-180 Cambridge University Press

[8] Ibid.

[9] Ibid.

[10] Ibid.

[11] Ibid.

[12] Ibid.

[13] Holberg, J. B. *Sirius: brightest diamond in the night sky*, pp.20-24

[14] Griaule, Marcel *Conversations with Ogotemmeli: An Introduction to Dogon Religious Ideas*, p. 19

[15] Ibid., p. 121

[16] Forde, Daryll *African Worlds: Studies in the Cosmological Ideas and Social Values of African Peoples*, pp. 84

[17] Ibid., p. 84

[18] Ibid., p.85

[19] Ibid., p.85

[20] Temple, Robert *The Sirius Mystery*, pp. 42-3

[21] Ibid., p. 64

[22] Ibid., pp. 42, 44

[23] Forde, Daryll *African Worlds: Studies in the Cosmological Ideas and Social Values of African Peoples*, pp. 86-87

[24] Scranton, Laird *The Science of the Dogon*

[25] van Beek, Walter E. A. *Dogon Restudied: A Field Evaluation of the Work of Marcel Griaule.* Current Anthropology, Volume 32, No. 2 (April 1991), pp. 139-167

[26] Campbell, Joseph and Toms, Michael *An Open Life: Joseph Campbell in Conversation with Michael Toms*, p. 22

[27] Campbell, Joseph and Moyers, Bill D. *The Power of Myth*, p. 40

Chapter Two
Lemuria: The Land of Mu

THE search for the first Cradle of Civilization will always intrigue and inspire many to set out in quest for the mythic Garden of Eden, as written about in the *Book of Genesis*. The written passages serve more of a metaphorical or allegorical purpose, which can be misleading to those seeking a literal meaning. Other tales resonate closely with the *Book of Genesis*, and thus should be examined under the same light. As human beings, everyone questions the past, present, and future conditions hoping to survive and maintain biological lineages. One must start from the beginning in order to understand present and future conditions. Fear of examining one's self can lead to avoiding knowledge concerning one's true nature. But for the sincere seeker there shines a light of hope. Following the ancient tales as an initial source of inspiration, one can travel to distant lands in hopes of entering a forgotten world.

Lemuria, the modern name for the lost continent of Mu, was established in an article entitled *"The mammals of Madagascar"* by zoologist and bio-geographer Philip Sclater, who theorized in 1864 that Madagascar and India once existed as part of a large continent.[1] Sclater used his theory to explain why certain fossils were found in Madagascar and India and not in Africa or the Middle East. Because of the growing interest of Darwinism, many theories use Lemuria as a means of explaining the absence and presence of fossils. One of these theories suggests that the absence of a so-called missing link resulted because of the evolutionary development that occurred on Lemuria. Many theories later became disproved after new theories of plate tectonics and continental drifts became accepted. Occult and clairvoyant writers of the time, such as Madame Helena Petrovna Blavatsky, claimed to have been given access to a pre-Atlantean book called *The Book of Dzyan* in the 1880's.[2] Blavatsky, who founded the Theosophical Society, claims that the Lemurians were once tall, hermaphroditic, egg-laying beings who resorted to bestiality; because of these acts, Lemuria sank to the bottom of the ocean. Author William Scott-Elliott expanded upon Blavatsky's theories, allegedly with astral clairvoyance, elaborating on the creatures of Lemuria with a bizarre account.[3] The stories given by the Theosophical Society offer no tangible information related to the ancient civilization of Lemuria; however, it is important to understand the historical context of the name Lemuria.

The legend of Lemuria spans Polynesian and Pacific cultures. In New Zealand, the indigenous Māori know the land as Hawaiki, while in Hawaii this mythical homeland is referred to as Kahiki. And on Easter Island, the Uoke natives refer to Lemuria as Hiva. There are a wide variety of descriptions of the mystical land of Lemuria: some place it in the Indian Ocean, while others place it in the middle of the Pacific Ocean. The mythical land ranges from a small mass of land to a very large continent that was once connected to Australia and California. The time in which this continent is said to have existed pre-dates the supposed world-wide flood, as written about in the Epic of Gilgamesh and biblical accounts of Noah's Ark. Given that the destruction of Lemuria took place long before this great deluge, it is reasonable to place Lemuria during the last Ice Age - if not prior. The actual determined date of destruction is difficult to determine because of the lack of substantial geological evidence and contradictory research. For the purpose of this book I will avoid evidence of "psychic" interpretations or accounts given by "Akashic travelers." I will focus my attention on the various accounts already set in motion by various societies and cultural groups in hopes of presenting a clear perspective on this ancient land. Mythic tales and accounts will be presented as one continuous story, preserving the original significance of this continual ageless myth.

Journey to Lemuria

The geographical time of Lemuria differs from that of today; it's almost unrecognizable. With the end of the climatic dinosaur era, new species began inhabiting the earth. The temperature of the planet increased, yet remained cooler than the preceding time period. In some areas, heat and humidity were intolerable. What is now known as the Arctic Circle consisted of lush subtropical vegetation and many animals as warm oceans circulated through all parts of the globe. The flora and fauna of that time period grew to tremendous sizes. This time period is referred to as the Paleocene geologic epoch, which lasted roughly 65 million years ago. It is supposedly during that time when a new species of humans emerged, unrelated to *Homo Sapiens*. As the continental plates shifted to where they are positioned today, the earth presented new challenges for all its inhabitants. Parts of the world consisted of swampy marsh lands, while others were occupied with persistent volcanic activity. The earth, in constant motion, eventually stabilized, and as a result, many of these early humans perished; life during this time was faced with extreme conditions. Based on certain ancient texts, theories propose that the cradle of civilization once lay where the Pacific Ocean is today. In other ancient accounts, the cradle of civilization is placed in either the Indian Ocean or above the Arctic Circle. I will explain later on in the book the reasons as to why these two other locations are thought to be the beginning of human civilization.

After a time, the people of this first civilization set out on quests for foreign lands in order to establish new colonies because of the population increase. These new communities established settlements in the east as well as in the west. Their civilization slowly began to expand and harmonize with the surrounding environment; these human beings were not primi-tive peoples. They spent generations developing intricately built houses with rectangular walls over ten feet high, using wood, leaves, and mud to cover the roof. Others built houses using stone blocks or carved their homes into the sides of mountains. Standing at an average height of six feet, they looked human but with many unique features. Their heads were disproportionate to their bodies and their foreheads were very high. The placement of their eyebrows was between six to seven inches below the hair on their heads. In the center of their foreheads about an inch and a half above the bridge of the nose was thought to be a walnut-sized gland. Their arms were much longer than ours, but their legs were of a stature similar to modern day humans, yet the arms and the legs remained quite muscular and developed. Their necks were a bit longer and thinner than normal, and their ears where much smaller. Their nostrils were rather large and the nose was broader and flattened. Their eyes were larger than humans today, and brown in color. Their skin color was tanned, but not very dark. They wore loose fitting clothes which flowed openly. Their hair was black, short at the top, and long toward the back.[4]

The inhabitants of this mystical land of Lemuria lived simple and peaceful lives. While mammals and birds (e.g. owls, pigeons, hawks, cranes, ducks, snakes, and turtles) came into existence during that time, the Lemurians did not hunt them. It is speculated that they ate small animals and fish, with

the bulk of their diet being fruits and vegetables. Their knowledge of breaking down and processing plants enabled them to
make foods such as breads and tortillas. With their skills, they
became masters of their environment, creating alternative methods to establishing a stable food supply. Living in widespread settlements throughout Lemuria, they often remained
within the bounds of their communities, rarely setting forth into
unknown territories.

Set apart from each other, homes kept families in solitude, unless they came together for communal activities.
While an abundance of gold and silver existed, they were solely used for decoration and were never exchanged as a means of
commerce. As time passed, they established communities
along river beds and streets, as well as large highways that offered access to the people. Allegedly, they rode on the backs
of large animals, while others rode animal-driven sleighs down
smoothed streets. Homes and communities alongside the river
and waterways were accessible by boats and rafts that used a
rock-like substance to propel them over the water at high rates
of speed.

The Lemurians built large temples and buildings intended for mystical and scientific studies. Times were hard for
the Lemurians with constant Earthquakes, volcanic eruptions,
tidal waves, and a fear of wild animals coming into the villages
to attack them. Over the centuries they learned to accept their
surroundings by achieving mastery over their psychic abilities.
The small gland on top of their foreheads helped increase a
heightened state of psychic perception. By closing their eyes,
they perceived anything they desired. This ability increased to
the point of being able to communicate with animals. Communication among themselves became unlimited because of
the lack of difference between somebody nearby and somebody
100 miles away. This 'sixth sense' enabled them to see beyond
what our common senses can detect. The visual and physical
sensations transcended three dimensions, leading to a cosmic

dimension. As advanced beings, the sociological accomplish-
ments of the Lemurians exceed anything today:

> The Lemurians must have enjoyed life to the fullest ex-
> tent, for they devised ways and means of producing all
> the necessities and luxuries required by them. Certainly,
> the present-day races of man have not reached this
> point. We have entered a cycle of artificialities, bring-
> ing forth artificial and unreal desires that can be satis-
> fied only with artificial things. We have developed the
> stage and the production of theatricals as an artificial
> means for the study of history and human problems.
> Having entered into this fictious manner of study, the
> stage has rapidly developed until we believe the theater
> plays and motion pictures are of educational value and
> a real necessity as a form of amusement.[5]

It is argued that the Lemurians did not suffer from diseases or illnesses because they cured themselves of physical
and psychic ailments by means of touch. Because of their high
level of mastery, they could choose the time and place of their
deaths. Once they felt they had achieved everything that they
needed in this life, they went into a deep meditative sleep and
transitioned over; age was inconsequential: once they felt that
they learned and did everything that was needed, they simply
engaged death. They could easily live to be 100 years old, but
there was no grief or remorse for death; it was understood as a
delicate balance of life that was very well accepted.

According to their standards, everything required a
communal effort. Lacking any system of commerce, they possessed few material items. Crime did not exist and nudity was
seen as completely natural, unrestricted by gender. Elaborate
ceremonies and rituals included marriage ceremonies in which
the man and woman appealed to the leader of the community,
seeking approval from the families prior to the ceremony. A

grand festival would occur in honor of their marriage but this was only the beginning for them: they would be led to the outer edge of the community, where the high priest demanded that they each give a piece of metal in honor of their leaving. If either one presented anything of a materialistic value, the ceremony would be halted until the following month. This test assured that neither of them did not conceal anything before departing into the wilderness. The couple then remained together for two months to fend for themselves, followed by a return to the temple. They each had to demonstrate that each one cared for the other and could provide clothing and shelter and protect themselves against fierce animals. If they failed to meet these expectations the marriage was not allowed and never again could they appeal for another marriage.

The community was the center point for all daily life. Everybody worked towards a common good: everything was shared, and everybody benefited. No standards existed for measuring labor, skills, and achievements. Everything was equal and everyone worked for the advancement of humanity:

> Those who were talented in various ways were given every opportunity to exercise that talent and to devote themselves to it, for if it was productive in any sense it afforded an opportunity for receiving all of the blessings of community life equal to those who produced more material of necessary requirements. This is why the arts and sciences among the Lemurians progressed to a high degree.

> The reverse of this condition is true today. Eminent artists and scientists capable of making the most valuable contributions to our knowledge and to our ethical development are forced to abandon their work and effort because they must resort to some occupation which pays them in money and enables them to live. If all of

the truly great artists and scientists in the world today were assured of an equal degree and form of living and the enjoyment of all the necessities of life while perusing their special professions, we would solve one of the great problems of the present and future development in our ethical culture.[6]

The End of Mu

It is believed that over the centuries many of the existing Lemurian colonies and communities lost contact with the original mainland. Times slowly changed as the planet experienced a series of glacial periods. Many of the various Lemurian groups developed their own languages, writing systems, and their physical features also began to change. Later expeditions taken to these communities reported seeing darker-skinned individuals wearing different clothing, speaking and acting completely differently. They appeared to have lost all sense of tradition and psychic understanding. It was especially hard for a group living in modern day Alaska: it seemed that the climate had made them lazy, causing their communities to remain desolate.

To the east of the continent was a small but growing colony of Lemuria known as Atlantis, which was thriving at this time. This land mass, in the middle of the Atlantic Ocean, was quickly forming and becoming another center of development in the world. Meanwhile, in Lemuria, generations passed and cultures either developed or disappeared. It is not fully known what actually took place before the great catastrophe that killed the millions of inhabitants of Lemuria. There are many theories as to why and how Lemuria was destroyed, but something of great intensity wiped out the continent. Located near the Pacific Ring of Fire, it is likely that an upheaval of the land suddenly occurred. Volcanoes may have erupted causing the earth to shake violently resulting in massive flooding until the continent submerged under the ocean and tidal waves to envelope the globe.

The few survivors endured the catastrophe by being in the higher ranges of mountain peaks. These mystics eventually descended down into what was left of their land and slowly began pilgrimages for new territories. Supposedly preceding the existence of modern day *Homo sapiens*, they remained in isolated communities across the northern, central, and southern Americas. It is estimated that the survivors of Lemuria were limited in number, and they remained while another civilization began to grow and thrive. It would be hundreds of generations before they would meet their distant relatives once again. Meanwhile, the Lemurians remained, quiet, peaceful, and mastering their sacred art and waiting...

---

[1] Sclater, Philip *The Mammals of Madagascar* from The Quarterly Journal of Science

[2] Blavatsky, Helena Petrovna *The Secret Doctrine, the Synthesis of Science, Religion and Philosophy*

[3] Scott-Elliot, W. *The Lost Lemuria*

[4] Cervé, Wishar S. *Lemuria: The Lost Continent of the Pacific*; Most of the section describing the continent of Lemuria and its inhabitants was paraphrased out of this book. Having read countless versions of the "supposed" Lemuria story, although it may be speculative, I believe Cervé's book best reflects a more tangible account of what may have taken place for reasons I will explain in following chapters.

[5] Ibid., p. 127

[6] Ibid., p. 109

Chapter Three
Atlantis

MODERN accounts about the fabled Island (or Continent) of Atlantis consist of theories based on historical accounts (primarily Plato's *Timaeus* and *Critias*). An array of evidence purports to link historical mythology to the land of Atlantis. Whether or not the most modern accounts of Atlantis are based on unfounded evidence is beside the point, as research should remain open to suggestions and new possibilities no matter how absurd they may seem.

As previously detailed, a devastating cataclysm fell upon the people of the ancient world, sealing the fate of Lemuria beneath the waves of the Pacific Ocean. The survivors of ancient lands scattered about various parts of the globe and evolved into their own separate colonies as Atlantis sprang into existence in the middle of the Atlantic Ocean. Centuries passed as the people of Atlantis developed their own technology and psychical advancements. As the Atlantean civilization's population increased, only a miniscule population of Lemurian survivors remained, continuing their mystical paths in isolation, uninfluenced by the changing world around them.

Exact dates surrounding Atlantis remain unknown, though they have been hypothesized in various books. In order to proceed in understanding the story of Atlantis, it is necessary to first understand the evolutionary context of humans during the time of Atlantis. Recent anthropological science points to evidence of a continual development of hominids throughout the ages, for example: *Homo floresiensis, Homo neanderthalensis, and Homo antecessor*; however, *Homo floresiensis* and *Homo neanderthalensis* are not genetically related to *Homo sapiens* but are of a 'different species.' Many of the *Homo* lineages may have evolved from common ancestors and eventually discontinued their evolutionary patterns and became extinct, with only current humans surviving. Questions remain as to the possibility that our human ancestors may have at one point in time coexisted with these more ancient people.

New Research Surrounding Human Evolution

New theories based on historical mythology and fossil records suggest that humans did not evolve from apes as previously believed. Resulting in the evolution of upright bipedalism in humans over long periods of time, apes evolved from humans through a distant common ancestor. Evidence suggests that we evolved from an upright bipedal creature that existed over twenty million years ago during the Miocene Epoch, and not five million years ago as previously understood, thus revolutionizing the way we view our evolution as a species. The first hominids that walked on two legs are known as *Morotopithecus bishopi*, located in present day Uganda, and dating back 21 million years.[1] From these earliest hominids an evolutionary separation emerges:

> Going forward from this point in time, we have the divergence of three separate lineages: one from the gorillas (split off at 8-9 million years ago); one for the

chimpanzees (split off at 5-6 million years ago); and one for the hominines (the dozens of species, including *Australopithecus* and *Homo*, that have humans, but no apes, as their descendants). [2]

Nearly seven million years ago, the earliest humans appeared in the tropical regions of Africa, as is evident with *Ardipithecus*, as they moved upward through Africa. The Pleistocene Era initiated a dramatic shift in climate approximately two and a half million years ago. The earth cooled, which dramatically decreased the rate of evolution of humans. With much of the world under ice and snow, humans survived in dry areas. Roughly 1.7 million years ago, humans colonized East Asia; one million years ago humans entered European lands. Evidence suggests that cycles of human variants (or hominids) spread throughout the world at various periods in time.

It is interesting to note that Neanderthals (*Homo neanderthalensis*) and humans are not of the same species, as indicated by mitochondrial DNA. Recent evidence shows that Neanderthals and humans - Cro-Magnons - did have interactions with each other within distinct regions of the ancient world. While Neanderthals demonstrated some capacity in developing their own culture, they ultimately faded into extinction. A similar fate applies to *Homo floresiensis* - known as "the Hobbits" - dwarf-like hominids, discovered on the Indonesian island of Flores. Remains date back 18,000 years, and stone tools unearthed in archeological sites date as far back as 94,000 years ago, during the Late Pleistocene. *Homo sapiens* did not reach these islands until 45,000 years ago, again fueling the debate of whether *Homo sapiens* interacted with other concurrent hominid species.

As modern *Homo sapiens* migrated to the outer reaches of the world, humans entered a new continent. It is still unclear as to the point in time that humans entered the Americas. While it is hypothesized as occurring 12,000 years ago, evidence suggests a continual wave of migration via the Pacific coastline on watercrafts - which helps explain the Monte Verde archaeological site in Chile which dates back to 14,500 BP (Before Present). The origins of people in the Americas continues to be debated; however, a new study released in 2008 indicates that mitochondrial DNA evidence concludes that 95% of the Native American population can be traced back to six women who lived in Beringia - a land bridge that once existed between Alaska and eastern Siberia 20,000 years ago.[3]

After thousands of years, humans gradually migrated throughout the world, and upon encountering other humans, they realized that they were not Neanderthals, but instead a different and more evolved culture: the Atlanteans.

Atlantis: The Antediluvian Mystique

After the fall of Lemuria, a new civilization began to arise. As the climate changed over the centuries, the poles froze, changing tropical wildernesses into frozen tundra. Various species of animals passed into extinction as great beasts inhabited the globe, such as the Woolly Mammoth, elephant-sized sloths called Megatherium, Woolly Rhinoceroses, Saber-toothed cats, and the giant short-faced bears of North America. During the glacial period, sea levels dropped to 300 feet lower than they are today. As a result, coastlines extended outwardly in the eastern United States by approximately 100 miles.[4]

The large island of Atlantis consisted of several surrounding islands that extended out to the Caribbean. The mainland of Atlantis consisted of numerous large mountains overlooking lush forests, lakes, and marshlands. Villages covered the beautiful landscapes among rivers and meadows. Food grew in abundance, as the fertile land sustained a large population and many wild animals, including a prodigious elephant population. Located on the island shores, various channels, ports, harbors, and canals cascaded from the top of the mountains down into the valleys, meandering through villages and outward into the seas. The active ports served sea merchants, traders, and naval stores. A variety of fruits, crops, and wood were carried down from the mountains into the ships waiting in the canals, and from there they were shipped into the city. Aqueducts provided the main source of water, across bridges and into occupied sections of the city.[5]

Surrounded by mountains, the main metropolis extended down toward the seas. The city consisted of a series of circular rings bridged together by roads, canals, aqueducts, and well-watered groves and sections given for the purpose of exercise and repose. Cisterns with royal and private baths - enclosed and open to the elements - contained temperature-controlled water, providing hot water for the winter and cold water for the summer. The same system of water temperature was applied to fountains laid around the city; around the fountains they planted trees and constructed buildings. On the last ring of the city, an immense wall completely enclosed the city, except for the open channel which led to the sea.[6]

The Atlanteans were very tall, had high cheekbones, slightly slanted eyes, and blonde or red hair. Exercise and a balanced diet maintained their healthy lives. During the Age of Leo - around 10,500 BCE to 8000 BCE - the Atlanteans opened their ports to trade with other civilizations, ranging from Europe to India. Increasing trade welcomed opportunities and intermarriages between the Atlanteans and the new humans who occupied the Eurasian and African continents.[7]

The Mythology and Mystical Practices on Atlantis

According to the mythology, a palace honoring Cleito and Poseidon stood within the walls of the city. Inaccessible to the people, the temple of Poseidon featured a gold statue of Poseidon, its height reaching the ceiling. Around the massive gold statue there were 100 Sea Nymphs (Nereids) riding on dolphins. The walls and pillars of the temple were decorated in gold and silver, while the roof was decorated with ivory, silver, gold, and orichalcum (a type of copper/gold metal). Gold statues of all the descendants of the ten kings and their wives decorated the outside of the temple. The Atlantean legend of Cleito and Poseidon is as follows:

> In the first ages the gods divided the earth among themselves, proportioning it according to their respective dignities. Each became the peculiar deity of his own allotment and established therein temples to himself, ordained a priestcraft, and instituted a system of sacrifice. To Poseidon was given the sea and the island continent of Atlantis. In the midst of the island was a mountain which was the dwelling place of three earth-born primitive human beings- Evenor; his wife, Leucipe; and their only daughter, Cleito. The maiden was very beautiful, and after the sudden death of her parents she was wooed by Poseidon, who begat by her five pairs of male children. Poseidon apportioned his continent among these ten, and Atlas, the eldest, he made overlord of the other nine. Poseidon further called the country *Atlantis* and the surrounding sea the *Atlantic* in honor of Atlas. Before the birth of his ten sons, Poseidon divided the continent and the coastwise sea into concentric zones of land and water, which were as perfect as though turned upon a lathe. Two zones of land and three of water surrounded the central island, which Poseidon caused to be irrigated with two springs of water-one warm and the other cold.[8]

In comparison to Atlantean culture, it must be understood that their scientific progress spans tens of thousands of years. In Atlantis, science and mysticism coexisted as a cosmic law governing everything in both a physical and spiritual con-

text. The study of art, science, and mystical crafts existed
among the adept and the neophyte through priestly ordinance.
Those initiated would have been trained in all the arts in a mo-
mentous fashion in order to encompass a diversity of knowledge and wisdom. Their understanding of life as a reflection
of a divine creation served to unite themselves with peace,
love, and compassion.

The high priests held detailed secrets that can only be
speculated upon, perhaps even possessing knowledge beyond
our own realms of understanding. It could be that beyond our
earth and in the heavens there exists a great influence on humankind, an ancient relationship that has always been in place.
The Atlanteans, similar to the Lemurians before them, carried
secrets regarding healing and were highly advanced in curing
the body with herbs and touch. They possessed knowledge of
anatomy and techniques on how to apply energy to specific
points on the body in order to heal the body of any ailment.

Advancements made during the Atlantean civilization
may have exceeded modern quantum technology. These advancements will remain a mystery until actual artifacts are located; until then, all that exists are speculative claims. Allegedly, the Atlanteans discovered a method to create perpetually
burning lights, possibly accounting for the stories of explores
who entered into tombs and found flames still burning in Egypt
and the Americas.[9] Others claim that they had mastered nuclear
technology and engaged in destructive warfare, ultimately leading to their demise.

Bull sacrifices were made to the god Poseidon in Atlantis by the ten kings who fulfilled an offering of a bull in accor-
dance to an oath invoking reparation toward those who plotted
against them.[10] As time passed, the Atlanteans deviated from a
path of light as they began to indulge in hedonistic pleasures,
hatred towards others, and corruption of power. "The Atlanteans instigated the first war; and it has been said that all sub-
sequent wars were fought in a fruitless effort to justify the first

one and right the wrong which it caused."[11] Materialism and greed corrupted the lives of the Atlanteans.

Fall from Grace

The following account demonstrates the horrible atrocities that occurred before the destruction of Atlantis as a young and beautiful Atlantean virgin woman stood on top of a monument and proclaimed the following:

> Oh, ye! Think ye that Incal will accept the blood of innocent animals for your crimes? Whoso sayeth this doth lie! Incal, God, will never take blood of anything, nor symbol of any sort which placeth an innocent in a guilty one's stead! And the Incalithlon, and the Holy Seat, and the Maxin Light are dishonored whenever a priest layeth an animal on the Teo Stone, and striketh a knife to its heart, tears it out and tosses it as sacrifice into the Unfed Light. Yea, the Unfed Light doth truly destroy it instantly. But think ye because of this that merciful Incal is pleased. O ye brood of vipers, ye priests that are charlatans and sorcerers! [12]

Her blasphemous proclamation held true for the people of Atlantis, and afterwards, a priest stoned her to death in the crowd whereby a human sacrifice was made of her. A bloodthirsty crowd gathered around her dismembered body, restless in their demands for another sacrifice: that of the priest who struck her down. Upon his removal and prior to being killed, a great vision of a human appeared: the Son of the Solitude. His words prophesied the end of Atlantis:

> Behold, the day of destruction is at hand which was foretold ages ago! Atlan shall soon be no more beheld by

the sun in his whole course, for the sea shall swallow you all! Attend ye! [13]

The Atlanteans lusted for more destruction. Their once pure and harmonious land now became polluted with vile substances. Chaos followed for many years, but it must be noted that not all Atlanteans continued down a path of decadence. A few wise mystics understood the signs and heeded the prophecy. Clandestinely, they gathered together the ancient histories of their people and relocated to previously established settlements. As explorers, these mystics extended their influence onto other inhabitants of the ancient world, preparing and waiting for their prophecy to be fulfilled.

While an exact date of the destruction of Atlantis remains unknown, many theories place it around 9600 BCE. [14] It is thought that powerful earthquakes shook the foundation of Atlantis, triggering a great flood that covered the land, "and in a single day and night of misfortune...the island of Atlantis disappeared in the depths of the sea." [15] It is also theorized that the ending of the Ice Age occurred as a sudden release of snow and ice into the oceans, which caused the sea level to dramatically rise. Stories of a great flood have been told all around the world. Millions lost their lives that day, not just on Atlantis, but also in other locations around the world. Others speculate that the relocated survivors of Atlantis were responsible for founding other great civilizations of the ancient world. The ancient survivors of Lemuria continued to embrace their long lost Atlantean descendants. They built monuments and cities which may still lay forgotten and undisturbed in dense jungles or under the deep sands of the desert.

The teachings of the Lemurians and Atlanteans existed in several places around the world, such as Egypt, Peru, and Central and North America. They were thought to be passed down in secrecy and developed into mystery schools that may still exist today as secret societies.

[1]   Choi, Charles Q. *Human ancestors walked upright, study claims* Special to LiveScience.com (October 9, 2007)

[2]   Filler, Dr. Aaron G. MD *The Upright Ape* (2007) , p. 222

[3]   Ritter, Malcolm *Native American DNA Links to Six "Founding Mothers"* Associated Press (March 13, 2008)

[4]   Heezen, Dr. Bruce Oceanographer with the Lamont Geographical Observatory of Columbia University; Taken from *Practical Atlantean Magic* by Murray Hope, pp. 58-63

[5]   Paraphrased from Plato's *Critias*

[6]   Ibid.

[7]   Hope, Murry *Practical Atlantean Magic*, p. 83

[8]   Hall, Manly P. *The Secret Teachings of All Ages*; interpretation of Plato's Critias, p. 33

[9]   Hope, Murry *Practical Atlantean Magic*, p.110

[10]   Spence, Lewis *The Occult Sciences in Atlantis*; Mithraic & Egyptian symbolism revolve similarly around the sacrificing of Bulls, p. 19

[11]   Hall, Manly P. *The Secret Teachings of All Ages*, p. 34.

[12]   Phylos *A Dweller on Two Planets*, p.418

[13]   Ibid., p. 421

[14]   Based on Plato's account

[15]   Plato's *Timaeus*

Chapter Four
Old World Accounts

TALES reminiscent of Lemuria and Atlantis are found throughout the Old World, perpetuated through myths and legends. Without supporting concrete evidence, analysis of these myths is limited to allegorical interpretations. Myths play a critical role in the development of culture, serving as significant moral stories and communal perspectives. Cultural interpretations are useful in understanding the foundations of a myth; over time, myths become distorted and interpreted differently. Insights contained within many accounts provide historical interpretations - or understandings - of a population during a given time period.

The mythical lands of Mu and Atlantis are merely conceptual realties, perhaps archetypal in origin. Psychologist Carl Jung coined the term 'collective unconscious' in the early 1900's, for an inherent set of ideas ranging from moral conduct to those of religious and systemic beliefs. These common ideas shared by humanity reside in our subconscious, serving as a foundation for all people. Jung also believed that archetypal values were associated with collective human uncons-

ciousness. These archetypal values are symbolic ideas or concepts related to universal experiences that may be expressed
through individual mediums. For example: stories from different cultures maintain the same key characteristics, such as the
wise elder (or mystic hermit), the hero, the villain, and the
trickster (or deceiver). The dilemmas, development, and success of the hero present a common theme in stories throughout
the world. Jung attributes this to a common, collective-
unconscious that is shared among everyone. It is possible that
the stories pertaining to the lost civilizations of Lemuria and
Atlantis stem from a collective-unconscious. Likewise, it is
possible that the stories are based on actual events, lingering as
distant memories still laying dormant in our unconscious.

Atlantean Tales from the Greco-Roman World

The main source for the legend of Atlantis is traced
back to the Greek philosopher Plato, who was born around 428
or 429 BCE, and was the student of Socrates. The account of
Atlantis can be found in Plato's two dialogues the *Timaeus* and
Critias, real people who lived during Plato's time; Timaeus
was an Italian astronomer, and Critias was an Athenian teacher
and poet. In Plato's dialogue, a discussion continues from the
previous day during which a "perfect society" is discussed.
Critias then tells a story passed down from his great grandfather, who had heard the story from Solon, an Athenian states-
man, nearly 150 years prior. According to Critias, Solon traveled to the Egyptian city of Sais where he was received by the
priests. Solon questioned the Egyptian priests regarding the
history of the world. Ultimately, Solon met an elderly priest
who said that the Greeks were children compared to the Egyptians who knew nothing of their ancient history. The priest
continued: "There have been, and will be again, many destruc-
tions of humanity arising out of many causes; the greatest have

been brought about by the agencies of fire and water, and other lesser ones by innumerable other causes."[1]

The Egyptian priest continued by mentioning great floods that swept the earth, purging it into water. After great cataclysms take place, a few survive to carry the responsibility of starting over again like children who "know nothing of what happened in ancient times." The priest describes several deluges, of which the Greeks knew only one and that the previous occupants of their land were "the fairest and noblest race of people which ever lived, and that you and your whole city are descended from a small seed or remnant of them which survived."[2] The Greeks did not know about this secret history because the survivors neglected to leave any written records. Where the city of Athens once stood, a city that was the first in war against Atlantis and "in every way the best governed of all cities, is said to have preformed the noblest deeds and to have had the fairest constitution of any of which tradition tells, under the face of heaven."[3] [4]

The priest explains that the patron goddess of Athens is the same as the Egyptian goddess, who established Athens before establishing Egypt a thousand years later. According to ancient records kept by the priests, the constitutional records themselves date back 8,000 years; therefore, Athens would date back to over 9,000 years ago. The priest discusses the laws that were set in place during that time, and that these were the same laws that both Greek and Egyptian cultures still adhered to; for example, the various castes maintaining obligations similar to those of the priests, artificers, shepherds, hunters, warriors, and over laws maintaining wisdom and order.

According to the priest, Athens was at war with Atlantis in the Atlantic Ocean, beyond the Pillars of Heracles (Strait of Gibraltar). The priest states that the island itself was larger than Libya and Asia combined and composed of other islands situated on its opposite side, facing the open oceans. The empire of Atlantis maintained control over the whole island, sev-

eral other islands, and parts of the continent reaching north to
Tyrrhenia (Italy) and east to Egypt. As the war continued,
parts of the land within the Pillars of Hercules became libe-
rated, until one day a great cataclysm occurred: "Afterwards
there occurred violent earthquakes and floods; and in a single
day and night of misfortune all your warriors in a body sank
into the earth, and the island of Atlantis in like manner disappeared in the depths of the sea."[5] In closing of the *Timaeus* dialogue, Critias says:

> I have told you briefly, Socrates, what the aged Critias
> heard from Solon and related to us...
> Socrates: And what other, Critias, can we find that will
> be better than this, which is natural and suitable to the
> festival of the goddess, and has the very great advan-
> tage of being a fact and not a fiction? How or where
> shall we find another if we abandon this? We cannot,
> and therefore you must tell the tale, and good luck to
> you; and I in return for my yesterday's discourse will
> now rest and be a listener.[6]

Critias continues to describe Atlantis, in Plato's *Critias*;
however, the dialogue abruptly ends because the rest was lost.
Continuing from the *Timaeus*, Socrates continues his discussion on the war between Atlantis and Athens; Critias also continues the story by repeating the tale that was told to him as a
child. Before he would begin, he mentions that Solon was
planning on writing the Atlantis tale in poetic form. The original names used by the Atlanteans were translated into Egyptian, using Egyptian gods who Solon later translated into Hellenic gods, which is why many of the gods mentioned in the
Atlantis narrative maintain Hellenic names. Critias's great-
grandfather, Dropides, obtained the original writings of Solon
and passed it on within his family. As a child, Critias studied
Solon's writings on Atlantis. The story describes Poseidon

creating Atlantis and populating it with five pairs of twin male children. Critias continues by mentioning the honorable family that lived on Atlantis, the geography and construction of Atlantis, including the majestic palace temple, the people of Atlantis, and their achievements. The story ends with the Atlanteans losing their divine nature, becoming unmoral beings consumed with greed. The dialogue ends with the people of Atlantis becoming unrighteous and straying from a path of peace and happiness. [7]

Other details of Atlantis can be found in the writings of other Greek and Roman accounts, including some that predate Plato's time. Greek historian Herodotus (c.484-425 BCE), often regarded as the "Father of History," mentions Atlantis twice in *The Histories* as he chronicles the history of everything around the ancient world. Scholars reference Herodotus to support their conclusions against Atlantis, claiming that he never once mentions Atlantis;[8] however, there is a written account of Atlantis by Herodotus written nearly 75 years before Plato:

> Now the Caspian Sea is apart by itself, not having connection with the other Sea: for all that Sea which the Hellenes navigate, and the Sea beyond the Pillars, which is called Atlantis, and the Erythraian Sea are in fact all one, but the Caspian is separate and lies apart by itself. [9]

> From the Garmantians at a distance again of ten days' journey there is another hill of salt and spring of water, and the people dwelling round it are called Atarantians, who alone of all human beings about whom we know are nameless; for while all taken together have the name Atarantians, each separate man and woman of them has no name given to them. This utter curses against the Sun when he is at his height, and moreover

revile the sun with all manner of foul terms, because it oppresses them by its burning heat, both themselves and their land. After this at a distance of ten days' journey there is another hill of salt and spring of water, and people dwell round it. Near this salt hill is a mountain named Atlas, which is small in circuit and rounded on every side; and so exceedingly lofty is it said to be, that it is not possible to see its summits, for clouds never leave them either in the summer or in the winter. This, the natives say, is the pillar of the heavens. After this mountain these received their name, for they are called Atlanteans; and it is said that they neither eat anything that has life nor have any dreams.[10]

Scholars attribute Plato to creating the legend of Atlantis through his writings; however, written a century before Plato, Hellanicus wrote a book entitled *Atlantis*. Unfortunately, only a small surviving fragment exists, which contains the following: "Poseidon mated with Celaeno, and their son Lycus was settled by his father in the Isles of the Blest and made immortal..."[11] It is believed that Hellanicus obtained this story from an earlier account. The surviving fragments of Hellanicus's tale of Atlantis possess similarities to that of Plato's Atlantis. The Isles of the Blest are thought to be west of Morocco, and are possibly the Canary Islands. [12] Another mention of the Isles of the Blest comes from the Greek historian Plutarch (46-120 CE), who stated that the islands were ten thousand furlongs off the coast of Africa, roughly 1,250 miles. The distance is the same length as the uninhabited Azores to the west from the Pillars of Hercules.

Here [Sertorius] met with sailors recently arrived from the Atlantic islands, two in number, divided from one another only by a narrow channel, and distant from the coast of Africa ten thousand furlongs. These are called the Islands of the Blest; rains fall there seldom, and in moderate showers, but for the most part they have gentle breezes, bringing along with them soft dews, which render the soil not only rich for plowing and planting, but so abundantly fruitful that it produces spontaneously an abundance of delicate fruits, sufficient to feed the inhabitants, who may here enjoy all things without trouble or labor.

The Seasons of the year are temperate, and the transitions from one to another so moderate, that the air is almost always serene and pleasant/ the rough northerly and easterly winds which blow from the coasts of Europe and Africa, dissipated in the vast open space, utterly lose their force before they reach the islands. The soft western and southerly winds which breathe upon them sometimes produce gentle sprinkling showers, which they convey along with them from the sea, but more usually bring days of moist bright weather, cooling and gently fertilizing soil, so that the firm belief prevails even among the barbarians, that this is the seat of the blessed, and these are the Elysian Fields celebrated by Homer.[13] [14]

The exact location of the Isles of the Blest remains unknown, either because they are misrepresentations of other islands in the Atlantic Ocean or because they too disappeared into the ocean. Greek historian Diodorus Siculus (first century BCE) mentions a story similar to that of Atlantis:

The Atlantides inhabited a rich country bordering upon the ocean, and were esteemed to excel all their neighbors in civil reception and entertainment of strangers; and they boast that the gods were born among them[15]...In a word, this island is so delightful that it appears to be the abode of the Gods rather than human beings.[16]

Proclus, a fifth century CE Greek philosopher and early advocate of Neo-Platonism, added commentary to Plato's *Timaeus*. His writings influenced various cultural accounts throughout the old world:

> The historians who speak of the islands of the exterior sea tell us that in their time there were seven islands consecrated to Proserpine, and three others of immense extent, of which the first was consecrated to Pluto, the second to Ammon, and the third to Neptune. The inhabitants of the latter had preserved a recollection (transmitted to them by their ancestors) of the island of Atlantis, which was extremely large and for a long time held sway over all the islands of the Atlantic Ocean. Atlantis was also consecrated to Neptune.[17]

European Tales

Tales of Atlantis also exist within European cultures ranging from Spain to Scandinavia. The Basques, a distinct cultural group located in southern France and northern Spain, claim themselves as descendants of Atlantis, which they call *Atlaintika*.[18] It is believed among the Celts, Welsh, and Gauls that they too descended from a continent that sank in the ocean. In the legend of King Arthur, the mysterious island where King Arthur obtained the magical sword Excalibur was known as Avalon. The Arthurian legend of Lyonesse makes reference to a submerged landmass located off the coast of southwestern England. Allegedly, Lyonesse was once an Atlantean colony connected by a series of islands. As time passed, the land of Lyonesse broke apart into the ocean and the people fled into England to later establish the Sacred Kingdom of Logres. [19]

An Irish myth details a group of people known as Nemedians who came from the sea and occupied Ireland. Celtic mythology contains tales of the Tuatha Dé Danann, who sailed from the ocean and drove out the Firbolg - the original inhabitants of Ireland. According to this Celtic myth, these Gods came from four lost cities: *Findias, Gorias, Murias,* and *Falias,* where they learned poetry and magic.[20] In the ancient Gaelic chronicles of *The Dirge of Four Cities*, poems are attributed to those lost cities now lying submerged in the ocean. The poem of *Murias* exudes an eerie mystique, reminiscent of many other legends:

> In the sunken city of Murias
> A golden Image dwells:
> The sea-song of the trampling waves
> Is as muffled bells
> Where He dwells,
> In the city of Murias.
> In the sunken city of Murias
> A golden Image gleams:
> The loud noise of the moving seas
> Is as woven beams
> Where He dreams,
> In the city of Murias.
> In the sunken city of Murias,
> Deep, deep beneath the sea
> The Image sits and hears Time break
> The heart I gave to thee
> And thou to me,
> In the city of Murias.
> In the city of Murias,
> Long, oh, so long ago,
> Our souls were wed when the world was young;
> Are we old now, that we know
> This silent woe

In the city of Murias?

In the sunken city of Murias
A graven Image dwells:
The sound of our little sobbing prayer
Is as muffled bells
Where He dwells,
In the city of Murias.[21]

Another comparison can be drawn upon the tale of the mythical island of Tír na nÓg, located beyond the seas west of Ireland. In Old Norse mythology, similar stories relate to mythical lands and great cataclysms that took place where people later migrated from. In traditional oral Norse mythology, everything originated from *Ginnungagap* (meaning "Great Void"), where a race of giants descended.[22] After the creation of *Búri* - the first God - in *Ginnungagap*, he had a son named Bor, who married a giantess and had three children: Odin, Vili, and Ve. In two Old Norse poems - *Poetic* and *Prose Edda* - cataclysms befell 'frost-giants' who originally descended from Ymir. The three brothers killed Ymir, causing his blood to overflow and consume the world in a great flood. A giant named Bergelmir escaped with his family on a raft (*lúðr*), echoing the Biblical tale of Noah. [23] Great battles ensued leading to the dramatic climax of *Rragnarök*, or the Twilight of the Gods.

Foretold to Odin, who is equivalent to the Greek god Zeus, a series of natural events would bring about the destruction of the gods. Odin was instructed to observe the animals foraging for winter food in early spring; the animals knew of the events to come. The winter would arrive and last for three seasons from autumn to the following autumn, becoming the coldest ever known, followed by three months of thawing. After the third winter, the end would come. Earthquakes would take place everywhere, causing the waters to rise, triggering massive floods. The earthquakes are the result of Loki - the giant evil one - breaking free after centuries of punishment for killing Odin's son Baldur. As this takes place, humans on earth would be killed by cataclysmic blizzards, floods, and quakes. Odin, unable to help the humans, would have to fight for his survival. A final war would then break out with fires devouring parts of the earth, blacking out the sun as stars fall from the sky. In the end, all the gods die and Alfadur, the great eternal god, is the only survivor. From this, Alfadur would create a new earth, creatures, and a man and woman to repopulate the world once more.[24] Other similar stories exist throughout Europe, suggesting that cataclysmic changes may have taken place on earth.

In addition to the myths and legends, other findings indicate the existence of previous advanced civilizations. Portuguese sailors discovered several uninhabited islands in the Atlantic Ocean called the Azores. In the middle of the ocean, they found animals, including rabbits, and land birds such as hawks which they named the islands after (Açores). There was no explanation for the presence of these animals being on the island. Two types of seals inhabited the islands: monk and siren seals which were common along the mainland shores and inland bodies of water. The monk seal is common in the Mediterranean and Caribbean; the siren seals originate from West Africa and eastern South America.[25] According to Claudius Aelianus, a third century Roman, "...the male [seal] has around his forehead a white band resembling the diadem of either Lysimachus or Antigonus, or some other Macedonian king. The inhabitants of the ocean shores tell that in former times the kings of Atlantis, who were descendants of Poseidon, wore on their heads, as a mark of power, the headband of male [seals], and that their wives, the queens, wore as a sign of their power, headbands of the female [seals]."[26]

In 1461, a statue marked with strange inscriptions on its base was discovered on the Azores high in the summits on the island of Corvo. The account was described by several historians, including the Arabic historian Sherif el Edrissi. *The Chronicle of the reign of the king of Portugal, Don João* by Damião de Góis in 1560 states in chapter nine that the statue was that of a man on an unsaddled horse. When word reached back to king Don Manoel, a painter was sent to paint the statue in its natural environment before it was removed. During a thunderstorm, the statue broke into pieces, leaving behind scattered fragments. According to de Góis, this report was a lie; according to contrary accounts, the statue broke while being removed by workmen. Several wax impressions made of the inscriptions yielded nothing because of being too badly worn.[27]

When the Canary Islands were discovered in 1395 by Jean de Béthencourt, a French explorer working for Spain, he came across inhabitants occupying the land. The native people, known as Guanches, spoke of a great disaster flooding their world, forcing the remaining survivors to retreat to the mountaintops. Investigations on the Canary Islands in 1981 unearthed large stone slabs 50 feet below the surface in an area 900-square feet in diameter. Steps were found laid out into a walkway down to where a dock once existed. They found symbols on some of the stones resembling those of the Guanches.[28] Investigators are unable to read the ancient writings, and even the ancient stone houses today lay in ruins. Strangely enough, the Guanches did not use boats, and were brutally killed by Spaniards which leaving no further ethnographical evidence. [29]

Sumer, Egypt and India

Located in present day Iraq, the ancient Sumerian civilization of Mesopotamia is one of the oldest known civilizations. Without being preoccupied with hunting and gathering, its agricultural stability and abstract philosophy led to the creation of some of the first advanced civilizations. Mythic tales evolved into complex belief systems. The earliest creation myths in Sumerian mythology contain a 'trickster-like' god named Enki, later known as Ea in Babylonian mythology. While different versions of the myth exist, the foundation of the story remains the same. Enki is asked to create workers on behalf of the gods so that they could be relieved of their work. After creating man out of clay, a series of events led to a quarrel which created several flawed creatures including giants. The gods in the Sumerian tale created agriculture, mankind, animals, and plants. The increasing human population began making too much noise for the gods so they devised a plan to wipe out mankind in a great flood. Thinking quickly, Enki warned Ziusudra, his favorite human, and instructed him to build a boat in which to place his family and various animals inside. Ultimately, Ziusudra survived the great flood and was granted eternal life by the other gods as a reward for saving all living things. [30]

The *Epic of Gilgamesh* is known one of the oldest written stories. Scholars believe that the flood story mentioned in the *Epic of Gilgamesh* derives from the ancient Akkadian tale of Atrahasis, who survived a great flood.[31] In the *Epic of Gilgamesh* a character by the name of Utnapishtim recalls how he survives a great flood by building a cube-shaped boat. As the waters subside, Utnapishtim sends out a dove, a swallow, and a raven to explore the land. Utnapishtim then emerges from the boat and makes an honorary sacrifice to the gods.[32] It is believed that the biblical account of Noah is based on this story; the tale of Noah is found in Judaic, Christian, and Islamic writings.

Ancient Egypt's flood myth is associated with the sun-god Ra. Ra was warned by his father, the Watery Abyss, that the people were becoming wicked and planning to rebel against the gods. Ra then sent the goddess Hathor to earth to punish the wicked people; however, Hathor went against Ra's original intent and killed good people as well. So many people were murdered that the Nile ran red with blood. Following the advice of the god Thoth, Ra devised a plan, and along with the help of the goddess Sektet, attracted Hathor with strong beer mixed with human blood. Ra instructed his servants to pour the liquid near Hathor in order to flood the dry land. Attracted by the smell of blood, Hathor drank the beer until she passed out, allowing the earth to repopulate. Unwilling to deal with the humans again, Ra left Thoth to govern the world. Thoth then instructed mankind how to read, write, compose poetry, and govern themselves.[33]

Evidence found at the ancient Egyptian Temple of Horus at Edfu lends support to the Atlantean tale mentioned by Plato.[34] The mythological stories involving Osiris, Isis, and Horus possibly take place on the lost land of Atlantis. British Egyptologist Dr. Eve Reymond spent years analyzing the writing found at the Edfu Temple, realizing that the inscriptions describe a mythical "homeland" of the ancient Egyptians, a land where the gods once lived. Found inside the temple, texts refer to a lengthy history of predynastic religions that once existed around Memphis. The ancient Egyptians considered these older religions to be the origin of their own. According to Reymond, "a well-known text on the inner face of the enclosure of the temple of Edfu tells us that the temple was built at the dictates of the Ancestors, according to what was *written in this book that descended from the sky to the north of Memphis*."[35] "The idea inherent in our myth is that a muddy island, that emerged from the primeval water by virtue of the activities of the nameless creative power, constituted the foundation ground for their domain. They seem to have created the actual land for their realm. In the first period of its existence the *Island of the Egg* was closely associated with the divine generation of the Primeval Ones. The nameless Creators of the Earth seem to have been regarded as its original inhabitants, who lived in it at first in a somewhat insubstantial form."[36] A secondary Island, known as the *Island of Trampling*, became a homeland for these original inhabitants who occupied the islands. The *Island of Trampling* later became submerged after a battle caused the inhabitants to perish.[37] According to the fifth section within the Edfu chronicles (VI, 182, 10-15), this did not bring about the end of these inhabitants; instead, the disappearance of these islands (under the primeval waters) resulted in a new territory.[38] "As a result of this action, a new domain came into existence, known as the *Blessed Island* and *Hareoty*."[39]

According to the Edfu chronicles, the original homeland remains beneath the ocean. The symbolic association, according to Reymond, concerned an underwater world becoming the place where the dead souls descended into. This Egyptian underworld is conceptualized as the place where the Ancestor gods dwell. After the great cataclysm, the world was emerged in darkness, which resulted in a new creation. The war and the great cataclysm are reminiscent of Plato's account describing the destruction of Atlantis.[40]

In ancient Indian epics, stories mention advanced forms of warfare. Ancient Sanskrit writings include airships (called *Vimanas*), with what would resemble missiles and atomic bombs. Several texts on the *Vimanas* focus on their construction and flight instructions.[41] Allegedly a war was fought between Atlantis and other civilizations around the world, including an unknown civilization possessing advanced technology. The following are excerpts taken from ancient Sanskrit epics alluding to advanced technology among the ancients:

> Gurkha, flying a swift and powerful vimana,
> hurled a single projectile
> charged with all the power of the Universe.
> an incandescent column of smoke and flame,
> as bright as ten thousand suns,
> rose with all its splendor.
> It was an unknown weapon,
> an iron thunderbolt,

a gigantic messenger of death,
which reduced to ashes
the entire race of the Vrishnis and the Andhakas.
The corpses were so burned
as to be unrecognizable.
Hair and nails fell out;
Pottery broke without apparent cause,
and the birds turned white.
…After a few hours
all foodstuffs were infected…
…to escape from this fire
the soldiers threw themselves in streams
to wash themselves and their equipment.

                              -The Mahabharata

(It was a weapon) so powerful
that it could destroy the earth in an instant-
A great soaring sound in smoke and flames-
And on it sits death…

                              -The Ramayana

Dense arrows of flame,
like a great shower,
issues forth upon creation,
encompassing the enemy…
A thick gloom swiftly settled upon the Pandava hosts.
All points of the compass were lost in darkness.
Fierce winds began to blow.
Clouds roared upward,
showering dust and gravel.
Birds croaked madly…
the very elements seemed disturbed.
The Sun seemed to waver in the heavens.
The earth shook,
scorched by the terrible violent heat of this weapon.

Elephants burst into flame
and ran to and fro in a frenzy...
over a vast area,
other animals crumpled to the ground and died.
From all points of the compass
the arrows of flame rained continuously and fiercely.
                    -The Mahabharata [42]

    In India, a unique culture known as the Tamil retain one of the most ancient languages. The Tamil claim to be descendants of an ancient land, of which India is a small remnant. Lemuria, according to the Tamil was known as *Kumari Kandam* and was situated south of India, expanding into the Indian Ocean; it was revered as the true cradle of civilization, and the birthplace of humanity. The Tamil claim to have descended from the original inhabitants of India, known as the Dravidian, who gave birth to Indus Valley Civilization dating back to 3,000 BCE. The destruction of the ancient land of 'kadal kol' (meaning 'land swallowed by the sea') was potentially caused by severe earthquakes that are common to the region, which would have triggered tsunamis that decimated the land of *Kumari Kandam*. [43] [44] Others suggest the land was destroyed by rising sea levels attributed to the end of the Ice Age. Tamil legends state that the people of *Kumari Kandam* lived 30,000 to 25,000 BCE (and possibly dating back millions of years prior)[45] and that they were also very advanced in technology and the arts. The land was said to be ruled by noble and fair leaders. Some people suggest that it was this ancient culture that influenced Vedic and Aryan societies much later.[46] *Kumari Kandam*, was a utopia where people lived in peace and harmony. The sacred healing practices, medicines, and knowledge are said to have originated from this lost land and continue to be used by the Tamil today.

    Controversy still surrounds the Tamil legends. Scholars believe that many contemporary Tamil writers use the tales of

Lemuria to support nationalistic ideals and to further justify their own existence. Mythological in origin, the legends lack validity; however, stories of the ancient land still exist throughout India. The Tamil recall the utopian Lemuria as a place where peace and harmony exceeded everything, a place where sacred wisdom originated. The following was presented by Tamil scholars R. P. Sethu Pillai, C. Mutthuvirasami Naidu and A. M. Paramasivanandam regarding the antediluvian homeland:

> O mischievous ocean! You consumed so many towns belonging to the Pandyan King! You drank up so many rivers! You swallowed so many mountains! Our Tamil poems recall that in ancient times the river Pahruli belonged to the Pandyan! The beauty of that river was praised by the poet Nettimaiyar. Where is that river? Where are its sprawling sands? Our Pandyan shed tears when he learnt that you had destroyed that river. Even today I can hear the sound of his crying in your breeze! Is this your only cruelty? You also swallowed up the river Kumari which had gloriously served as the southern limit of our ancient Tamil land…Where is that river Kumari? That river which served as the southern boundary of the fine land where Tamil is spoken, you destroyed it and destroyed our limit! You utterly destroyed with your cruelty all the towns and villages which had flourished in the land between the Pahruli and Kumari! The vast range of Kumari that rose high and lofty on that land also became prey to your cruelty! Alas! You ate up our land! You drank up our rivers! You consumed our mountains!…
>
> Alas! What can one say about the suffering heaped upon the ancient Tamil land which gave birth to the arts and to world civilization? What can one say about the cruelty the ocean that caused all this? What can we say

about the state of the Tamil-speaking land that today stands shrunken and emancipated...How much distress and loss has all this caused? Can we even measure this? If today our ancient Tamil land and ancient Tamil learning had survived, we would have ruled the world from Kumari to the Himalayas! We have instead become the laughing stock of others! Is this not your doing? ... If it had not been for your actions, we would have ruled the world! Why were you angry with Tamil Nadu and the Tamil language and the Tamil people? [47]

The Orient

During a diplomatic excursion to what is now Sri Lanka, Roman historian Gaius Plinius Secundus (23-79 CE), otherwise known as Pliny the Elder, gave a descriptive account to Emperor Claudius regarding a people found in Seres, in what is now northwestern China. Pliny the Elder learned from the native inhabitants of a people from Seres who "exceeded the ordinary human height, had flaxen hair, and blue eyes and made an uncouth sort of noise by way of talking, having no language of their own for the purpose of communicating their thoughts."[48] The natives spoke of these people being encountered beyond the Emodian Mountains (the Himalayas) by means of establishing trade.

Ancient Asian cultures contain stories of floods from which only a few survived. One of the oldest existing Chinese legends pertains to a goddess named Nü Gua (or *Nüwa*), the creator serpent goddess of mankind, and Fu Xi, the creator god and first emperor. The legend begins with a man working out in the fields who notices a large thunderstorm in the distance and tells his two children to go inside. The man hangs a cage in his house and stands guard with a large fork. As the thunder and lightning arrived, the thunder god descended from the clouds, attacking the man with a gigantic battle axe. Thrusting his fork into the god, the man pushed him into the cage and quickly locked it. Following the capture of the thunder god, the storms subsided. The next morning, the man headed toward the market to buy herbs and sauce to pickle the thunder god. He instructed his two children not to give the thunder god water under any circumstances. But as soon as the man left, the thunder god pleaded with the children for a drop of water, and they agreed. The thunder god then burst through the cage and pulled out his tooth to give to the children to repay them. The thunder god presented an ultimatum to the children: plant the tooth, or die. As soon as the god left, the children planted the tooth, which quickly became a gourd plant; rains violently returned, flooding the earth. When the man returned home, he told the children to climb up the giant gourd. Meanwhile, he built a boat so that he could travel to the Lord in heaven and plea for him to stop the flood. The Lord listened to the man's pleas and ordered the water god to stop the flood. The rain stopped instantly, and as a result, the man's boat crashed back to earth and killed him. Safe in their gourd, the children realized they were the only survivors left; they married in order to re-establish humanity.[49] Other Chinese flood myths feature a human or half dragon named Yu the great, who was sent from heaven to control the flood.[50] Variations of flood myths exist throughout China, as well others in surrounding regions in the present time.

On the island of Japan, a unique group of people once occupied the region in vast numbers. Known as the Ainu, their genetic traits, such as their hairy bodies, are unusual for Asian populations. They are the original indigenous peoples of Japan and are considered to have Caucasian-like traits. The Ainu also have a flood myth, in which only a few people survive by fleeing to mountaintops. In Ainu mythology, the Ainu originate from a couple who descended to earth, bringing forth their creation.[51] Similar to the Ainu, several cultural groups maintain "Earth-Diver Creation" myths, in which a god or animal is sent by the creator to retrieve back a substance from the depths of the primeval waters. This substance becomes earth in its full manifested glory. These stories are common in Native American tales as well as in other cultures, such as Birhor people in India, Hinduism, and Central Asian groups like the Buriat, the Samoyed, and Altaic people.[52]

Ancient Chinese philosopher Lao Tzu (sixth Century BCE) talked extensively about the sacred wisdom of ancient masters. He wrote the *Tao Te Ching,* which deals with the philosophy of Taoism. Toward the end of his life he left China and traveled west to the land of *His Wang Mu.* According to legend, this mystical place is where the ancient ones lived. He wrote the *Tao Te Ching* before crossing the Chinese border near Dunhuang, after a border guard persuaded him to do so, and was never heard from again. Key parts in his writings offer hints related to the sacred wisdom of the ancient masters which he so eagerly sought out.[53] An excerpt from the *Tao Te Ching* is as follows:

> The Ancient Masters were subtle,
> mysterious, profound, responsive.
> The depth of their knowledge is unfathomable.
> Because it is unfathomable,
> All we can do is describe their appearance;
> Watchful, like men crossing a winter stream.
> Alert, like men aware of danger.
> Courteous, like visiting guests.
> Yielding, like ice about to melt.
> Simple, like uncarved blocks of wood.
> -*Lao Tzu, Tao Te Ching, Chapter 15*

[1]   Plato's *Timaeus*; Translated by Benjamin Jowett (1817-1893)

[2]   Ibid.

[3]   Ibid.

[4]   Ibid. "before the great deluge of all, when the city *which now is* Athens was first in war…" Implying it was not Athens, but rather a continuum of civilizations prior to Athens that once existed in the same area. Athens can be only traced back over 7,000 years, making it the most continual occupied city in the world.

[5]   Plato's *Timaeus*; Translated by Benjamin Jowett (1817-1893)

[6]   Ibid.

[7]   Plato's *Critias*; Translated by Benjamin Jowett (1817-1893)

[8] Feder, Kenneth L. *Frauds, Myths, and Mysteries*, pg 201; "The best-known Greek historian, Herodotus, who lived 100 years before Plato, never mentions Atlantis."

[9]   Herodotus *The History of Herodotus*, Volume 1 translated by G. C. Macaulay; Book I: Section 203, p. 100

[10] Ibid. Book IV: Section 184, p. 364

[11]   Castleden, Rodney *Atlantis Destroyed*, p. 164

[12]   Ibid.

[13] *Ancient Sources for the Atlantis Story* Rosicrucian Digest,Volume 84 Number 2 2006 ; Taken from Plutarch, "Life of Sertorius," *Plutarch's Lives*, trans. John Dryden, ed. and rev. A.H. Clough (1859)

[14]   It is interesting to note that the most fertile type of soil is that of volcanic soil due to its high rate of nutrients.

[15] *Ancient Sources for the Atlantis Story* Rosicrucian Digest, Volume 84 Number 2 2006 ; taken from Diodorus Siculus, *The Library of History*, bk. 3, chap. 4, trans. George Booth (1700; London: W. McDowall for J. Davis, 1814), 194-201

[16] Ibid.; taken from Diodorus Siculus, *The Library of History*, bk. 5, chap. 15 (selection)

[17]   Baldwin, John D. *Pre-historic Nations; or, Inquiries concerning some of the great peoples and civilizatins of antiquity, and their probable relation to a still older civilization of the Ethiopians or Cushites of Arabia*, pp. 396-7

[18] Berliz, Charles *Atlantis: The Eighth Continent*, pp.19-20

[19]   Andrews, Shirley *Atlantis: Insights from a Lost Civilization*, pp. 212-3; taken from Roberts, Anthony *Atlantean Traditions in Ancient Britain* , pp.9,16)

[20] Squire, Charles *Celtic Myth and Legend Poetry and Romance*, p. 46

[21] Sharp, William *From the hills of dream: threnodies, songs and later poems*, p. 110

[22] Page, Raymond Ian *Norse Myths*, p. 57

[23] Ibid., p. 57-8

[24] Bierlein, J. F. *Parallel myths*, p.246-8

[25] Berliz, Charles *Atlantis: The Eighth Continent*, p. 175

[26] Ibid. Quote taken from Claudius Aelianus's *The Nature of Animals*

[27] Braghine, Colonel A. *The Shadow of Atlantis* (1940) , pp. 154-5

[28] Berliz, Charles *Atlantis: The Eighth Continent*, pp.54, 91-2

[29] Ibid., p. 54

[30] Jacobsen, Thorkild *The Treasures of Darkness: A History of Mesopotamian Religion* , pp. 113-4

[31] Tigay, Jeffrey H. *The Evolution of the Gilgamesh Epic*, p. 237

[32] Willis, Roy G. *World Mythology*, p. 63

[33] Bierlein, J. F. *Parallel Myths*, p.135

[34] Zitman, Willem H. *Egypt: "Image of Heaven": The Planisphere and the Lost Cradle*, p.223

[35] Ibid., p. 213

[36] Reymond, E.A.E. *The Mythical Origin of the Egyptian Temple*, pp.74-5

[37] Ibid., p.109

[38] Zitman, Willem H. *Egypt: "Image of Heaven": The Planisphere and the Lost Cradle*, p. 216

[39] Reymond, E.A.E. *The Mythical Origin of the Egyptian Temple*, p.17

[40] Zitman, Willem H. *Egypt: "Image of Heaven": The Planisphere and the Lost Cradle*, pp.217, 223

[41] Childress, David Hatcher *Lost Cities of Ancient Lemuria and the Pacific*, pp.71-2

[42] Ibid., pp.72-3

[43] Ramaswamy, Vijaya *Historical Dictionary of the Tamils*, pp. xli -xlii

[44] Gupta, Om *Encyclopaedia of India, Pakistan and Bangladesh*, p. 1328

[45] Weiss, Richard S. *Recipes for Immortality: Medicine, Religion, and Community in South India*, p. 93

[46] Ibid., pp. 90-4

[47] Ramaswamy, Sumathi *History at Land's End: Lemuria in Tamil Spatial Fables*, The Journal of Asian Studies, Vol. 59, No. 3 (Aug., 2000), pp. 575–602

[48] Pliny (the Elder) *The Natural History of Pliny*, Volume 2, p. 55

[49] Willis, Roy G. *World Mythology*, p.93

[50] Ibid., p.92

[51] Leeming, David Adams *A Dictionary of Asian Mythology*, pp.10-11

---

[52] Ibid., p. 55

[53] Childress, David Hatcher *Lost Cities of Ancient Lemuria and the Pacific*, p. 48

Chapter Five
Native American Myths and Legends

TRADITIONS of the Native American Indians are among the most diverse in the world. Their traditions spread from the Americas to the Arctic regions, the Great Plains, the Tropical Rainforests, down through the Andes Mountains, and to the tip of Patagonia. The cultural groups were so diverse that a member from a California tribe could walk ten miles in any direction and encounter another tribe with a different language and culture. The Native American languages were unique in that members of one tribe would not be able to understand another tribe; as a result, some tribes developed a form of universal communication akin to sign language. The religious aspects of the Native Americans centered on the idea of a divine creator, sometimes being represented by the Sun, whose presence they worshipped.

Until recently, researchers believed that most indigenous groups remained isolated because of natural obstacles related to the geography; however, the discovery of trails indicates that trade routes intertwined through much of the Americas. Archaeologists have traced obsidian found in North

America to a volcanic origin in Mexico, in addition to sea shells found in regions hundreds of miles inland. Trade in the ancient pueblo village of Acoma - in northwestern New Mexico - consisted of Aztec and Mayan artifacts from over a thousand miles south. An example of the use of trails is that of the Inka Empire: every day, relay runners retrieved fresh fish from the sea for the emperor to eat. These relay runners would run over 200 miles from the Pacific Ocean, across the Andes Mountains, and into Cuzco in the Sacred Valley. The lengths of the trails and roads of the Inka Empire surpassed those of the Roman Empire. The Inkas had 25,000 miles of paved roads connected by stations. These played a crucial role during the conquest; upon the arrival of the Spanish, stories of their arrival spread quickly throughout the Americas. The Quechua language was to the Inka Empire as Latin was to the Roman Empire.

Much discussion concerning Native Americans over time and their level of achievements - everything from Inka cosmology to what type of plant the Native Californians used as toilet paper - point to the idea that an endless amount of information can be studied and learned from Native American anthropology. The bulk of what scholars identify as 'mythology' should not be dismissed as mere fantasy; these timeless stories hold the sacred value of the long deceased elders and the people who still pass them on today. These stories also serve as clues to an unknown prehistory in the Americas, the common ties of which may one day lead to further discoveries within historical anthropology.

Native American Accounts of a Lost Paradise

Oral narratives have been passed down since the beginning of time. These tales deal with ethical and moral lessons, offering descriptive accounts of how one's ancestors came to be and what is considered important for a unique cultural group. Several stories around the world contain the same symbolic ideas as to how the people and stories originated. Some stories tell of the world being covered with darkness followed by a God (or gods) creating light and mankind. As these stories are analyzed, new ways of understanding history emerges; for example, many native cultures do not view the concept of time as being linear, but rather in terms of cyclical motions.

In the 1940's, anthropologists and linguists began studying the Hopi lexicon. The western concept of time establishes past and future abstractions: such as 'it was,' 'it is,' and 'it will be.' Time exists on a linear scale and becomes quantified. The Hopi do not follow a western concept of time. When the Hopi set out to create a basket, they do not think about when it will be completed; it just exists in its current state. In other words, "it belong[s] to a state of becoming,"[1] weaving the basket will take weeks, and when a person feels tired they stop, and later continue on a project. "The essence of Hopi life, therefore, is preparing in the present so that those things that are capable of becoming can in fact come to pass. Thus weaving a mat is preparing a mat to become a mat; it will reach that state when its nature so ordains- whenever that will be."[2] The reason for this is that their culture is based on agriculture, with seasons passing in a continual motion. Their harvests are critical to sustaining life, influencing their view of planting as a state of unknown potential and focus, and not on the result of planting itself. This came to be known as the Sapir-Whorf Hypothesis: "It is comparable in some ways to Einstein's theory of relativity. Just as Einstein said that how people saw the phenomena of the universe was relative to their point in observation, so Worf said that a people's world view was relative to the language they spoke."[3]

Oral traditions are not the only forms of communications passed down in Native American culture. In Mesoamerica, certain texts still exist today. Though written in both pre and post-conquest times, the texts sustain the continuation of traditions. These texts are often referred to as the Aztec codices, and are written in Nahuatl, Spanish, and Latin. Among the Mesoamerican writings is the infamous Mayan Popol Vuh (the Popol Vuh was discovered in the 1700's by Father Ximinez) which serves as a source for Mayan cosmology and mythological dramas. According to these ancient texts; "Those who gaze at the rising of the sun...had but one language before going west. Here the language of the tribes was changed. Their speech became different. All that they had heard and understood when departing from *Tulan* (translated from Nahua as "place of Reeds") had become incomprehensible to them... Alas, we have abandoned our speech. Our language was one when we departed from *Tulan*, one in the country where we were born."[4]

Aztlán, the mythical ancestral homeland for the Aztecs, is mentioned in the Boturini Codex, the Codex Telleriano-Remensis, and the Aubin Codex. Aztlán is also mentioned in the *History of Tlaxcala* by Diego Muñoz Camargo, a mestizo, who was born in the 1500's, and in a 16th century manuscript entitled the *Historia Tolteca-Chichimeca*. The importance of Aztlán did not gain notoriety until a Dominican-born Friar by the name of Diego Durán, who was fluent in Nahuatl, in 1581 made known the land of Aztlán. Friar Duran described Aztlán as a utopian paradise that was reminiscent of the Garden of Eden in his book *Historia de las Indias de Nueva-España y Islas de Tierra Firme*. This fueled the imaginations of Spanish explorers who set off in search of this mythical land in what is present day California.

From *Chicomoztoc*, a mythical place meaning 'the place of the seven caves,' the Aztecs emerged from the womb through caves deep within the earth and later departed to Aztlán (the lost homeland meaning 'place of cranes' but can also be translated 'place of whiteness').[5] A sixteenth century drawing in the Boturini Codex places Aztlán on an island to the west of Mexico. Atlantean researchers place Aztlán to the east

Leaving Aztlán, by an unknown Aztec artist shortly after the conquest (taken from the 16th Century Boturini Codex)

(in support of Atlantis), but the depiction indicates the location as being to the west. The land of Aztlán may tie in more appropriately with the land of Lemuria in the Pacific Ocean, as opposed to Atlantis in the Atlantis Ocean. Careful interpretation as to the actual location of Aztlán would place it in the far north and to the west. The Chicano movement later used this interpretation to justify its location in Los Angeles, California. However, in a biographical ethnography written by a Yurok woman belonging to a secret ancient order within the Yurok tribe known as the "Talth," she mentions a homeland, or Garden of Eden, and gives the same directions as described by the Aztecs: 'from the far north and to the west.' While similar in location, she provides a detailed account as to the location of this mystical homeland:

> In our recollections of the past we left the land of our birth (*Cheek-cheek-alth*) many thousands of years ago with our leaders, the Talth, who were given the true name of God in the old land, and carried with them the forked root, or walth-pay. With this divine rod they commanded food, comfort and peace during their long years of weary wanderings. After we left the beautiful valley of *Cheek-cheeck-alth*, for years we wandered down a European land, always moving toward the south, having our origin in the far north. Over this land we wandered like exiles, we know not how long, as it might have been centuries until we reached the rolling waves of the ocean. Upon reaching this salt water we made boats or canoes, and paddled over the waves until we reached the opposite shore, having crossed the straits in safety. [6]

If this account is correct, it places this ancestral land in the Arctic region, but the Pacific Ocean cannot be ruled out as a possibility.

Tales of Destruction

Tales of a great war continue to exist in many of the Native American groups. Such stories include accounts that can be interpreted as aerial warfare, vast destruction of cities by weapons, and the destruction of a continent followed by the coming of a new age afterwards.[7] In Mexico, indigenous accounts provide clues as to what might have happened to the lost lands of Lemuria and Atlantis. The few remaining books from Mesoamerica mention the destruction of these civilizations. Within the *Chilam Balam*, *Popul Vuh*, *Codex Tro-Cortesianus*, and *Codex Troanus* there are references to great disasters that the academic sciences of today dismiss as purely mythology. Those within academia may be correct, but behind every myth there is reason for its existence, regardless of its allegorical, metaphorical, or symbolic content. Within the mythological dramas, there are lessons vital to the survival of the future generations of all cultures.

Author Manly P. Hall theorizes that the ancient mysteries practiced by the Atlanteans spread throughout the Americas. Priesthoods were created and cloaked with dark wisdom, similar to those of Atlantis. Blood scarifies found in the Mesoamerican cultures might be attributed to the ancient Sun Mysteries that became perverted by those on Atlantis. Black magic, necromancy, and sacrificial rites became entangled with the original teachings of the Mystery Schools. The left-hand path of the mystical arts might have been a logical remaining factor that spread throughout Mesoamerica. This led to the destruction of Atlantis, and may also be attributed to the symbolic fall of the Aztec Empire.[8]

The Mayan books of the *Chilam Balam* were transcribed from memory in the 18th century. While some written texts date back to the time of the actual conquest, the Spanish burned all of the ancient Mayan records. The following account describes volcanic explosions that triggered massive floods on the earth:

> Ah Mucencab came forth and obscured the face of the Heavens… the Earth began to awaken. Nobody knew what was to come. Suddenly subterranean fires burst forth into the Sky, and fire rained down from above, and ashes descended, and rocks and trees were thrown down, and wood and stone smashed together.
> Then the Heavens were seized and split asunder. The face of the Heavens was buffeted to and fro and thrown on its back… [the people] were all torn into pieces; their hearts failed them while they yet lived. Then they were buried in the sands, in the sea.
> In one great sudden rush of water the Great Serpent was ravished from the Heavens. The Sky fell and the Earth sank, when the four gods, the Bacabs, arose who brought about the destruction of the world.[9]

The *Popol Vuh* mentions the creation of previous forms of humans, almost symbolic of the prehistoric humans who evolved over time only to become extinct. Similar to the books of the *Chilam Balam*, the *Popol Vuh* mentions a great flood reminiscent to the destruction of Atlantis:

> Then the waters were agitated by the will of Hurakan, and a great inundation came upon the heads of these creatures…. They were engulfed, and a resinous thickness descended from the heaven;… the face of the Earth was obscured, and a heavy darkening rain commenced- rain by day and rain by night….There was heard a great noise above their heads, each other, filled with despair; they wished to climb upon their houses, and the houses, tumbling down, fell to the ground; they wished to climb upon the trees, and the trees shook

them off; they wished to enter into the caves, and the caves closed themselves before them....Water and fire contributed to the universal ruin at the time of the last great cataclysm which preceded the fourth creation.[10]

Stories of destruction continue in the two existing Mayan codices: the *Codex Troano* and the *Codex Cortesianus*, also known as the Madrid Codex (or *Codex Tro-Cortesianus*). Insight into the codices may provide some accounts explaining what happened to Lemuria (known as Mu in the ancient world). The following translations are by no means accurate, but different translations of the same passages contain similar messages. The *Codex Cortesianus* include the following passages which were translated in James Churchward's *The Lost Continent of Mu* (please refer to the footnotes for insight into the actual validity):

> By his strong arm Homen caused the earth to tremble after sunset and during the night Mu, the country of the hills of earth, was submerged.
> Mu, the life of the basin (seas), was submerged by Homen during the night.
> The place of the dead ruler is now lifeless, it moves no more, after having twice jumped from its foundations: the king of the deep, while forcing his way out, has shaken it up and down, has killed it, has submerged it. Twice Mu jumped from her foundations; it was then sacrificed by fire. It burst while being shaken up and down violently by earthquakes. By kicking it, the wizard that makes all things move like a mass of worms, sacrificed it that very night.[11]

A second passage found in the other surviving part of the Madrid codex (specifically the *Codex Troano*) details the destruction of the continent of Lemuria. The following excerpt is tak-

en from the Mayan researcher Augustus Le Plongeon's book
Queen Moo and the Egyptian Sphinx:

> In the year six Kan, on the eleventh Muluc, in the
> month Zac, there occurred terrible earthquakes, which
> continued without intermission until the thirteenth
> Chuen. The country of the hills of mud, the *'Land of
> Mu,'* was sacrificed. Being twice upheaved, it suddenly
> disappeared during the night, the basin being continual-
> ly shaken by volcanic forces. Being confined, these
> caused the land to sink and rise several times and in
> various places. At last the surface gave way, and the ten
> countries were torn asunder and scattered in fragments;
> unable to withstand the force of the seismic convul-
> sions, they sank with sixty-four millions of inhabitants,
> eight thousand and sixty years before the writing of this
> book.[12]

Some of the earliest translations of ancient Mayan and Aztec
writings were completed by ethnologist Abbé Brasseur de
Bourbourg. His early writings inspired Augustus Le Plongeon's translations. It was de Bourbourg's contributions to the
study of Mayan writings that made the later decipherment
possible. Ultimately, his personal beliefs and research on Atlantis stigmatized him as a pseudo-scientist. In one of de
Bourbourg's translations of the Aztec *Codex Chimalpopoca*, a
similar tale of a cataclysm emerges (comparable to Plato's description of Atlantis's demise):

> This is the sun called *Nahui-atl*, '4 water.' Now the wa-
> ter was tranquil for forty years, plus twelve, and men
> lived for the third and fourth times. When the sun *Na-
> hui-atl* came there had passed away four hundred years,
> plus two ages, plus seventy-six years. Then all mankind
> was lost and drowned, and found themselves changed

into fish. The sky came nearer the water. In a single day all was lost, and the day *Nahui-xochitl*, '4 flower,' destroyed all our flesh.

And that year was that of *cé-calli*, '1 house,' and the day *Nahui-atl* all was lost. Even the mountains *sunk into the water*, and the water remained tranquil for fifty-two springs.[13]

Various mythological accounts pertaining to the destruction of Lemuria exist throughout the Americas as well as Micronesia. Many islanders claim that their homelands were destroyed by explosions and tidal waves. On the island of Hawaii, the legend states that "our motherland rests... at the bottom of the Royal Ocean."[14] Hawaiian's regard the deity Pele with such great admiration and respect that she is known as the fire and lightning who fled from her homeland and came to Hawaii. Was she a survivor from Lemuria or Atlantis? Or maybe she was just a regular person? Clues perpetuate the idea of a great flood causing Pele to search for new land – in what is now known as Hawaii. Three times, the water level rose to the tops of mountains and then receded. This is reminiscent of the great flood myths that tie the destruction of Atlantis to the melting of ice in the Arctic region. These tales can also be found around North America in variations existing from tribe to tribe. Native American tales describe whole tribes being washed away by rising waters, while in other tales only one or two people survive the catastrophe. There are also tales of visionary prophets forewarning of the events to come, and in other symbolic tales animals took on actual roles during the great flood. In other myths, people survived in great canoes (similar to the tale of Gilgamesh). An example that illustrates a Native American flood myth is that of the Maidu Native Americans from the Sacramento Valley in Northern California:

Long, long ago the Indians living in Sacramento Valley were happy. Suddenly there came the swift sound of rushing waters, and the valley became like Big Waters, which no man can measure. The Indians fled, but many slept beneath the waves...Only two who fled into the foothills escaped. To these two, Great Man gave many children, and many tribes arose. But one great chief ruled all the nation. The chief went out upon a wide knoll overlooking Big Waters, and he knew that the plains of his people were beneath the waves. Nine sleeps he lay without food, and his mind was thinking always of one thing: How did this deep water cover the plains of the world?

At the end of nine sleeps he was changed. He was not like himself. No arrow could wound him. He was like Great Man for no Indian could slay him. Then he spoke to Great Man and commanded him to banish the waters from the plains of his ancestors. Great Man tore a hole in the mountain side, so that the waters on the plains flowed into Big Waters. Thus the Sacramento River was formed.[15]

And in South America, the Inka describe a similar event to the North American Native Americans:

In 'Ancient times,' when 'very early people' lived, the world wanted to come to an end. A young llama was sad and would not eat because it knew that the ocean was about [to] flood the earth. The herder did not understand this llama buck and threw a maize cob at the animal. The llama said that in five days, the ocean would overflow and the whole world would come to an end. The llama said to go to the mountain Villcacoto and to take food for five days. On their arrival, all varieties of animals were already amassed on the moun-

tain. The llama and the herder huddled together and escaped the flood. The floodwaters covered all of the land
with only the peak of Villcacoto remaining dry...After
five days, the waters receded and the ocean retreated all
the way down again, exterminating all the people. Afterward, the one remaining herder began to multiply
again.[16]

The destruction attributed to the ancient civilizations of
Lemuria and Atlantis may be also found in the mythology of
the Hopi, who are located in northern Arizona, surrounded by
the Navajo (*Diné*) Reservation. The Hopi, in their cosmology,
revolve around the notion of different 'worlds' that once existed, similar to what is found among the Aztec and Maya. The
Hopi believe that prior to this world, they dwelled in what is
known as the Third World. Dan Katchongva, a Hopi *Sun Clan*
leader of Hotevilla, recalls the following regarding the Hopi's
emergence into the Fourth World:

> Somewhere down in the underworld we were created
> by the Great Spirit, the Creator. We were created first
> one, then two, then three. We were created equal, of
> oneness, living in a spiritual way, where the life is ever-
> lasting. We were happy and at peace with our fellow
> men. All things were plentiful, provided by our Mother
> Earth upon which we were placed. We did not need to
> plant or work to get food. Illness and troubles were un-
> known. For many years we lived happily and increased
> to great numbers.
> But eventually evil proved to be stronger. Some people
> forgot or ignored the Great Spirit's laws and became
> materialistic, inventing many things for their own gain,
> and not sharing things as they did in the past. This re-
> sulted in a great division, for some wanted to follow the
> original instructions and live simply.

The inventive ones, cleaver, but lacking wisdom, made
many destructive things by which their lives were dis-
rupted, and which threatened to destroy all the people.
Many of the things we see today were known to have
existed at that time.[17]

...Children were uncared for. Sorcerers directed their
energies into harming those they were jealous of or dis-
liked. The people became so enamored by their suc-
cesses and self-importance that many decided they had
created themselves.[18]

Finally, immorality flourished. The life of the people
became corrupted with a social and sexual license
which swiftly involved the leader's wife and daughters
who rarely came home to take care of their household
duties. Not only the leader, but also the high priests
having the same problems.[19]

"People had no respect for anything. Life had become *koyanis-
qatsi*- a world out of balance."[20] The legend continues on with
Maasaw, the Guardian of the Earth, whom the Hopi asked if
they could enter the Fourth World. Upon several requests,
Maasaw allowed a few to enter into the Fourth World, and so
the priests planted a tree that extended into the upper world in
which they would climb out of the Third World.

All this was kept secret from the corrupt majority of the
population. Only good-hearted people were informed of
the plans to leave. As soon as they knew the project was
successful, they began to climb up on the inside of the
reed, resting between the joints as they worked their
way up. The bamboo did not have sections in it during
their long climb skyward. Finally, the pointed end of
the bamboo pierced the sky and the people climbed

through the emergence hole, or *sipapuni*, into this, the Fourth World.[21]

Further investigation into the Hopi myth reveals a description of what might have happened. Frank Waters, in 1968, wrote *Book of the Hopi* with Oswald 'White Bear' Fredericks. In his book, Waters describes the people growing corrupt and becoming consumed with greed, resulting in several wars. There were many large cities, nations, and civilizations in existence at the time as the people created *patuwvotas* (flying shields) in which destroyed each other's cities. In the end, the great lands were destroyed by a vast flood, not by rain, but from within the earth itself.[22] [23]

> "See," said Sotuknang, "I have washed away even the footprints of your Emergence; the stepping-stones which I left for you. Down on the bottom of the seas lie all the proud cities, the flying *patuwvotas*, and the worldly treasures corrupted with evil, and those people who found no time to sing praises to the Creator from the tops of their hills. But the day will come, if you preserve the memory and meaning of your Emergence, when these stepping-stones will emerge again to prove the truth you speak."[24]

Although most stories about the great flood have commonalities in them, the Hopi state that after the great flood took place, another group of people emerged from the Third World: the *Pahana* (also spelled *Bahana*) meaning Elder White Brother. The Hopi were given a sacred tablet inscribed with Maasaw's "road plan of life" by Old Spiderwoman, who then broke it in half and gave it to the Hopi and *Pahana*. The *Pahana* departed to the land of the East vowing to one day return after the time of *koyaanisqatsi*. It is said that during *koyaanisqatsi*, a great day of purification will overcome all the people of the land and those who are as righteous as the Hopi will survive. This era is prophesized by many different groups throughout the Americas, including the tales involving "white-skinned gods," who shared their wisdom and vowed to return one day.[25]

Ancient Mystics

There are several accounts regarding giants mentioned by Native American people. One ethnographical account states that before "ancient white people" arrived to this continent, there was already in existence a race of giants: "These giants were represented…as being very swarthy in complexion, and they used implements so large that no ordinary man could life them. It was an age when large animals roamed the earth, and it seems the birds and fowls were all very large in size." These giants were considered "cruel and wicked" and god became displeased with them and informed the "ancient white people" that they would become the new inhabitants of the world. The ancient giants were then destroyed and the "ancient white people" began to inhabit several regions of the continent. This is why these giants were known as *Pah-pel-ene* to the Yurok, which translates to 'the people who have passed away.' The Yurok ethnography mentions a few having found stone relics including huge stone bowls, and slabs used by these giants of which nobody could move. As time passed, these large artifacts sank into the ground, forever sealing their secrets from the world.[26]

There are in existence a few known examples of 'white people' visiting the Americas prior to European contact. They are usually described as tall, intelligent, and white in skin color. The most well-known of these stories is that of Quetzalcoatl, a Toltec king portrayed as a plumed serpent, well-known in Toltec, Mayan, and Aztec mythology. Worshiped as a god, Quetzalcoatl is said to have been very wise in the mystical arts and was associated with learning and knowledge within sacred priesthood traditions. Quetzalcoatl was revered as a mystic who helped jump start agriculture, science, and the arts. He was, by Mesoamerican means, the closest thing to god. There are many versions of the myth, many of which entangle various other gods into a dramatic story. Quetzalcoatl was often described by the Aztecs as a bearded white male who relinquished materialistic things in order to become an enlightened being. He is said to have departed into the sea toward the direction of the rising sun from which he originally came, vowing to one day return. Similar stories exist in various Native American communities. Other Mayan groups know the same description as *Kulkulkan* or *Voltan*, while the Chibchas from Colombia know this deity as *Bochica,* and as Viracocha by the Inka.

In Inka mythology, Viracocha rose from the depths of Lake Titicaca and brought forth light into this world. He was the creator of giants, who according to legend did not meet Viracocha's expectations. As a result, he flooded the world and destroyed these ancient giants.[27] Viracocha then created a new race of man, causing civilization to spring into existence. Viracocha, disguised as a poor man, traveled around as a mystic healer spreading wisdom wherever he went.[28] Once this was completed, Viracocha departed to the west across the Pacific Ocean vowing one day to return. An early Spanish historian described Viracocha as "a man of medium height, white, and dressed in a white robe like an alb secured round the waist, and that he carried a staff and a book in his hands."[29] Another Spanish historian and conquistador in Peru states that "this Inca was called Viracocha because he came from other parts and brought with him a different dress, and that in his features and aspect he appeared like a Spaniard, because he had a beard."[30] Various writings mention that perhaps these exceptional individuals were not alone, that in fact they were the leaders of tribes or groups of white people.[31] Though the authenticity regarding some of these accounts may be speculative, they match up with independent ethnographical accounts.

Amazing Legends of the Mysterious Ancients

Investigations into Native American accounts regarding a race of giants living in the Americas can also be found through various sources. Author Ross Hamilton's research has produced several Native American accounts portraying an ancient "white," tall, and "intellectually sophisticated" race of people who existed prior and during the Native Americans. Hamilton believes that a massive cover-up by the Smithsonian Institute occurred under the security of government officials. Hamilton reports on several people uncovering the remains of "giant" humans (up to eight feet tall) which were later confiscated. An interesting account of these beings comes from the collection of James Mooney (1861-1921) who states the following:

> James Wafford, of the western Cherokee, who was born in Georgia in 1806, says that his grandmother, who must have been born about the middle of the last century, told him that she had heard from the old people that long before her time a party of giants had once come to visit the Cherokee. They were nearly twice as tall as common men, and had their eyes set slanting in their heads, so that the Cherokee called them *Tsunil' kalu'*, "the Slant-eyed people," because they looked like the giant hunter *Tsul' kalu'*. They said that these giants lived far away in the direction in which the sun goes down. The Cherokee received them as friends, and they stayed some time, and then returned to their home in the west...[32]

Hamilton gives mention to the possibility of two races of giants who once existed in the United States (through the discovery of ethnographical statements that were largely ignored by the government upon the desecration of burial remains). Oral traditions state that one of the giant races occupied a majority of territories until another race of giants violently overtook their land:

> In this connection I would say that Mr. Jonathan Brooks, now living in town, stated to me, that his father, Benjamin Brooks, who lived with the Indians fourteen years, and was well-acquainted with their language and traditions, told him and others that it was a tradition of the Indians that the first tribe occupying this whole country, was a black-bearded race, very large in size, and subsequently a red bearded race or tribe came and killed or drove off all the black beards, as they called them.[33]

The Native American historical and oral research presented has been only one aspect of the findings. The topic of the physical remains themselves is controversial within the Native American community today, as will later be discussed in depth. One of the most valuable bio-ethnographies ever written is that of Native American Lucy Thompson. Her book, entitled *To the American Indian: Reminiscences of a Yurok Woman*, was published in 1916 because she felt that the true stories of her people were not being recorded by anthropologists. The Yurok community at that time was headed for cultural destruction and she took it upon herself to tell her side of the story. Thompson was born of noble blood among her people, and was initiated into a secret society within the community (which very much was based on a Priest and Priestess system). The Yurok are located in North California, almost 90 miles east of Mount Shasta on the banks of the Klamath River. Ancient stories of

One of the last initiates of the Talth tradition;
Che-na-way Weitch-ah-wah, Lucy Thompson
(U.S. Library of Congress, c. 1916)

white predecessors have long existed within the Yurok tribe, as well as surrounding tribes. Among the Yurok, these white people are known as *"Wo'ge"* (or *Wa-gas* according to Lucy Thompson); the Hupa know them as *"kixunai,"* and the Karok know them as the *"ikhareyev."* All of the tribes describe them as immortal inhabitants.[34]

Lucy Thompson explains that when Native Americans first arrived on the Klamath River, they found it already occupied by a mystical white race who occupied the entire continent. Moral and civilized, they shared with the Native Americans their arts and sciences and coexisted peacefully for several generations. There were intermarriages between the two races, and as Thompson explains, they were seen as non-promiscuous. During the time they occupied the land, there were no wars, no violence, and kindness and love exceeded everything. It is not known why the *Wa-gas* left, but it was a sad time for the Yurok: "They went toward the north from whence we came, and disappeared from our land beyond the northern seas." The *Wa-gas* left behind stone monuments on top of mountain peaks and in various locations throughout the land. Before the *Wa-gas* left, they assured the Yurok that they would one day return. According to some Yurok legends, they departed to *Cheek-cheek-alth*, the land of their birth in the far north: "All the half-castes with the exception of a few went away with the *Wa-gas*, and nearly all those that were three-quarters Indian remained with our people." It is said that when they return "peace and happiness will reign supreme again over this great land, and evil will be cast out." The exodus of the *Wa-gas* was said to take place before the great flood that ensued. Waiting for the *Wa-gas*, the Yurok encountered another white race coming to inhabit the land. They greeted them with open arms and praises until realizing that they were not the *Wa-gas*; they then drove them out of their homes, violated their women, took their lands, and gave whiskey to the men.[35] The term *Ken-e-ahs* (meaning literally "white people") was given to the white race instead of *Wa-gas,* meaning "ancient" or "holy ones." [36] Some of the amazing descriptions given by Thompson in her book can be verified today. The descriptions of the Klamath River and Redding Rock in ancient times are among the few verifiable clues into the accuracy of their oral traditions over time.

Other Yurok accounts state that when the Native Americans first arrived and settled on the Klamath River the *Wo'gey* "took refuge in trees, rocks, springs and other places." The Yurok also state that the *Wo'gey* did everything they could to help them, giving them medicine because it is said that they felt pity on the humans because they themselves were "immortal."[37] The Yurok attempted to live in peace and harmony as the *Wo'gey* did. Knowing that there would always be a struggle to keep the world in harmony, the *Wo'gey* taught the Yurok what to do to help keep the world in balance through the use of dances and prayers.[38] The high priest (or medicine man) quoted the *Wo'gey* as saying "we and the world, well, we pretty much support each other."[39] The following is what the *Wo'gey* instructed the Yurok on how to contact them:

> If a person wants to tell me something, let him come up (into the hills) and stay all night. Let him take tobacco with him and angelica root, only those two. And he must be careful of himself before he does that: he must get sweathouse wood, and drink no water, and go with no women. Then I shall answer him; and if I answer him he will have what he tells me that he wants. And he may not eat in the house with others. He will have to eat his food (separately) for ten days. [40]

It is also said that the *Wo'gey* cried, according to the Yurok, because they were leaving this world; in other words, the *Wo' gey* will no longer be in physical form on the earth and will transcend into another plane of existence.[41] They asked that people remember them and feel profound sentiments when they are remembered.[42]

    If history serves us as a guide, we should one day look forward for the arrival of these people. It poses many questions which persist in every culture across the Americas: are they still alive, or are they hiding? Perhaps hidden within prophecy lay an allegorical sequence of events that are to teach us valuable lessons about the course we are heading towards as a society. We each must learn what we can from these stories and hopefully think critically and reflect upon their meanings. Our decisions today shape our future; these tales of ancient mystical lands and people are in turn lessons for each of us to carry as they have been passed down through the generations.

---

[1] Thompson, David S. *The Sapir-Whorf Hypothesis: Worlds Shaped by Words*

[2] Ibid.

[3] Ibid.

[4] Berliz, Charles *Atlantis: The Eighth Continent*, p. 62; Found in various translations of the Popol Vuh.

[5] Anaya, Rudolfo and Lomelí, Francisco A. *Aztlán: Essays on the Chicano Homeland*, pp. 22-3

[6] Thompson, Lucy *To the American Indian: Reminiscences of a Yurok Woman*, p. 76

[7] Berliz, Charles *Atlantis: The Eighth Continent*, p. 108

[8] Hall, Manly P. *Secret teaching of All Ages*

[9] Berliz, Charles *Atlantis: The Eighth Continent*, pp. 184-5

[10] Ibid., p. 185

[11] Churchward, James *The Lost Continent of Mu*, pp. 78-9; It is clear that Colonel James Churchward obtained the translations from Augustus Le Plongeon.

---

[12] Le Plongeon, Augustus *Maya/Atlantis: Queen Moo and the Egyptian Sphinx*, p. 147; According to Lewis Spence, Augustus Le Plongeon's translations "were of the most fantastic description and manifestly imaginary" (Spence, Lewis *The Problem of Lemuria*, pp. 92-3). The authenticity of the previous "translations" by LePongeon (and later borrowed by Churchward) may be more speculative than actual fact.

[13] Donnelly, Ignatius *Atlantis: The Antediluvian World*, p. 100

[14] Berliz, Charles *Atlantis: The Eighth Continent*, p. 71

[15] Judson, Katharine Berry *Myths and Legends of California and the Old Southwest*, p. 70

[16] Steele, Paul Richard and Allen, Catherine J. *Handbook of Inca Mythology*, pp. 69-70

[17] Katchongva, Dan *Hopi: A Message for All People*

[18] Peterson, Scott *Native American Prophecies*, p. 159

[19] Katchongva, Dan *Hopi: A Message for All People*

[20] Peterson, Scott *Native American Prophecies*, p. 160

[21] Ibid., p. 161

[22] Berliz, Charles *Atlantis: The Eighth Continent*, p. 196

[23] Williams, Mark R. *In Search of Lemuria*, p. 221

[24] Wilson, Terry P. *Hopi: following the path of peace*, p. 57

[25] Peterson, Scott *Native American Prophecies*, pp. 162-3

[26] Thompson, Lucy *To the American Indian: Reminiscences of a Yurok Woman*, pp. 83-4

[27] Steele, Paul Richard and Allen, Catherine J. *Handbook of Inca Mythology*, p. 53

[28] The mythological accounts themselves, regarding Viracocha, change slightly through various indigenous narratives. In the *The Huarochirí manuscript* (Salomon, F., Urioste, J.and de Ávila, F. *The Huarochirí manuscript: a testament of ancient and Colonial Andean religion*, p. 46), Viracocha travelled as a poor beggar later establishing villages, creating complex masonry, and irrigation canals. And in some versions Viracocha emerged from Lake Titicaca, while in others Viracocha came from the western shores of the Pacific Ocean.

[29] De Gamboa, Pedro Sarmiento *History of the Incas*, p. 35

[30] de León, Pedro de Cieza *The second part of the Chronicle of Peru* (Hakluyt Society/ Sir Clements Robert Markham Translations), pp. 120-1

[31] Wilkins, Harold T. *Mysteries of Ancient South America* pp.102-103; two mentions are made by Wilkins regarding mythological stories regarding Quetzalcoatl and a preexisting white race. Though I have not been able to find Wilkins original source, I found it also in Churchward's *The Lost Continent of Mu*, though he is not mentioned in Wilkins bibliography.

In Guatemalan mythology recorded during the Spanish Conquest, according to Wilkins and Churchward, "When King Quetzalcoatl, of the very white race, was conquered by an invading race with dark skins, he refused to surrender. He said he could not live as a captive, not submit to savagery. So, with as many of his white people as could crowd into his ships, he sailed to a far distant country towards the rising sun. He reached it, and with his people, settled down there. They prospered and became a great race. During the great battle (in old Central America) many escaped into the forests and were never again heard of; but the rest were taken prisoners, and enslaved by the dark-skinned men." And in Aztec tradition: "in a time to come, this white people shall return and again master this land (of Central America and old Mexico)."

[32] Mooney, James *Myths of the Cherokee and Sacred Formulas of the Cherokees*, p. 391

[33] Crane, WM. H. *Memoirs of Townships.-Vermillion* The Fire-Lands Pioneer Volumes I & II, Firelands Historical Society. November 1858, pp. 38-9

[34] Heizer, R.F. and Whipple, M.A. *The California Indians*, p. 479

[35] Thompson, Lucy *To the American Indian: Reminiscences of a Yurok Woman*, pp. 81-7

[36] Buckley, Thomas *Standing Ground: Yurok Indian Spirituality, 1850-1990*, p. 282

[37] Keeling, Richard *Cry for Luck: Sacred Song and Speech Among the Yurok, Hupa, and Karok Indians of Northwestern California*, p.57

[38] Buckley, Thomas *Standing Ground: Yurok Indian Spirituality, 1850-1990*, pp. 214-5

[39] Ibid., p.217

[40] Kroeber, A.L. *Yurok Myths* (1976), p. 291

[41] Ibid., p. 310

[42] Keeling, Richard *Cry for Luck: Sacred Song and Speech Among the Yurok, Hupa, and Karok Indians of Northwestern California*, p. 298

Chapter Six
Early Explorers

Before Columbus

THERE are many stories regarding the first people to make contact between the Old World and the New World. New claims have been made within the last half century, but many are based on unfounded speculations and half-truths used to support absurd theories.

Archaeological evidence indicates that the Norse arrived in North America in what is modern day Newfoundland; however, they retreated because of conflict with the indigenous people. The Viking colony was short lived and evidence indicates their presence reaching as far south as Maine. There have been attempts to prove their presence in other regions in America such as The Newport Tower in Rhode Island and The Kensington Runestone in Minnesota; however, all have been proven false.

Many speculate that ancient druids or Irish monks settled in Salem, New Hampshire, and Gungywamp in Connecticut. Archaeological evidence indicates that they were not made by pre-Columbian settlers, but by colonist settlers. Some theories involve Africans being among the first visitors in the Americas, based on the presence of so-called black Indians, pre-Columbian skeletons with negroid features, and the infamous Olmec heads. This theory has also been proved false by many archaeologists. Others propose that the Chinese discovered the New World in 1421. While capable, no archaeological evidence has been found to indicate their presence in the Americas. Prior to the Knight Templar persecution in 1307, it is documented that they possessed a large fleet of ships that mysteriously vanished during the initial disbandment on Friday the 13th in 1307. Several sources claim that the Knight Templar made it to the Americas. However, the archaeological record shows no evidence to support that the Knight Templars ever made it to the Americas.

The Journey into a New World

In 1492, Spain managed to end the long reconquest (or reconquista) and drove out the last Muslim ruler from Granada, in southern Spain. Since the early eighth century, southern Islamic (or Moor) influence dominated the outer reaches of the Iberian Peninsula of the southern European kingdom. In 1238, the Spanish drove out most of the occupying Moors, but it was not until January, 1492, that they expelled the last remaining Muslims. After their successful campaign, Ferdinand II of Aragón and Isabella I of Castile decided to outflank the Portuguese, who were expanding toward the Indies in hopes of establishing secure trade routes. The idea of Portuguese procurement of Eastern riches seems to be the prime motive of Ferdinand and Isabella's funding of Italian navigator Christopher Columbus.[1] A few months after the victory of Granada, Christopher Columbus set sail on August 3, 1492. On October 12, contact was made between the Old World and New World. The island they landed on was named San Salvador, and according to the log of Christopher Columbus, the natives were friendly "well-built people, with handsome bodies and very fine faces...and their skin is the color of Canary Islanders or of sunburned persons... [and] tall."[2] Columbus noticed scaring on some of their bodies and the explanation conveyed to him was that tribes from neighboring islands were trying to capture them. And more importantly, it became evident to Columbus "that people from the mainland come here to take them as slaves."[3]

According to Christopher Columbus' son Fernando, Columbus was "exceptionally interested in reports of sunken lands under the ocean."[4] Columbus researched as much as he could about the uncharted ocean he was about to venture on. It had also been advised that he might be able to visit some of the islands that survived the sinking of Atlantis.[5] "When Columbus sailed to discover the new world, or to rediscover an old one, he took his departure from a Phoenician seaport, founded by that great race...This Atlantean sailor, with his Phoenician features, sailing from an Atlantean port, simply reopened the path of commerce and colonization which had been closed when Plato's island sank into the sea."[6] Ultimately, Christopher Columbus died believing that he had truly reached the east.

Stories began to spread among the first Spanish colonizers. Explanations for the existence of indigenous people revolved around religious doctrine by making historical connections through the Holy Bible. They thought that these people must be ancestors of the mysterious Ten Lost Tribes of Israel, as mentioned in the Holy Scripture. Their reasoning later revolved around the lost land of Atlantis as an explanation for their existence. The indigenous people viewed the Spaniards as the gods who had once brought peace and balance to the land, now returning from the lost land to the east in order to declare their due inheritance.

Expeditions were held into the unknown world in what is now Florida. Hearing legends from the natives, Juan Ponce de León, in 1513, headed to Florida in search of the fabled

'Fountain of Youth.' The next expedition was that of Francisco Hernandez Cordova, who sailed with 110 men from Cuba to the coast of the Yucatan. Shortly thereafter, they were attacked and driven further up the coast. Some of the sailors left the ships to refill the water and were approached by about fifty Mayans. According to Bernal Diaz del Castillo, "they then made signs with their hands to find out whether we came from the direction of the sunrise" to which they replied: "yes." [7] In another instance, they were asked the same question by a group of natives, which puzzled the Spaniards. They were then attacked by the same indigenous tribe, resulting in the loss of forty-eight men, causing them to sail back to Cuba. A year later, Captain Juan de Grijalva returned to the same location to avenge the attack. Following a battle, they continued on their expedition, only to be attacked and driven to retreat back to Cuba. By this time, word had spread of the mysterious people who came from the direction of the rising sun. One person who listened carefully to the descriptions of these men and urged it to remain a secret was the Aztec emperor Moctezuma. [8]

In 1519, Hernán Cortés and 508 soldiers acted against the royal crown by sailing toward the Yucatan Peninsula. On a nearby island, they met a Franciscan friar named Gerónimo de Aguilar. Friar Aguilar had been shipwrecked there eight years prior, along with other survivors. According to Cortés, Aguilar "learnt that the others who were shipwrecked with him were scattered throughout the land…and it would be impossible to rescue them without spending much time there." [9] He was captured along with another survivor, named Gonzalo Guerrero, by the Mayans in order to be sacrificed. They escaped and were later recaptured by another Mayan tribe. Friar Aguilar states that Gonzalo Guerrero became a well-known and high ranking Mayan warrior (who later fought against the Spanish), and after marrying, had the first Mestizo children. During this time, Friar Aguilar learned the Chontal Mayan language, which played a vital role for Cortés. In April of 1519, another transla-

tor emerged, named Doña Marina (otherwise known as La Ma-
linche), she spoke Chontal Mayan, and Nahuatl, the language
of the Aztecs. A translation for Cortés was made by Friar
Aguilar and then by Doña Marina.

This was during the Aztec year of One Reed, the prophetic year that Quetzalcoatl was prophesized to return. Montezuma sent gifts to Cortés, hoping he would return from where
he came; however, as more gold was offered, Cortés became
more enticed. Along their journey, Cortés and his army came
across many followers who were oppressed by the Aztecs. As
Cortés advanced, Montezuma became fearful and contemplated
a new plan of action. Cortés and his army were attacked by the
Tlaxcalans, who the Spaniards completely defeated - something the Aztecs never accomplished. As they traveled to Tenochtitlan - the heart of the Aztec empire - they became impressed with the surrounding feats of achievement. In November, 1519, they reached Tenochtitlan with a massive army
alongside indigenous warriors; they were escorted into the
middle of Tenochtitlan. Built in the middle of a lake, Tenochtitlan featured causeways extending from the shore and into the
city itself. Larger than any other city in the world at that time,
Tenochtitlan had homes equipped with private bathrooms, public bathrooms on the streets, and sophisticated garbage removal
systems.

Cortés held Montezuma hostage as they remained inside Tenochtitlan. In April, 1520, word reached Cortés that
more Spaniards had arrived on the coast to arrest him, under
the order of Pánfilo de Narváez. Cortés, along with some of
his men, left to fight Narváez and succeeded. During Cortés'
departure, there was an Aztec festival at the main temple. Under the command of Pedro de Alvarado, a massacre escalated
into a large revolt by the Aztecs. Upon returning to Tenochtitlan, Cortés decided to cut off the main causeways to the city,
completely isolating the city, which signaled the end of the
great Aztec empire.

After the fall of the Aztec empire, the Aztec and Mayans became deculturalized. Catholic missions where built around Mexico for the purpose of converting the Mayan and Aztec 'savages' into Christians. Many indigenous people replaced their old gods with the symbolism of the new Catholic Saints. Many people faced punished if caught deifying their old gods in secret. In some cases, missionaries would discover miniature ancient pagan statues hidden behind Saints, which to the people conveyed the same meaning. This was also evident in the accounts of Juan Diego in 1531, who claimed that he was visited by the Virgin Mary. The parallels between the Aztec goddess and the Virgin Mary caused the indigenous population to convert to Catholicism. The Virgin's holy image was portrayed with brown skin. A message of masticate - the mixing of indigenous and European - was ensured among the people, creating a sense of dignity tied to who they were and for the new race that was coming into being. This, however, did not prevent the further destruction of Mayan and Aztec culture. The most famous incident was in 1562 when Diego de Landa ordered the burning of Mayan codices and anything else considered pagan. Similar to the fire that torched the Library of Alexandria by invaders, the Spanish decimated the culture of the Aztec and Maya. Only four codices exist today, located in European libraries. All records of their history and those concerning the ancients and the lands of Lemuria and Atlantis were lost forever.

In Spain and Portugal, tales spread of other empires and civilizations embarking many on the conquest for gold (which later became the inspiration for Colonel P. H. Fawcett).[10] Stories of secret cities existing deep in jungles and cities of gold and mysterious tales of "white Indians" living in remote regions of the Americas became widespread. The story of Aztlán fueled their imaginations: a Garden of Eden existing in the Americas begged to be searched for in a vast and unknown foreign land. The stories of "white Indians" existed through various accounts; the most interesting was that of the natives in Panama. Written accounts of the indigenous tribes with "white Indians" in Panama date as far back as 1679.[11] It was there in Panama that one of the greatest expeditions started in 1524 toward the undiscovered lands to the south.

Conquest of the Inka, the Children of the Sun

As time progressed early Spanish explorers searched for better trade routes. In the 1520's, Ferdinand Magellan, a Portuguese born navigator, set out on a voyage around the world. He sailed along the coasts of South America, through narrow straits, and across the Pacific Ocean. During this voyage, many sailors claimed to have encountered giants in the area of Patagonia. Their descriptions of these alleged giants were exaggerated, claiming that they stood double the height of the average European. "The man of the ship, led this giant to a small island where the captain awaited him. And where he was before us, he began to marvel and to be afraid, and he raised one finger upward, believing that we came from heaven. And he was so tall that the tallest of us only came up to his waist."[12] While the true meaning of the name Patagonia, or Patagão, itself is unclear, many believe it refers to the root word *pata,* meaning foot: "Land of the Big Feet." Other sailors, including Sir Francis Drake, spoke of the now extinct tribe of indigenous giants (believed to be of the Tehuelche tribe). Examinations revealed that the tallest natives were only about five feet and ten inches, as opposed to twelve feet, as claimed by earlier voyages.[13]

The first Spanish explorer to sail to the continent of South America was Pascual de Andagoya in 1522. Andagoya reported back stories of a wealthy land full of gold called "Birú," the later derivative being Perú, which would later form the foundation for the legends of El Dorado. The actual story of El Dorado was recorded by Gonzalo Fernández de Oviedo y

Valdés (1478-1557), who heard stories from the Muisca natives in Columbia about a chief who Oviedo referred to as "El Dorado."[14]

> The great lord...goes about continually covered in gold dust as fine as ground salt. He feels that it would be less beautiful to wear any other ornament. It would be crude and common to put on armour plates of hammered or stamped gold, for other rich lords wear those when they wish. But to powder oneself with gold is something exotic, unusual, novel and more costly-for he washes away at night what he puts on each morning, so that it is discarded and lost, and he does this every night of the year. [15]

These stories caught the attention of Francisco Pizarro, an illiterate pig-farmer from Spain who sought wealth in the New World. In Panama, Pizarro drew a line in the sand and told his men: "Friend and Comrades! On that side are toil, hunger, nakedness, the drenching storm, desertion and death; on this side, ease and pleasure. There lies Peru with its riches; here, Panama, and its poverty. Choose each man, what best becomes a brave Castilian. For my part, I go to the south."[16] Following those words, Pizarro and his men set off to conquer the new land in the south.

At that time, a great civil war broke throughout the Inkan Empire in South America. Two sons, Atahualpa and Huáscar, fought over their rightful heir to the throne, following the death of Huayna Capac, the eleventh Sapa Inka ruler. Huayna Capac died from smallpox, which had already spread down from Mexico into South America. Pizarro, by this time had made several attempts to enter the great Inka Empire, but failed miserably; however, in 1532, Pizarro and his men succeeded and ventured into Peru. News of their arrival quickly spread and Atahualpa soon learned of the white bearded men who came. As their arrival continued, Atahualpa received nightly updates about these new visitors and where they were staying along the Inka trails. The indigenous people were ordered by Atahualpa to feed the visitors. It is here that they had the first taste of an unknown root that we now know as the potato.

The tales of Viracocha held value among indigenous people. Similar to the Aztec perception of Quetzalcoatl's return, the Inka embraced the return of the mythical bearded men. Atahualpa soon realized that these were not gods, but ordinary men who did not posses god-like qualities as mentioned in the Inka legends. In Cajamarca, a meeting was set up between Atahualpa and Pizarro's men, aided by their translator Felipillo. During the meeting between Atahualpa and Pizarro's men, the Spaniards insisted that they came in peace and wanted to serve Atahualpa. Atahualpa knew that they were being dishonest and he refused their gesture and demanded to meet with their leader, Pizarro himself.

In November of 1532, Pizarro's army was outnumbered by the thousands; he carefully placed men in specific locations around the place where Pizarro and Atahualpa were to meet. Nearly 7,000 men marched alongside Atahualpa into the center plaza in Cajamarca. In the plaza, Friar Vincente de Valverde approached Atahualpa and demanded him to convert to Catholicism. Friar Valverde then presented Atahualpa with the Holy Bible, following his claims that it spoke to him. Atahualpa took the Bible and examined its pages; unimpressed, he threw it to the ground. That act was the justification Pizarro needed to attack. The hidden Spanish soldiers emerged, fully clad in armor, armed with guns, cannons, and horses - which the Inka had never seen and were unprepared for. A brutal massacre resulted in the capture of Atahualpa, who bargained to fill a large room with gold and silver in exchange for his release. Then, as promised, gold and silver arrived from Cuzco (the heart of the Inkan Empire) and was melted down. On August

29th 1533, Atahualpa was killed, bringing an end to the Inka Empire.

Knowing that there was more gold to be found, the Spanish invaders moved southward to the mythical center of Tawantinsuyu (the Inka Empire), Cuzco. Many legends surround the creation of Cuzco, the most common being that of Manco Cápac, who rose from the depths of Lake Titicaca and traveled to Cuzco through underground caves, and established a new kingdom. During the rule of Manco Cápac, he abolished human sacrifice and put forth a code of ethics (similar to the tales of Quetzalcoatl and Viracocha). Cuzco was later ransacked and usurped by the invading Spaniards. Expeditions to find other cities of gold precipitated the search for El Dorado, as tales ran rampant several expeditions continued as far as the Amazon.

As the Spanish ventured into new territories, they came across new places and people. One account details the structures of Tiahuanaco. In Inca Garcilaso de la Vega's *Comentarios Reales de los Incas*, he asks the indigenous people if they had built it the structures; the Inka laughed and said that it was built thousands of years before their time. Similar to the ruined Sphinx in Egypt, the Inka did not know who built many of the structures in Peru and Bolivia. The natives stated that the structures were built by gods "who caused enormous rocks weighing hundreds of tones each, to fly into position across the mountain ranges, deep valleys, and rivers."[17]

In 1547, an expedition discovered an interesting group of natives known as the Chachapoyas, which means 'warriors in the clouds.' Early accounts describe them as having white skin. According to Pedro Cieza de León:

> They are the whitest and most handsome of all the people that I have seen in Indies, and their wives were so beautiful that because of their gentleness, many of them deserved to be the Incas' wives and to also be tak-

en to the Sun Temple...The women and their husbands always dressed in woolen clothes and in their heads they wear their llautos, which are a sign they wear to be known everywhere.[18]

Pedro Cieza de León provided additional accounts of white people. In both of his *Chronicles of Peru*, he describes a tribe that once inhabited an island on Lake Titicaca which was later decimated by the Inka. He heard from various indigenous sources that the 'white people' had originally come from the valley of Coquimbo (present day Elqui Valley, Chile):

> Before the Incas conquered the country, many of the Indians declare that there were two great lords in Col- loa, one called Sapani, the other Cari. They conquered many of the fortresses called *pucaras*. They say that one of these chiefs, Cari, entered the large island where it is swampy, in the Laguna de Titicaca, and found there a white people, who had beards. They fought with them in such a manner that all were killed.[19]

Pedro Cieza de León also discovered ruins at a location in Peru called Guamanga (now called Ayacucho). When he asked the indigenous who had built the sites, they responded "a bearded and white people like ourselves were the builders, who came to these parts many ages before the In[k]as began to reign, and formed a settlement here."[20]

As the Spanish ventured deep into the uncharted jungles of the Amazon, there were similar reports of tribes of white Indian women warriors who were described as being "very white and tall." The name 'Amazon' originates from these warrior women in South America, when a connection was made to that of the ancient Greek myths of Amazonian warriors:

>These women are very white and tall, and have hair
>very long and braided and wound about the head, and
>they are very robust and go about naked, [but] with
>their privy parts covered, and their bow and arrows in
>their hands, doing as much fighting as ten Indian men,
>and indeed there was one woman among those who
>shot an arrow a span deep into one of the brigantines,
>and others less deep, so that our brigantines looked like
>porcupines.[21]

Other tribes found had similar characteristics of being tall and
white. The Yurucares, meaning literally "white men," from
eastern Bolivia, the Yanomami of the Amazon were also described as "white," and the Wai-Wai of Guyana.[22] Early Jesuit
Missionaries venturing into the various reaches in South America through Brazil and Peru heard similar tales of "white-
bearded men" and some of the men in fact claim to have encountered these mysterious people. [23]

Sailors navigating the Pacific Ocean came upon tribes
of "white Indians." In 1576, the Spanish explorer Juan Fernandez sailed between Callao in Peru and Valparaiso in Chile.
During his journey, he unintentionally sailed off course into the
unexplored Pacific Ocean. Sailing past present day Easter Isl-
and, and discovered what he thought to be the coast of a previously unknown land. According to Fernandez, he saw "the
mouths of very large rivers…and people so white and so well
clad and in everything different from those of Chile and Peru."[24] He kept this discovery secret, but died before being able
to return.

In Peru, the Inka hid their most precious treasures in an
isolated city called *Paititi*. Massive amounts of gold, silver,
and gemstones were taken to *Paititi* to prevent the Spanish
from obtaining them. While tales of *Paititi* coincide with those
of El Dorado, it has never been found. Some legends claim
that Inkarrí, another mythical being thought to be Viracocha,

came to discover Cuzco and a group of natives known as the
Q'ero. After creating the Q'ero, Inkarrí retreated to the jungles
of Pantiacolla, founding the city of *Paititi*. Another legend
states that as the Spanish began to destroy the Inkan Empire, a
group of high ranking mystical priests and priestesses fled into
the mountains, maintaining their secret traditions and kept
them hidden from the world. According some accounts, the
Q'ero (who Inkarrí founded) are the last remaining descendants
of the secret Inka tradition spanning back to the original high
priests and priestesses from Cuzco. In the Sacred Valley of
Peru, it is also believed that a series of Mystery Schools (e.g.
Písac), similar to those found in Egypt, existed with limited
membership. The sacred knowledge of the Mystery Schools
may be related to the Lemurian and Atlantean culture; these
Mystery Schools found in the Andean Mountains and Egypt
are reminiscent of these ancient teachings. Investigations of
the Andean Inka and pre-Inkan masonry can be closely associated with that of Egypt, as will be mentioned in detail later.

North America

One of the earliest expeditions into the heart of North
America happened as an accident. Beginning in 1527, the
Narváez expedition intended explore the Gulf regions into
Florida; however, after a hurricane several storms ripped
through the Gulf of Mexico, the surviving members of the expedition were forced to land in Florida, near present day Tampa Bay. The 400 men who survived faced starvation, disease,
and possible attacks by natives. Having no other choice, they
resumed their expedition down into Mexico where they knew
there were other Spaniards. Only four men returned as the rest
were either killed or captured along the way. Among the four
survivors was the infamous Álvar Núñez Cabeza de Vaca, who
pretended to be a mystic healer in order to pass freely between
tribal territories. What made the group more unique was the

fact that they still had an African slave among them. Also, the indigenous population thought they were gods and referred to them as *children of the sun*. Later, Cabeza de Vaca converted to the native traditions and formed a large following of indigenous disciples (similar to Quetzalcoatl) until they reached Mexico City in late 1536, almost eight years later. His writings are considered among the most important accounts related to early Spanish exploration of the New World. Cabeza de Vaca also claimed to have heard stories about the infamous cities of gold, similar to the legend of Quivira and Cíbola, also known as the Seven Cities of Gold.

Concurrently, on the other side of the continent, the first Spaniards set foot in 1533 in what is present day California, fifty years before the British attempted to colonize Virginia.[25] The name California originates from a 1510 novel by Garci Rodríguez de Montalvo entitled *The Labors of the Very Brave Knight Esplandián*. In the novel, de Montalvo mentions an island named California, which is ruled over by the Amazonian Queen Califa. The island of California exists without men, but is rich with gold and other precious stones.[26] Two accounts by Christopher Columbus and Hernán Cortés mention places populated exclusively by women, explaining why the Spaniards who landed in Baja California made a connection between the novel and real life. Early Spanish maps depict California as an island; however, it was not until much later that they realized it was not an island at all. Though fueled by both Spanish and Native American myth and fantasy, it did not stop the Spanish from searching for the mythical lands, gold, and other riches. Even much later with tales of the Aztec homeland Aztlán, written about by Diego Durán who regarded it as the Garden of Eden, many of the Spanish explorations were focused around California during the following years. Various other expeditions ventured into the unknown regions of North America in search of wealth, such as the Coronado and De Soto expeditions.

After arriving in California in 1542, Juan Rodríguez Cabrillo began exploring the California coast. As Cabrillo entered the Channel Islands off the coast of southern California, he noticed something unique among the indigenous population living on the islands. Some Native Americans remained hostile and violent toward them, while other tribes embraced them, as if expecting their arrival. He describes the islands as being "densely peopled by a superior race," describing the children as being "white, with light hair and ruddy cheeks," and the women as having "fine forms, beautiful eyes, and a modest demeanor."[27] The Channel Islands continue to provide fertile research beneficial to analyzing the ancient coastal migration routes of Native Americans; however, retrieved artifacts point to a different perspective. Some believe that a colony of ancient "Caucasian" people once occupied the islands and engaged in racial mixing. If this can be proven, then their existence may point to the possibility of them being the last descendants of the ancients from Lemuria or Atlantis.

In a letter by Sebastián Vizcaíno to King Felipe III of Spain, he mentions his discovery of Monterey, California, and describes the indigenous people as having "strong bodies and white faces."[28] Vizcaíno also states that "they are very knowledgeable about silver and gold and said that these metals can be found in the interior."[29] There are also accounts of early Carmelites and Rosicrucian mystics being among the earliest of settlers in the Monterey region, more specifically in Carmel (between 1602 and 1603). If this is true, then secret traditions passed down from Atlantis and the Egyptian Mystery Schools - the Essenic traditions, and later European Rosicrucianism - may have helped establish a continuing secret movement in California. Thus, the secret Mystery School traditions from the Old World finally met with the New World teachings from Lemuria and Atlantis.[30]

In the southwest territories among the Zuni and Hopi, they anticipated the return of the White Brother. It was not until 1540 that Francisco Vasquez de Coronado, with an army of 336 soldiers and numerous Native Americans, ventured into Zuni territory in New Mexico. The Zuni allegedly knew of seven villages, which Coronado thought might be the fabled seven cities of gold. Coronado sent off a few men, among them Don Pedro de Tovar, in search of the gold. For the Hopi, the return of the white brother was supposed to take place in the year 1519, similar to the Aztec return of Quetzalcoatl. The Hopi encountered by Don Pedro de Tovar were frightened of the men, having heard stories of men who captured the Zuni, traveled on animals, and ate people.[31] Following a brief encounter, Don Pedro de Tovar was taken to Oraibi, a nearby Hopi village, followed by a gathering of all the clan leaders. Four lines of sacred corn were laid on the floor, and then the leader of the Bear Clan came forward putting out his hand palm facing up to Tovar. "The Hopis knew that if the Spaniard was their true White Brother, he would hold out his own hand, palm up, and clasp the elder's hand to form the *nakwach*, the ancient symbol of brotherhood."[32] Tovar assumed it was a gesture for them to offer something; the Hopi were shocked, wondering if the *Pahana* had forgotten the ancient pact. "It was understood that when the two were finally reconciled, each would correct the other's laws and faults; they would live side by side and share in common all the riches of the land and join their faiths in one religion that would establish the truth of life in a spirit of universal brotherhood. The Spaniards did not understand, and having found no gold, they soon departed." [33] As time passed, many Spaniards arrived, instilling an everlasting impression on the Hopi. The elders grew older and realized that they would not see the true *Pahana* in their life time. It was understood that when they returned there would be only peace forever:[34]

> So if he ever did come they must be sure to ask him
> about his books, which they thought would contain his

secrets, and it was said that the book of truth would not be on top, but at the very bottom, after all the other books. If he asked the Hopi for the privilege of teaching them his language and taught them how to write, they must be sure to ask that they would like to be taught in the book of truth, because if he was a true Bahana he would quickly consent to teach them of this book. For their belief is, that if he is not the one they are looking for he will refuse to teach them his religion. Now if they learned his religion they would compare it with their religion and ceremonies, and if these were alike they would know that the Bahana had been with them in the beginning.[35]

In 1762, mega-fauna remains thought to date back to the late-Pleistocene epoch were discovered in Big Bone Lick, Kentucky. Two samples of wood contained within the fossil deposits dated to modern times, suggesting that these large mega-fauna existed up until fairly recently.[36] [37] However, it was not the mega-fauna that caught historians' eyes, but instead the fossilized human remains located alongside the animals:

In 1762 John Bartram, the Philadelphia Quaker who supplied Linnaeus and other European naturalists with descriptions and specimens of American plants and animals, heard that a large tooth and a fragment of a tusk had been brought to Fort Pitt by some Indians. He requested his friend James Wright to make inquiries among the Indians concerning the place where these objects had been found. Though an interpreter, Wright secured an account of the site which came to be known as Big Bone Lick. According to Wright's informants, the lick contained five entire skeletons, the heads pointing toward a common center. The bones were of enormous size and were accompanied by tusks ten or twelve feet long. No such creatures as these had ever been seen alive by the Indians, but legend said that they had once been hunted though the forests by men of gigantic stature and that when the last of these men had died, God had destroyed their mighty prey in order to protect the present race of Indians. [38]

A notable case is that of Llewellyn Harris, a Mormon Missionary of Welsh descent who had visited the Zuni tribe in January of 1878. Harris concluded that several Welsh words were similar to that of the Zuni and held the same meaning. The Zuni, according to Harris, claimed that they had occupied a region in Mexico preceding the conquest of the Spanish. The Zuni later fled to present day Arizona, near the Diné (Navajo) tribe. Harris also states that many of them claim to be descended from the Aztec ruler Montezuma. The Zuni provided Harris with insight into secret traditions that intrigued Harris:

> Before the conquest of Mexico by the Spaniards, some white men landed in Mexico and told the Indians that they had come from the regions beyond the sea to the east. They say that these white men [be]came the ancient kings of Mexico, from whom Montezuma descended. These white men were known to the Indians of Mexico by the name of *Cambaraga*; and are still remembered so in the traditions of the Zuni Indians. In time those white people became mixed with Indians, until scarcely a relic of them remained.[39]

It was known that many tribes in North America awaited the arrival of the ancient white people. The Yurok in California believed the arrival of the white settlers to be the long awaited return of the ancient white peoples. The Yurok, along with many other tribes, rejoiced upon the white peoples' arrival, believing them to be the *Wa-gas* returning. "But soon the sad mistake was discovered, to our sorrow, when the men began to debauch our women, give whiskey to our men, and claim our land that our forefathers had inhabited for so many thousands of years… We no longer termed them as *Wa-gas*, but as *Ken-e-ahs*, which means foreigners, who had no right to the land and could never appreciate our kindness, for they were a very different people from the *Wa-gas*. They had corrupt morals that brought dissolution upon our people and wrought the horrors of untold havoc."[40] Many of the tribes who looked forward to a time of peace were greeted with just the opposite: their own destruction. Some of the tribes were incorporated into Missions, others died from smallpox and other diseases, and others became isolated on reservations. Genocide has taken place since the arrival of the Europeans, enough to cause indigenous cultures throughout the Americas to become extinct. Today, the passing of an elder within a tribe often means that nobody is left to maintain the language or learn the old sacred practices. The Yurok's ancient order of Talth, consisting of an American Mystery tradition of high priests and priestesses, no longer exists. The last of the initiated Talth, Lucy Thompson (*Che-Na-Wah Weitch-Ah-Wah*) presumably, passed away in 1932, bringing an end to the ancient secrets passed down for countless generations. The secrets of the ancients rest among ruins on the Yurok Reservation in Northern California, forgotten with the passing of time.

The Pacific Ocean Cultures and Polynesia

Further investigations into accounts around the Pacific Ocean reveal encounters with other 'white' tribes. These accounts can be found near Polynesia, including the early discovery of Easter Island. New Zealand ethnologist Percy S. Smith states the following, regarding the Maori who are indigenous to New Zealand:

All through the race, everywhere me meet with it, we find a strain of light-coloured people who are not Albinos but have quite light hair and fair complexions. With the Maoris this strain often runs in families for many generations; at other times it appears as a probable reversion to the original type from which this strain was derived. There are also traditions amongst the Maori of a race of 'gods' called Pakahakeha, who are said always to live in the sea, and are white in complexion-hence the name Pakeha they gave to the white man on first becoming acquainted with us in the eighteenth century.[41]

Legends of blond or red haired people exist throughout much of Polynesia and Micronesia. On the Gilbert Islands, blond people are known as *Matang*, while people on the islands surrounding the Solomon Islands are known for their light-colored hair and light-colored skin.[42] The gods worshipped by the natives of the Pacific Ocean regions characteristically have sandy red hair and white-colored skin in many of the legends. When the British Captain James Cook landed on Hawaii in 1778, the indigenous Hawaiians believed it was their god Lono returning, suggesting the gods from their myths were perhaps descendants of the ancient Lemurian or Atlanteans and that these early explorers were those gods.

After learning the stories of Captain John Davis and Juan Fernandez discovering a large land mass in the Pacific Ocean, Dutch navigator Jacob Roggeveen set out in 1721 to find this mysterious land. While he did not find the land described by Captain John Davis, he did in fact discover Easter Island on Easter Day. Easter Island was nothing like the descriptions given by Juan Fernandez and John Davis who suggested that part of the lost continent submerged only after being seen. Similar tales emerged and people theorized that a narrow land mass that stretched from Easter Island to the Galapagos Islands had vanished. According to Roggeveen, the indigenous people of Easter Island had light skin and red hair, similar to Europeans. He estimated that there were about 5,000 inhabitants living on the island. He investigated the island and found the gigantic statue monoliths made of solid rock. According to the natives, there is a legend of Hotu Matu'a, who first arrived on Easter Island from the unknown land of Hiva (archaeological evidence suggests the first people colonized Easter Island around 300 to 800CE). The mythical land of Hiva, according to the natives, lies underneath the Pacific Ocean as a result of a great cataclysm. It is still unclear as to the actual cultural influence of the native Rapanui on Easter Island, and whether it is exclusively a Polynesian or South American influence. Other anthropologists suggest that the indigenous Rapanui are descendents of the Maori people of New Zealand, based on their similar physical characteristics such as being tall and white-skinned. The evidence as to their true origin remains inconclusive. Many of the islanders were wiped out by warfare and disease. All that remains on the island are the gigantic Mo'ai monoliths staring out into the Pacific Ocean, serving as a reminder of the long lost land of Hiva, or perhaps eagerly awaiting the return of the ancient ancestors.

---

[1] Beebe, Rose Marie and Senkewicz, Robert M. *Lands of Promise and Despair*, pp. 3-4

[2] Ibid., p. 6

[3] Ibid., p. 8

[4] Berliz, Charles *Atlantis: The Eighth Continent*, p. 56

[5] Ibid., pp. 57-8

[6] Donnelly, Ignatius *Atlantis: The Antediluvian World*, p. 311

[7] Peterson, Scott *Native American Prophecies*, p. 42

[8] Ibid., p.43

[9] Cortes, Hernan *Letters from Mexico*, p.17

[10] Berliz, Charles *Atlantis: The Eighth Continent*, p. 112

[11] *White Indians Seen in Panama in 1679* ; The Science News-Letter, Vol. 9, No. 274, (Jul. 10, 1926), p. 9

[12] Pigafetta, Antonio (Translation by Raleigh Ashlin Skelton) *Magellan's voyage: a narrative of the first circumnavigation* , p. 46

[13] Smith, Bernard *European vision and the South Pacific*, p. 36

[14] de Oviedo y Valdés, Gonzalo Fernández *Historia General y Natural de las Indias, Islas y Tierra Firme del Mar Oceano*

[15] Grann, David *The Lost City of Z*, pp. 148-9

[16] Prescott, William H. *History of the Conquest of Peru*, pp.152-3

[17] Berliz, Charles *Atlantis: The Eighth Continent*, pp. 149-50

[18] de León, Pedro de Cieza *The second part of the Chronicle of Peru*; Conquest of Chachapoyas

[19] de León, Pedro de Cieza *First and Second Chronicles of Peru* [mentioned in both chronicles]

[20] de León, Pedro de Cieza *The Travels of Pedro de Cieza de Léon, A.D. 1532-50, Contained in the First Part of His Chronicle of Peru*, p. 309

[21] De Carvajal, Gaspar *Discovery of the Amazon*, 1542

[22] Grann, David *The Lost City of Z*, pp. 138-9

[23] Wilkins, Harold T. *Mysteries of Ancient South America*, p. 117

[24] Spence, Lewis *The Problem of Lemuria: The Sunken Continent of the Pacific*, p. 22

[25] Beebe, Rose Marie and Senkewicz, Robert M. *Lands of Promise and Despair*, p. 3

[26] Ibid., pp. 9-10

[27] Heizer, R.F. and Whipple, M.A. *The California Indians*, p. 273

[28] Beebe, Rose Marie and Senkewicz, Robert M. *Lands of Promise and Despair*, p. 45

29 Ibid.

30 Schultz, Richard *Essene Lineage in California* Rosicrucian Digest,Volume 86 Number 2 2007

31 Peterson, Scott *Native American Prophecies*, pp. 159- 192

32 Ibid. pg 172 and Waters, Frank *The Book of the Hopi*, p. 252

33 Waters, Frank *The Book of the Hopi*, p.252

34 Nequatewa, Edmund *Truth of a Hopi: Stories Relating to the Origin, Myths and Clan*, pp. 47-8

35 Ibid., p. 47

36 Deloria, Vine Jr. *Red Earth White Lies: Native Americans and the Myth of Scientific Fact*, p.120

37 Martin, Paul S. "Prehistoric Overkill," in *Pleistocene Extinctions*, ed. Paul S. Martin and H.E. Wright, Jr. (New Haven: Yale University Press, 1967) , p. 88

38 Letter from James Wright to John Bartram, August 22, 1762, quoted by George Gaylord Simpson, "*The Discovery of Fossil Vertebrates in North America*," Journal of Paleontology 17 (1943): 36.

39 McClintock, James H. *Mormon Settlement in Arizona*, p. 72

40 Thompson, Lucy *To the American Indian: Reminiscences of a Yurok Woman*, p. 84

41 Smith, Stephenson Percy *Hawaiki: the original home of the Maori; with a sketch of Polynesian history*, p. 96

42 Spence, Lewis *The Problem of Lemuria: The Sunken Continent of the Pacific*, p. 75

Chapter Seven
Modern Accounts

IN March of 1882, an incident occurred in the Atlantic Ocean involving the *S.S. Jesmond* as it headed to New Orleans from Messina, Sicily. The ship's cargo consisted of 1495 tons under the direction of Captain David Robson. On the first of March, the ship crossed the Straits of Gibraltar, the famous Pillars of Hercules that Plato described as beyond the seas where Atlantis once laid. Upon reaching 31 ° 25' N, 28 ° 40' W - roughly 200 miles west of Madeira, and about 200 miles south of the Azores - the crew of the *S.S. Jesmond* came across something unusual. As they sailed, they observed the ocean surface as being muddy and full of dead fish, as if an underwater volcanic eruption had taken place. This continued into the evening when the Captain saw smoke in the distance and presumed it was from another ship. The following morning, the amount of dead fish in the ocean increased. The Captain noticed that the smoke was coming from mountains on an island to the west. According to the maps, there were no islands for several hundred miles. As the ship was within 12 miles off the shore of the island, they dropped anchor to investigate. Maps indicated that the depth of the ocean was thousands of fathoms in depth; however, the anchor hit bottom at only seven fathoms.

As Captain Robson and some crew members landed on the island, they observed no trees, no sandy beaches, no signs of life, as if the island had just risen from the ocean. The sailors saw volcanic debris littering the landscape and a plateau with smoking mountains in the distance. As they marched toward the direction of the mountains, they discovered several deep chasms; reaching the mountains would take several days. The crew decided to head back and investigate a partially broken embankment. One of the sailors then came across an unusual arrowhead in the crumbling rock. The Captain then sent people back to the ship to retrieve several picks and shovels. For the next two days, they dug into the gravel and unearthed many unusual things such as the "crumbling remains" of "massive walls," and a variety of artifacts including "bronze swords, rings, mallets, carvings of head figures of birds and animals, and two vases or jars with fragments of bone, and one cranium almost entire." Along with "what appeared to be a mummy enclosed in a stone case... encrusted with volcanic deposit so as to be scarcely distinguished form the rock itself." The hardest task was hulling the large rock sarcophagus from the island to the ship. As the weather changed, they had no choice but to abandon their efforts and go back on their course. Upon reaching New Orleans, the crew reported their findings to the *Times Picayune* and to other reporters on the scene. Captain Robson revealed plans to take the artifacts to the British Museum; however, the British Museum claims to have never received any such artifacts from Captain Robson. The ships log was destroyed during the September 1940 London Blitz in the offices of Watts and Company.

Further investigation reveals that the Captain and crew of the *S.S. Jesmond* were not alone in reporting a mysterious island in the middle of the Atlantic Ocean. Captain James Newdick of the schooner *Westbourne*, sailed from Marseilles

in France to New York during the same time, also reported
having seen an island at 25 ° 30' N, 24° W. Captain Newdick's
report of the island was featured in the *New York Post* in April
of 1882. Countless other ship captains also reported having
come across large quantities of dead fish spanning miles across
the ocean surface, some of these reports even made it into *The
New York Times*. The British Institute of Oceanography concluded that the number of dead fish covered an area of 7500
square miles and weighed at least half a million tons. Some
sailors on ships reported eating the dead fish and reported no
illnesses.[1]

This was not the first story of a mysterious island sur-
facing in the Atlantic. A notable case is that of Sabrina Island,
near São Miguel Island in the Azores. During June and July of
1811, underwater volcanic eruptions caused a large land mass
to surface. Captain James Tillard on the *HMS Sabrina* claimed
the island for Great Britain. It then sank, returning underneath
the waves of the Atlantic Ocean. Three years prior, in 1808,
volcanic eruptions on São Jorge Island (in the Azores) caused
thousands of feet of land to suddenly rise up.[2]

The Quest Begins

In 1868, a young man named James Churchward was
stationed in Central India to help with famine relief in the area.
According to Churchward, this is where he met a high priest
(or Rishi) in a Temple School Monastery. The Rishi gained the
trust of Churchward and decided to reveal to him ancient tablets hidden for thousands of years deep within the monastery's
vaults. They taught Churchward how to interpret some of the
basic symbols on the tables so that he could decode its mysterious inscriptions. Churchward desired to learn more, so the
Rishi eventually taught him the new language thought to be the
first language of man. For twelve years he continued learning
the secret history inscribed on the tablets and shortly thereafter

learned the story of Mu, the cradle of civilization. Churchward then departed around the world to seek out more evidence on this mysterious land and its people.

Using what he remembered from the tablets, he set out to find more proof of Mu (or Lemuria). Along the way, he investigated rock carvings, manuscripts, and tablets depicting the lost civilization. Churchward traveled all over Central Asia, Tibet, and Egypt where he decoded ancient inscriptions which had been lost for generations. He traveled to Siberia, then down to Australia and New Zealand as he studied natives living in the Polynesian islands. In Polynesia, he found clues about the lost civilization and what caused its destruction. The people of Mu spread throughout the world, but their civilization came to an abrupt end. The people of Mu resorted to savagery, from which our modern day culture later emerged from. Churchward gathered several inscriptions that he claimed to be evidence of Mu. He also headed numerous expeditions around the world and wrote several books dedicated to the study of Mu. As a Freemason, he theorized that the ancient teachings of Freemasonry could be traced back to Mu in partial fragmented teachings or expressions.[3] The Freemasonry link can also be found in Lucy Thompson's book *To the American Indian*, where she makes a connection between her husband's Freemasonic association to that of the Yurok Talth mystery tradition. Thompson concluded that the Freemasonic mystery tradition and the Yurok Native American Talth tradition have the same origins, dating back to the cradle of civilization.

Only a few people at that time had speculated about Mu/Lemuria. Of course others had different motives in proving the existence of the lost civilization. A British soldier named Colonel Percy Harrison Fawcett set off into the Amazon in search of the lost cities. Driven by stories of El Dorado and the existence of a great civilization whose remnants exist in Amazon, he ventured into the jungles of South America in April of 1925, never to return. Fawcett believed that large stone pyramids existed in the jungles of eastern Peru. According to Fawcett, these cities preceded those of the Inka and were superior to anything that could have been imagined at the time. These mysterious cities in the Amazon were built by people who came from the east, the survivors of a lost land now submerged in the ocean. He believed that these ancient cities were thousands of years old, more ancient than any in the Americas. Lewis Spence, author of *The Problem of Atlantis* and *The Problem of Lemuria: the Sunken Continent of the Pacific*, corresponded with Colonel P. H. Fawcett. Colonel P. H. Fawcett stated the following in a letter to Lewis Spence before his disappearance:

> I have good reason to know that these original (white Atlantean) people still remain in a degenerate state. . . They use script and also llamas, an animal associated with Andean heights above 10,000 feet, but in origin a low country, hybrid animal. Their still existing remains show the use of different coloured stones in the steps leading to temple buildings and a great deal of sculpture in demi-relief.[4]

Fawcett was aware of the Spanish and Portuguese expeditions where they reported seeing white tribes (one living in a city called Atlán).[5] The natives told stories to Fawcett about great cities that existed deep in the jungles, and large stone houses and streets that would be illuminated at night. The natives also spoke of an ancient people who still occupied the cities and how tribes still protected these cities from intruders.[6] It is unknown what exactly happened to Fawcett during his expedition. All that remains are his last words before disappearing:

> Whether we get through, and emerge again, or leave our bones to rot in there, one thing is certain. The answer to the enigma of Ancient South America...and

perhaps to the prehistoric world...may be found when those old cities are opened up to scientific research. That the cities exist, I know...

A Dweller on Two Planets

In 1886, a book entitled, *A Dweller on Two Planets*, was written by eighteen year old Frederick Spencer Oliver. Oliver lived in the remote town of Yreka in northern California near Mount Shasta, where he wrote the book over a three year period. According to Oliver, he was channeled by Phylos, the Tibetan, and completed the book through automatic writing. Completed in 1886, the book was published in 1905 by Oliver's mother, Mary Elizabeth Manley-Oliver, six years after his death in 1899. In the book, Oliver describes the different incarnations of Phylos through the times of Lemuria and Atlantis. The book is divided into three sections (or books). In *Book I*, Phylos is described as being his past reincarnation Zailm, who lived in Atlantis in 11,160 BCE. Phylos also mentions advanced technology that once existed, including antigravity machines, x-rays, televisions, wireless phones, air conditioners, high speed monorails, and voice-operated typewriters. At that time, the descriptions were considered to be extreme science fiction (though many of the technological and scientific inventions would not surface until many years later). *Book III* reflects on the past incarnations of Phylos's Atlantean lives and what he learned. The karmic retributions he lived through were played out vividly and in great detail. Phylos describes the destruction of Atlantis, known in ancient times as Atlan, *Queen of the Seas*, and the people of Atlantis as *Children of Incal* (Incal roughly translating to God). Further statements made about Atlantis indicate around 300 million people living on Atlantis as well as in various colonies abroad. And like Plato's description, he describes the ultimate end of Atlantis by tidal waves, floods, and a great earthquake that collapsed Atlantis into the bottom of the ocean. The fate of Atlantis, according to Phylos, was due to corruption and lust for power and riches.

An intriguing section in the book is *Book II* which describes a modern day reincarnation of Phylos as an American. Phylos was incarnated as Walter Pierson, a Civil War veteran, who lived in California during the Gold Rush. In the story, he befriends a Chinese laborer named Quong who seemed to deeply fascinate Pierson. Pierson then finds out that Quong is actually an "adept" of a secret order of mystics who dwell inside Mount Shasta, called the *Lothinian Brotherhood*. Quong later instructs Pierson to follow him into an isolated canyon where they are confronted by a Mountain Lion, whom Quong quickly subdues. Quong takes Pierson to a very large quadrangular block of stone and with a simple touch, Quong opens a passage into the mountain. They enter a tunnel that led them into a large chamber with a dome ceiling about 60 feet wide. The walls were illuminated and polished and the floors were covered in a carpet that had oriental characteristics. The chamber was known as *Sach*, where others throughout the western hemisphere would meet. Pierson later found out that he was chosen to join the ancient order, and began on his path down a long and arduous journey of mystical unfoldment into the hidden mysteries of eternal life.

> Once I was there, friend, casting pebbles in the stream's deep pools; yet it was then hid, for only a few are privileged. And departing, the spot was forgotten, and today, unable as anyone who reads this, I cannot tell its place. Curiosity will never unlock that secret. Does it truly exist? Seek and ye shall find; knock and it shall be opened unto you. Shasta is a true guardian and silently towers, giving no sign of that within his breast. But there is a key. The one who first conquers self, Shasta will not deny.[7]

Lemuria: The Lost Continent of the Pacific

One of the most important books regarding Lemuria was published in 1931 entitled *Lemuria: The Lost Continent of the Pacific*. The book was written by Dr. Harvey Spencer Lewis under the anagrammatical penname Wishar S. Cervé. According to the book, several secretive manuscripts from Tibet and China were handed to the Rosicrucian Order, A.M.O.R.C., by representatives from China. During that time, political and social unrest began in China by revolutionary actions committed by the Communist Party. The manuscripts given to Dr. Harvey Spencer Lewis described the ancient continent of Lemuria and its inhabitants. Lewis made no effort to prove the authenticity of the translated statements presented in the book, instead he left it up to the imaginations of readers to discover the truth for themselves. Prior to the release of that book, an article was published in a 1925 issue of *The Mystic Triangle*, a publication by the Rosicrucian Order, which mentioned unusual incidents around Mount Shasta, as well as in other places. The book provides details about the strange occurrences that have taken place in Northern California, stirring up new interest in ancient civilizations.

The interesting stories regarding the existence of mystical beings in the vicinity of Northern California can be traced through the Native American legends; however, most tribes claim that these ancient mystics left. Several accounts mention prior knowledge regarding these living inhabitants that date back to the 1800's. Strange lights would be seen on top of Mount Shasta at night, which some attributed to secret rituals. The lights were described as a red glow while others described a beaming white light. It is said that only four or five people ever "penetrated the invisible protective boundary of this Lemurian settlement; but no one has ever succeeded in entering the village; at least, no one has ever returned to tell the tale."[8]

Many people in the vicinity of Mount Shasta have tried to get near to the mysterious lights and sounds. "After having reached a certain point in his progress toward the center of the lights and sounds, one of two things would happen. On one hand, he might come in contact with a heavily covered and concealed person of large size who would lift him up and turn him away from the district, as though forcibly impressing him with the idea to hurry away as rapidly as possible. On the other hand, a strange and peculiar set of vibrations or invisible energy would seem to emanate toward the investigator and force him to remain fixed in his position, so that he could move in no other direction than away from the place of his inquiry."[9]

In many instances these beings have been known to visit the surrounding towns of Mount Shasta. They are described as very tall, always barefoot, the men having very short hair, very noble looking, and white spotless robes resembling high-caste East Indian garment.[10] But in other instances they are described as wearing sandals, having long curly blond or gray hair, slightly larger heads, and talking with a slight British accent. They are sometimes seen on isolated roads at night, as well as in the day. In every attempt to photograph or get close enough to talk to them, they simply vanish.[11] This might be the reason why Native Americans living around Mount Shasta thought that there was a race of invisible people living on the mountains.[12] These mystics have been known to go into several of the stores and purchase odd items, such as large amounts of sulfur and salt. They have also been known to purchase large quantities of lard, in which they always bring their own container (being described as almost transparent bladders).[13] Living as simple as possible, they do not try to attract attention; these gentle and peaceful people do not care much for the advancements of modern technology. Payments for these items are always paid for in gold nuggets, with the value of the gold nuggets always exceeding their purchased items. If they do not find what they are looking for, they travel store to store until they find what they are looking for. During times of crisis, many of the stores would have American Red Cross donation boxes, during which the beings were observed donating large sums of gold to the relief aid during World War I and the Japanese earthquake.[14]

One particular incident reported was of an "official" visit made by these mysterious people to San Francisco (though it certainly was not the last). The visit was made when a delegate came walking barefoot from Mount Shasta to San Francisco (almost 300 miles away) and was described as wearing a white robe who was escorted by younger men. The group presented themselves at the Ferry Building and was then escorted up Market Street and into City Hall. The motive behind their appearance: "to bring greetings and an assurance of goodwill upon the anniversary of the founding of their sacred retreat."[15] The delegate then met in the Mayor's office and was given the Key to the City.[16] And just as mysteriously as they had appeared, they returned to their village.

During the early times when the automobiles were first being introduced, drivers on the roads near Mount Shasta would describe seeing a bright flash of light glimmering in front of them. Without warning, the electrical system inside the car would malfunction and turn off. The drivers would then get out of the car and push the car down the road from whence they came, and just as mysteriously as the car had stopped working it would start up again.[17] As frightening as some encounters may seem, these mystics have been known to help during different times. California has endured severe fires over the course of its history. In some instances, fires can reach too close to Mount Shasta, and a strange white fog or cloud is seen taking form in the vicinity. Slowly, the circular cloud rises and travels to the location of the fire where it slowly encloses the fire and extinguishes it. Some of the locals in the area are clear to show the circular burnt indication on trees, demonstrating how suddenly the fire ceases in a straight line, as if by some mysterious force.[18]

The Mystery Continues...

There have also been findings of strange petroglyphs in nearby Castle Crags. On a sunny Sunday, two high school students from nearby Dunsmuir were hiking along a remote region in Castle Crags and came across some petroglyphs. They then ran back to notify Frank Bascom, who was with the U.S. Forest Service and known to be closely involved in archaeology and geology in the region. They hiked back through Castle Creek canyon, through Mount Bradley road, and continued down into the banks of Castle Creek. They had found two Maltese cross designs, two "E-like" characters, what looked like an Egyptian ankh, a double triangle inscription, and the palm of a male and female hand. Further investigations conducted by the U.S. Forest Service produced more petroglyphs in the surrounding area (the largest measuring eight feet in height). Bascom writes the following about the petroglyphs that he investigated:

> The fact stands out that the petroglyphs or symbols chiseled in the coarse granite rocks up Castle Creek show greater skill and symmetry and a higher degree of culture than any found elsewhere in different places of southwestern United States. The petroglyphs have been colored a reddish hue with some unknown liquid solution, and it was evidently used to keep any growth of vegetation from covering the symbols.
> The people who did this work were no doubt artists possessing great skill. On what is now two large boulders there was at some remote time, one huge rock, which at some time was cleft asunder. The symbols are on the east side of these two rocks. Those on the rock to

the south reveal a large man's hand, painted with some unknown stain. In the palm of the hand is chiseled the "all-seeing eye" and on the rock to the north is a beautifully-shaped woman's hand in whose palm is chiseled a form of the swastika.

Were the symbols placed on the two rocks before or after the rock broke and separated? On the rock to the north, the woman's hand is at the side and not in the center of the rock. In chiseling the rock, the natural thing would be to place such work in the center and not at the side of the rock. This might indicate that the symbols were cut into the rock prior to its separation.[19]

Investigations were conducted by various Anthropology Departments in Universities, including Stanford University, and Academy Press in New Jersey. The only explanation the universities could give was that the petroglyphs were carved in by local Indians. Bascom later wrote: "This I doubt. In talking with the highest type of the older local Indians, they state this work was not chiseled by Indians. Therefore, we have to turn to another source." [20] After reading Colonel James Churchward's, *The Lost Continent of Mu*, Bascom determined that the petroglyphs had been carved during the prehistoric era and that they resembled the symbols found in Churchward's book. "Churchward, in his 'Lost Continent of Mu' lists six of the symbols found at Castle Crags: the swastika, a form of the Maltese cross, the triangle, the all-seeing eye, the serpent and the three steps to the throne. He found these symbols engraved on clay tablets in the temples of India as they had existed in the sunken continent of Mu and I'd consider them authentic."[21]

Near the outskirts of the forests surrounding Mount Shasta there are other strange petroglyphs, as mentioned in Cervé's book; carved on a stone and written in English: "*Ceremony of Adoration to Guatama*." The name *Guatama* is considered to be the Lemurian name for America.[22] This ceremo-

ny honors the time when their ancestors arrived on this continent in order to escape the catastrophe that befell the people of
ancient Lemuria. This celebration, or adoration, of their presence on this land, is said to take place each night at midnight
throughout the entire year.[23] The ceremony can be observed
with is array of brilliant lights throughout parts of California.
In his book, Cervé mentions similar strange lights being seen in
the Santa Clara Valley, from Mission Peak, only a short distance away from Mission San Jose. Bright lights coming from
different mountain peaks in California were seen for years during certain times of the month. In the east foothills of San Jose
a strange light was observed in 1880 for about 30 years until it
was not seen again. In 1931, the mysterious bright light reappeared bright enough to be viewed all around parts of the San
Francisco Bay. Because the lights were seen during the United
States prohibition, police suspected that the light was a signal
to illegal moonshiners waiting in the bay. The police made the
effort to pinpoint the exact location of these mysterious lights.
The following morning, a search led investigators to a remotely
dense grove in Mission Peak, and because of its remote location, no electricity was available. What puzzled investigators
most were that they found no signs of people in the area. Mission Peak, in Fremont California, features mysterious anomalies which I will address at a later time. My investigations led
to published reports of an incident dated Wednesday, June
17th1931; mentioned by the San Jose Evening News as well as
the San Jose Mercury:

Mystery Light Is Unexplained

MISSION SAN JOSE June 17. - Authorities
today sought the source of the mysterious bright light
which has again made its appearance on Mission Peak
recently and is believed to have been used several times
during the past few years as a signal to rum runners op-

erating in boats in the lower regions of San Francisco Bay.

A transit aimed at the spot from which the unusually bright flashes of light, evidently in code signals, came from the slopes of the peak failed to obtain the location. When daylight came it was found that the location given by the transit was a clump of trees, but there was no evidence of any light having been there or of even a blade of grass trampled on.

There have also been strange accounts of strange dirigible or vimana (ancient Sanskrit accounts of "flying ships") in various locations throughout California, and other places around the Americas. In the book *A Dweller on Two Planets*, Oliver describes a blimp-shaped craft hovering over the oceans. Similarities emerge between that craft and the ones described by Dr. Lewis in some of his writings. "Many testify to having seen the strange boar, or boats, which sail the Pacific Ocean, and then rise at its shores and sail through the air to drop again in the vicinity of Shasta. This same boat was seen several times by the officials employed by the cable station located near Vancouver, and the boat has been sighted as far north as the Aleutian Islands…It is generally believed that there is another Lemurian settlement in that locality which is regularly visited by this boat which has neither sails nor smokestacks."[24] There have been numerous legends ranging from indigenous Polynesian to Native Californian myths regarding "flying canoes" or "crafts." One of these stories of flying ships comes from a Paiute Native American named Oga-Make:

> You ask me if we heard of the great silver airships in the days before white-man brought his wagon trains into the land? We, the Paiute Nation, have known of these ships for untold generations. We also believe that we

know something of the people who fly them. They are called The *Hav-musuvs*... They are a people of the Panamints, and they are as ancient as Tomesha [Death Valley] itself.

When the world was young, and this valley which is now dry, parched desert, was a lush, hidden harbor of a blue water- sea which stretched from half way up those mountains to the Gulf of California, it is said that the *Hav-musuvs* came here in huge rowing-ships. They found great caverns in the Panamints, and in them they built one of their cities. At that time California was the island which the Indians of that state told the Spanish it was, and which they marked so on their maps...Living in their hidden city, the *Hav-musuvs* ruled the sea with their fast rowing-ships, trading with far-away peoples and bringing strange goods to the great quays said still to exist in the caverns...

When the *Hav-musuvs* could no longer use their great rowing-ships, they began to think of other means to reach the world beyond. I suppose that is how it happened. We know that they began to use flying canoes. At first they were not large, these silvery ships with wings. They moved with a slight whirring sound, and a dipping movement, like an eagle...The passing centuries brought other changes. Tribe after tribe swept across the land, fighting to possess it for awhile and passing like the storm of sand. In their mountain city still in the caverns, the *Hav-musuvs* dwelt in peace, far removed from the conflict. Sometimes they were seen in the distance, in their flying ships or riding on the snowy-white animals which took them from ledge to ledge up the cliffs. We have never seen these strange animals at any other place. To these people the passing centuries brought only larger and larger ships, moving always more silently...They are a beautiful people.

Their skin is a golden tint, and a head band holds back
their long dark hair. They dress always in a white fine-
spun garment which wraps around them and is draped
upon one shoulder. Pale sandals are worn upon their
feet...
He had been in the giant underground valley of the
Hav-musuvs, he said, where white lights which burn
night and day and never go out, or need any fuel, lit an
ancient city of marble beauty. There he learned the language and the history of the mysterious people, giving
them in turn the language and legends of the Paiutes.
He said that he would have liked to remain there forever in the peace and beauty of their life, but they bade
him return and use his new knowledge for his people...
 How many *Hav-musuvs* could live in their eternal
peace away from the noise of white-man's guns in their
unscaleable stronghold? This has always been a land of
mystery. Nothing can change that.[25]

There are several accounts in regards to these flying
crafts heading to various locations, where Dr. Lewis states other Lemurian colonies are still in existence today. At one point
in time, these ancients inhabited most of the Americas; however, they soon came together to form tight communities (or colonies) that still remain. As previously mentioned, the stories
contain traveling crafts, which might suggest that the colonies
of these mystics are in communication with each other. Question remains as to why have not we seen any today, while reports of incidents of "elongated" flying crafts throughout the
1930's were common, prior to the U.F.O./"flying saucer" craze
that followed after 1947. A 1931 account states the following:

Recently a group of persons playing golf on one of the
golf links of California near the foothills of the Sierra
Nevada range, saw a peculiar silver-like vessel rise in

the air, float over the mountaintops and disappear. It was unlike any airship that had ever been seen and there was absolutely no noise emanating from it to indicate that it moved by motor of any kind.[26]

It is possible that our advancements in technology have discouraged these ancients from traveling outside their own community due to fear of being discovered. These colonies remain in isolated regions, according to several sources, and perhaps that is how they remain so elusive.

As mentioned previously, the location of one of the alleged colonies is thought to exist in the general vicinity of Vancouver. Dr. Lewis also mentions Santa Barbara and the Channel Islands as locations previously occupied by these beings; this is where the Spanish explorer Juan Rodríguez Cabrillo described seeing an advanced race of "white" Indians. Not to mention one of the oldest skeletons found in the United States was found on one of those islands, and maintains "Caucasian" features. Other current Lemurian colonies allegedly exist around isolated areas in California, Baja California, and Mexico. Albert Van der Naillen (author of *In the Sanctuary*) claims to have visited one of the supposed Lemurian colonies existing in Mexico. Van der Naillen was given sacred manuscripts by these mystics and told to take them to his sanctum. His son returned to try and establish contact with them; however, he came across other mystics instead.[27] Another notable case is that of Jose Carmen Garcia who, in 1947, claimed he was held captive inside an underground city in a nearby extinct volcano in Irapuato, Mexico. In captivity he was given a "magic formula" that these people used to grow giant vegetables. When he came to, he planted some of the most gigantic vegetables ever recorded in that area.[28] Another unusual account comes from Mount Sombrero in the Tampico region of Mexico. Deep inside the caves, explores claim to have heard strange noises similar to a "hydroelectric plant."[29] There have been many claims of subterranean interlinking cavern systems spanning around the world, also known as the "Hollow Earth Theory," by various conspiracy theorists. In the region of Mount Shasta (and other extinct volcanoes), there is evidence of cavern systems created by old lava bed flows; however, there is no evidence to suggest that they may lead to a vastly populated subterranean city (e.g. Telos) or connect with another underground city further away.

In 1904, J.C. Brown was hired by the Lord Cowdray Mining Company in London, England, to search for gold in the mountains of Northern California. Brown traveled to Mount Shasta where he noticed a cliff face that did not match the surrounding rocks. He also noticed debris and vegetation blocking a hole that upon digging out revealed a small entrance leading into what appeared to be a cave. He soon realized that it was actually a large tunnel leading down into the mountain. Exploring the large cave, he continued for about three miles into the tunnel and discovered bits of gold. He came across several cross-sections and intersecting parts of the tunnel system. Eleven miles into the mountain he came across what he described as a village. He discovered two rooms filled with gold and copper tablets, and in rooms adjacent, he found rooms filled with more tablets; the golden tablets were inscribed with drawings and hieroglyphs. In other rooms he found spears, gold statues, a temple chamber, and a vast chamber filled with 27 skeletons - the smallest being 6'6" and the largest spanning over 10 feet. There were also two mummies in colorful robes.

He spent the next several days exploring and taking notes. Brown decided to leave everything undisturbed, and upon leaving the entrance he covered it well and marked its location on a map. From 1904 through 1934, he researched various texts and esoteric books on the subject of Lemuria, concluding that the remnants he found inside Mount Shasta were of Lemurian origin. In 1934, 30 years after his discoveries, Brown shared his story with the world.

Brown, at the age of 79, lived in Stockton, California, where he gathered the people needed for an expedition. Eighty people showed up, including a newspaper editor, museum curator, retired printer, and several scientists. Together, they spent six weeks planning the expedition where he revealed the secrets of what he had found 30 years prior. Some people in the group gave up their careers and sold their property with the hopes of becoming rich. Meanwhile, the editor and curator demanded Brown to tell them more in order to determine the facts. And Brown did everything he could to help explain his story. After it was settled, they met one last time to ensure that the final preparations of the expedition were set; that was the last anybody saw of him.

Many suspect that he was abducted, having previously stated that he had barely escaped with his life after being captured. The Stockton police investigated, but in the end found nothing. J.C. Brown vanished, and theories abounded with suspicions as to his whereabouts. Those present with the group still believe that the caves hold vast treasures of an ancient race waiting to be discovered. However, Brown never revealed the exact location of the secret entrance. The area of wilderness surrounding Mount Shasta is so vast that it would be nearly impossible to locate the hidden entrance. There seems to be no solid evidence for his disappearance seeing as there was no personal gain involved.

Since J.C. Brown's story there have been many claims by people having found entrances into the actual Lemurian settlement inside Mount Shasta. For example, Abraham Mansfield, who in 1934, claimed he was taken into the city inside the mountain by seven-foot tall Lemurians. Other stories began to emerge during the Lemurian craze, ranging from meeting Saint Germain on Mount Shasta, to reptilian aliens roaming the land. Many of these stories are based on imaginative creations, and many have successfully gained publicity toward their own agendas.

Death Valley

Death Valley Men, written by historian Burke Lee and published in 1932, presents a similar story to that of J.C. Brown. The story takes place in Death Valley, instead of Mount Shasta, yet the artifacts found within the cave are very similar to those in J.C. Brown's story. Lee mentions two miners, Jack and Bill, who encounter three people after entering their cabin. They are having car trouble and decide to wait while one of them goes to the Los Angeles area for parts. The conversation then centers on old Paiute legends, as they decide to share with them the reason they were in Death Valley. They said that Mr. Fred White was in the area of Wingate Pass searching for gold when he accidentally fell through a shaft into a huge cavern. Moving around inside the darkness, he noticed manmade impressions in the rocks. Thinking he had stumbled into a mine, he pressed on for several hours in darkness as he inched his way along the wall until it came to an end and he fell forward. Feeling the ground he noticed that it was unusually polished. Lighting a candle, he realized he was in a vast chamber filled with preserved mummies surrounding a stone table inlaid with jewels. White moved around until he accidentally triggered a lever that ignited lights all around the room. Now he saw that there were over a hundred mummies in the room; some had golden spears, shields, and wore unusual leather clothing, golden armbands and jewel aprons. Some of the mummies stood upright, while others lay on the floor. Towering over him was an 89 foot gold statue of a man.

Fred White returned to the site twice, accompanied by his friend and his wife. There were stone doors that would open upon the slight push of a finger, passages leading to parts of the mountains, and widows that overlooked Death Valley. They concluded that the city was built by ancient people. The location of the city, high in the mountains, was once a port where ships would come in. White brought the cavern to the attention of the Smithsonian Institute who then offered a million and a half dollars for their findings. White had previously left some of the artifacts, jewels and gold they had collected to a friend, whom afterward, denied having anything. Angrily, they returned to the location to find more artifacts, only to realize that the landmarks marking the entrance into the city were gone after a storm ravaged the area. The three of them were last spotted near the area where they mentioned, however, they were never seen again. Many of the local miners searched in vain for years, but never found White or his group again.

In 1931, another man stumbled into the ancient city in Death Valley. Dr. F. Bruce Russell, a retired Cincinnati physician, came to Death Valley to try his luck at mining. On one occasion, he fell into a tunnel that led to a series of other tunnels and made a discovery. Over the years, Russell tried to find other people to help him explore what he had discovered, but nobody believed him. It was not until 1947 that Russell brought in Howard E. Hill and Dr. Daniel S. Bovee - who helped establish the New Mexico cliff dwellings site. They met in private and Russell disclosed his discovery to the men. Russell had found the mummies of people who had stood between eight and nine feet tall; Bovee determined them to be 80,000 years old. The men later conducted an expedition into the cavern system, estimated at over 180 square miles and consisting of 32 caves extending from Death Valley into Nevada and Arizona. They discovered an ancient ritual hall with various symbols and objects similar to those used by Freemasons. In another tunnel, they found preserved animal remains ranging from elephants to saber-toothed tigers and dinosaurs, which were displayed in niches. Unique hieroglyphic writing covered the surface of the polished stone granite walls. They noticed that the mummified remains were exclusively male and described the odd clothing they wore: "These giants are clothed in garments consisting of a medium length jacket and trouser extending slightly below the knees…The texture of the material is said to resemble gray dyed sheepskin, but obviously it was taken from an animal unknown today." Hill describes other things "including household utensils and stoves which apparently cooked by radio waves." This was before people knew what microwave ovens were, but the Los Angeles County Museum quickly lost interest because of the mention of 'extinct animals on display.' Newspapers refused to publish the story and eventually it faded into obscurity. While it is a questionable account, it is notable. There are also Native American legends that speak of labyrinths and a city that lays hidden within the mountains in Death Valley.[30][31]

[1] Berliz, Charles *Atlantis: the eight continent*, pp. 78-80

[2] Ibid., p. 77

[3] Churchward, Col. James *The Lost Continent of Mu*, p. 136

[4] Wilkins, Harold T. *Mysteries of Ancient South America*, p. 88

[5] Berliz, Charles *Atlantis: the eight continent*, p. 112

[6] Ibid., p. 113

[7] Phylos *A Dweller on Two Planets*, p. 258

[8] Spence, Lewis *The Problem of Lemuria: The Sunken Continent of the Pacific*, p. 105

[9] Cervé, Wishar S. *Lemuria: The Lost Continent of the Pacific*, p.179

[10] Spence, Lewis *The Problem of Lemuria: The Sunken Continent of the Pacific*, p. 108; Taken from an article by Edward Lanser, *A People of Mystery*. The Los Angeles Times, May 22, 1932

[11] Cervé, Wishar S. *Lemuria: The Lost Continent of the Pacific*, p. 182

[12] Eichorn, A.F., SR. *The Mount Shasta Story*, p. 58

[13] Ibid.

[14] Ibid.

[15] Spence, Lewis *The Problem of Lemuria: The Sunken Continent of the Pacific*, p. 108

16 Selvius, Frater. *Descendants of Lemuria: A Description of an Ancient Cult in California* The Rosicrucian Digest, May 1931
17 Walton, Bruce *Mount Shasta: Home of the Ancients*, p. 25
18 Ibid., p. 25
19 Frank, Emilie A. *Mt. Shasta California's Mystic Mountain*, pp. 80-81
20 Ibid., p. 81
21 Ibid., p. 81
22 Cervé, Wishar S. *Lemuria: The Lost Continent of the Pacific*, p.183-4 and Spence, Lewis *The Problem of Lemuria: The Sunken Continent of the Pacific*, p. 107
23 Spence, Lewis *The Problem of Lemuria: The Sunken Continent of the Pacific*, p. 107
24 Selvius *Descendants of Lemuria:A Description of an Ancient Cult in California* The Mystic Triangle, Aug, 1925
25 Oga-Make *Tribal Memories of the Flying Saucers* FATE magazine, Sept. 1949
26 Walton, Bruce *Mount Shasta: Home of the Ancients*, p. 26
27 Lewis, Dr. Harvey Spencer *The New Lemurian Mystery* The Rosicrucian Digest, Sept. 1936
28 Walton, Bruce *Mount Shasta: Home of the Ancients*, p. 26
29 Ibid., p. 27
30 *Trace of Giants Found in Desert* San Diego Union Aug. 4, 1947
31 *Expedition Reports Nine-Foot Skeletons* Hot Citizen Aug. 5, 1947

Chapter Eight
The Evidence

IF civilizations once existed in the Atlantic and Pacific Oceans, then there should be proof of the submerged lands. Speculative accounts have always existed; however, without further investigative proof, the theories cannot be justified. The location for the submerged land of Lemuria allegedly exists in three separate locations: the Pacific Ocean, Indian Ocean, and the Arctic Ocean. Potential locations given for the submerged land of Atlantis include the Mediterranean Sea, Caribbean Sea, and Atlantic Ocean. Analysis can rule out locations using known scientific evidence. Vast collections of data should not be ignored and through interpretive evidence, more knowledge can be gained of the lost civilizations.

A massive supercontinent known as Pangaea existed nearly 250 million years ago. As time passed, the continents shifted and broke into the continents we know today. Evidence exists in the form of many rare species of fossil that can be found on either side of the oceans today. Region specific fossils found along the coast of Brazil, in South America, are also located along the coast of West Africa, matching an area of land on Pangaea. The land of Lemuria can be accounted for on the map of Pangaea if one is to simply add in the missing continent on any of the surrounding sides; the missing land of Atlantis is a little harder to explain because of the small gap between North and South America, and Europe and Africa. The coastlines are indicative of the changes that have occurred. Over time, land masses distort, some sink, and others rise. Plate tectonics can provide an understanding of the lost continent of Lemuria and Atlantis through knowledge of volcanic eruptions, seismic movement, and subduction of land. The earth's crust is divided into fourteen plates: half minor and half major. Within the gaps of the plates, those spaces are occupied by hundreds of microplates. The different convergent movements of the plates cause the subduction zones to completely transform the landscape.

Ocean floor topography may provide evidence of the submerged lands in question. Studies show that the Pacific Plate was created during the Jurassic Period, occurring 200 to 145 million years ago; therefore, any newly submerged landmass cannot be attributed to once having existed in the Pacific Ocean. Some research concludes that active regions of magma formed new land, specifically basalt. The Tamil Indian legend of *Kumari Kandam* to the south of India may also be proved by ocean seafloor dating; however, there is much objection against this. Seafloor dating can be inconclusive when trying to prove the existence of submerged lands. Carbon dating of rocks cannot be done; however, through analysis of the sedimentary layers on the ocean floor, a rough sequence of time can be determined. The dating of the Hawaiian Islands can be traced through the gradual movement of the Pacific plate. The Hawaiian Islands have shifted over 3,700 miles, giving it an approximate age of 70 million years.

In the analysis of Atlantis, the islands in the Azores may provide another perspective into destruction of Atlantis. In 1898, the transatlantic cable snapped nearly 500 square

miles north of the Azores. A ship set out to retrieve the cut
lines and discovered an underwater plateau named Telegraph
Plateau. In their investigation, they discovered submerged
lands containing high mountain peaks and valleys on the seafloor, approximately 1,000 miles north of the Azores. The crew
collected rock samples that covered the seafloor. It was not
until 15 years later that Paul Termier, director of the Oceano-
graphic Institute, analyzed the rock and determined the following; 1.) The rock was of volcanic origin and formed as part of a
lava flow resulting from eruptions in the Telegraph Plateau. 2.)
The rock contained amorphic, vitreous, and non-crystalline
structure, therefore it was solidified in the open air and not underwater. 3.) The whole region must have sank 6,560 feet at
either the same time as the volcanic eruption or shortly afterward. Thus, the specimen was evident of a prehistoric catastrophe in the middle of the Atlantic. 4.) Due to the mineralogical
nature of the specimen (a tachylite). And the fact that tachylites
dissolve in sea water within about 15,000 years, along with the
contours in the specimen appearing intact, the Atlantic catastrophe most likely occurred less than 15,000 years previously
and probably considerably later than 13,000 BCE.[1] Other rock
samples have been collected around the Azores, including
some that were collected 6,600 feet underwater, north of the
Azores, by the Soviet Academy of Science. Dr. Maria Klenova
examined the rocks and concluded they were formed 15,000
years ago by atmospheric pressure. Granitic rocks were collected north of South America between Venezuela and the Virgin Islands by a Duke University expedition. Dr. Bruce Heezen, a leading United States oceanographer stated the following: "Up to now, geologists generally believed that light granitic or acid igneous rocks are confined to the continents and that
the crust of the Earth beneath the sea is composed of heavier,
dark-colored basaltic rock... Thus, the occurrence of light-
colored granitic rocks may support an old theory that a continent formerly existed in the region of the eastern Caribbean

and that these rocks may represent the core of a subsided lost continent."[2]

Sea levels at the time of Atlantis's supposed demise were around 300 feet lower than what they are today. Furthermore, archaeological evidence shows that around 12,000 years ago, there may have been cities based around the coast and islands of the Caribbean before the sea level rose. Sightings of underwater pyramid-like structures in the region have also been reported by individuals, including Ed Wilson who, on June 7, 1948, was flying over the Caribbean. Forty-five miles northeast of Miami and about 250 feet above sea level he "noticed something big under the water and thought it was a wrecked ship. Not far from the surface, something was causing the water to rush past it at a fast rate. It curled around it and made a deep channel. The ocean appeared to be opening up... I suddenly realized that what I was looking at was not a ship at all, but it seemed to be a huge building below down in the water. The water seemed to get shallower around it. I could see a slanting side of a building that looked like a mountain. I was down about fifty feet from the surface and could see the water. I circled around it for about a minute and a half. I could even see barnacles on it and water running past the top of it. At my point of angle and from my position I could clearly see a monstrous building. The sun was radiating in such a way that in its rays I could see this huge building clearly visible down under the water. I thought I saw other buildings around it but I could not see them well. The one I was looking at must have been 100 to 250 feet high according to the pattern I could get."[3] Before he could get readings of the location, a bright reddish hue enveloped his plane at 600 feet above the water causing engine failure and the electronics to malfunction. He glided for about 2 miles until he finally regained control and went back to the airport. "Over the past years I have been back many times, but I could never sight it again. A lot of damned Miamians made fun of my story. But I know I am right."[4]

The mystery of the Bermuda Triangle is often associated with stories of Atlantis in the western Atlantic Ocean. One of the most reasonable theories that offers an explanation for the disappearance of crafts relates to evidence of frozen methane gas in the vicinity of the Bermuda Triangle. Temperature shifts in climate and seismic oceanic activity cause this methane gas to release into the water and atmosphere. The result is a complete loss of buoyancy in the water, causing ships to sink. And once the gas reaches the air it can cause planes to lose control over their engines, and in extreme cases a spark from the engine can ignite the flammable gas. Methane gas is found throughout most of the world's oceans in the layers of seafloor (though presumably preserved at colder temperatures). If global temperatures continue to rise, these gasses would be able to melt and release into the atmosphere, which would speed up the overall temperature of the earth (Methane gas is 10 times more potent than Carbon Dioxide in global warming).

Among Atlantean researchers, one of the most interesting cases for underwater ruins is that of the Ampere Seamount near Madeira. In 1974, Russians conducted underwater explorations deep in the Atlantic Ocean on the *Academician Petrovsky*. Crew members included a scientist from the Russian Institute of Oceanography and photographers specializing in underwater photography. Photographs taken in 1978 at the Ampere Seamount reveal platforms, square blocks, walls, and long stairways. Researcher Egerton Sykes believes that the Russian ship was a spy ship scouting out locations to station submarines in the event of a war, and that it happened to stumble across the site. He believes that the exact location of the photographs was not reported and that the photographs were taken in the Azores between Santa Maria and São Jorge. Sykes compared the ruins in the photographs to structures created by the Aztec and Maya.[5]

Similar structures can also be found on island of Yonaguni, Japan. A stone pyramid with a flat top over 80 feet high was discovered underwater. Some archaeologists claim that it was created naturally (based on amateur photographs), while photographs clearly show evidence of a manmade presence. A team of scientists led by marine seismologist Masaaki Kimura was sent out to survey the underwater structure and to determine if the structure was created naturally. Using scientific equipment, they surveyed the underwater structures and re-created a three dimensional model. They concluded that it was likely made by humans. Upon learning of the results, American geologist Dr. Robert M. Schoch, professor of science and mathematics at Boston's University, flew out to investigate the structure. "I believe that the structure can be explained as the result of a natural process," accounting for the wave and currents that might have been responsible for the formations.[6] He determined it to be a natural structure; however, it clearly had artificial characteristics. "I cannot totally discount the possibility that the Yonaguni monument was at least partially worked on and modified by the hands of humans."[7]

Further investigations produced evidence suggesting a manmade construction. Several holes were found along various parts of the structure (more specifically found on the uppermost section), similar to what many ancient civilizations used to create their massive blocks. In a straight line they would drill holes and with a hard pull they would break off the stone slab. Hieroglyphs carved alongside the structure may perhaps be the lost symbols of Mu, as mentioned by Colonel Churchward. Carved structures were also found at the Yonaguni monument; the most well-known is of the enormous human face discovered by Tom Holden, during a filming for the History Channel. Several of the structures found later underwater resemble the ruins found in Peru, more specifically in Sacsayhuamán.

Ruins and Remnants of the Ancient Descendants

Many researchers have developed theories over the exact location of Atlantis. In recent times, many attribute the civilization described by Plato, as those similar to the Minoan civilization in the Aegean Sea. The Minoan civilization was advanced and idolized the use of bulls in a ritual manner. Several parallels can be made between the Minoan and Atlantean civilization, which leads researchers to believe that it is the fabled civilization described by Plato. The Minoan civilization came to an abrupt end when a volcanic explosion on the island of Santorini triggered a tsunami that destroyed the Minoans. The ancient Antikythera mechanism, dating back over 2,000 years ago, is just one of the many examples of advanced Greek knowledge about mechanics. In no way do I doubt that these advanced technological achievements could have been constructed without the aid of an advanced civilization; I suggest that there could have been a transference of knowledge from an advanced civilization that might have taken place at some point in time and whose evidence might still exist to this day.

In Egypt, the first excavation on the Sphinx was undertaken by Thutmose IV around roughly the 14th century BCE. The great Sphinx was a forgotten enigma, even for the Egyptian Pharaohs. Accounts describe the antiquity of the Sphinx: Pharaoh Amenhotep II of the 18th dynasty described the Sphinx as being older than the pyramids themselves. Many legends portray the Sphinx as a sacred monument in honor of Atlantis, while others believe that there is a hall of records underneath. In Egypt, the great pyramids are also believed to have been created either by aliens or the Atlanteans themselves; however, there is plenty of evidence showing that there were several failed attempts at building pyramids. The massive pyramid structures we see today were attempted after various false starts. Such evidence can be found at the Pyramid in at Meidum and the Bent Pyramid at Dahshur after the weight of its own structure collapsed on itself.

Several technological techniques in the construction of Egyptian monuments are found to be used around the world. Various structures around the world were erected by each of the civilizations corresponding to its verified cultural authenticity. As unique as each monument stands as a testament to great achievement, one cannot help but wonder if the techniques themselves contain knowledge passed down from an alternative source. If the stories regarding Lemuria and Atlantis are true, then the disbursement of these populations should have ultimately left some remnant knowledge along with various other groups occupying the vast lands of the world. Lastly, the focus primarily should be placed on ancient ruins found around the world and the commonality between them through the format in which they were erected. Over time knowledge becomes dispersed, changed and in time dissipates further from the root source. In Peru, knowledge in the building of magnificent temples can be attributed to a source found near Lake Titicaca. The Tiahuanaco culture was the primary source for the future construction of Inkan architecture. The advanced knowledge in masonry in Peru and Bolivia is far superior in many ways to the architectural knowledge we have today. Gigantic stone monuments testify to the superior knowledge of these people. Throughout Peru, many of the ancient ruins consist of fitted stones that interlock so precisely that a person cannot stick a needle through a crack.

Three types of stone were used by the Inka for the construction of public buildings found in the heart of the ancient Inkan Empire in Cuzco. Black andesite turns a deep reddish brown color as it ages. A greenish-grew diorite porphyry, most common in Sacsayhuamán, and Yucay limestone, a hard grey stone is used throughout Sacsayhuamán and Cuzco itself.[8] The symmetrical designs on each of the interlocking stones found in Cuzco are unique, making each one completely different (resembling a jigsaw puzzle). It is not known how the Inka accomplished the task of building some of the larger monuments. The precision involved would have taken a great amount of time and effort for the Inka to test each stone, remove it, make the adjustments, and repeat until the stone became a perfect fit.[9] Many of the sacred sites and temples around Peru rely on the use of water, which still flows year round as naturally as it did before the conquest. Parts of the terraces maintain their own unique ecosystem. Depending on the amount of sunlight or water a given species of plant would need, they would be placed within the terraces accordingly.

The Inka themselves had knowledge on how to construct their buildings according to the natural landscape. At many of the sites, the masonry is based on already existing natural rock formations. At the very tip of the peak of Huayna Picchu in Machu Picchu there are houses, terraces, tunnels, caves, and steep stairways. The level of skill and courage required to construct these buildings at the top of a mountain peak continue to impress visitors today.

It is noticeable that in some of the ruins in the Andes, particularly in the Sacred Valley, resemble the ancient Tiahuanacan civilization. In several instances, the masonry constructed in the lower portions of buildings are superior to the upper portions of the building. It appears that a group of highly skilled stone masons constructed the monuments. It is evident that the Inka civilization, which existed much later, built upon established foundations and structures. For example in Peru, there once stood a massive structure known as the Temple of Viracocha (also spelled Wiracocha) in the archaeological site of Raqchi. The foundation, or base of the columns, feature similar advancements in stone masonry similar to those located near Lake Titicaca; however, they appear as if they had never been completed. The upper construction of the temple, built on top of the existing stone masonry, is made out of adobe stretching up two stories in length.

What little remains of the Temple of Viracocha in Raqchi, Peru
after being looted and destroyed by invading Spanish forces.

Machu Picchu

Doorway to Huayna Picchu

Keystone Cuts

Four different styles of masonry found within a
single street corner in Cuzco, Peru

The stone masonry found around Cuzco, Sacsay-huamán, and Ollantaytambo, in Peru, can also be attributed to having the same constructional techniques as those found in Egypt. For example, in Abydos, Egypt, the masonry is similar to what is found in Peru. Stone blocks found in the Osireion and the Valley Temple in Egypt have nitches, oddly polygonal shaped (yet perfectly fitted) stone blocks, and irregular bulks notches that stick out from the blocks - all characteristic of the ancient masonry found in Peru. Some of the stone blocks found in Egypt and Peru twist around the corners and interlock perfectly with the other blocks. In Peru, while the Spaniards destroyed most of the cities, the larger structures could not be destroyed. As a result, the Spaniards built on top of the preex-isting Inka structures. During earthquakes, the only parts of the structure that would topple over were the ones created by the Spaniards. Unique masonry found near Lake Titicaca in the remarkable *Pumapunku* (meaning the Door of the Cougar) site in Bolivia can also be found in Temple of the Sun, in Cuzco, Peru. Great engineering and precision went into the construc-tion of these two sites. Finely cut straight lines, perfectly carved round holes, complex shaped angles, everything down to the smallest detail was exact.

The most interesting technique found in the building of these massive monuments (found in Egypt and Peru) are what David Hatcher Childress refers to as "keystone cuts." In Peru and Bolivia, these T-shaped carvings connected the stones with a bronze metallic filling. It is believed that their true purpose was to hold together the massive stone blocks during earth-quakes; however, after many years, these structures toppled and many of the indigenous people collected these metallic clamps for other practical uses. Metallurgy in Peru predates the Inka. Evidence of metallurgy found among the pre-Inkan as well as Inkan sites consists of copper, bronze, lead, zinc, an-timony, bismuth, silver, and gold. The aforementioned keys-tone cuts were also used in ancient Greek architecture, in Dendera, Egypt, and as far away as the sacred site of Angkor Watt in Cambodia.

Other evidence of an ancient civilization having an impact on cultural groups around the world can also be found within their languages and writings. Among the large Moai statues on Easter Island, hieroglyphs inscribed on tablets have been found. The decipherments of these hieroglyphs have been unsuccessful; however, researchers have found similarities between the Rongorongo hieroglyphs on Easter Island and those found in the Indus Valley in India (more specifically the writing discovered at Mojenjo Daro and Harappa in Pakistan). The Indus Valley civilization is believed to be one of the most ancient civilizations in the world, dating back to 3,000 BCE. In 1932, Guillaume de Hevesy theorized that the Rongorongo language originated in the Indus Valley, which he determined through comparative linguistics. However, many scholars have dismissed the authenticity of the research as being pseudoscience.

Further investigations reveal that a majority of ancient civilizations around the world followed a 360-day year. Classic writings of the Hindu Aryans use the 360-day year. The *Aryabhatiya*, an ancient Indian mathematical and astronomical work written in Sanskrit, describes a year as being twelve months, each month being thirty days; Ancient Babylonians also used those measurements for months and years. Many of the structures located in Babylonia indicate that they followed a 36 decan zodiac system, each one following the sun for a period of ten days in relation to the stars. Many of the walls in Babylonia were 360 furlongs in circumference - a reflection of their year. In the ancient Egyptian culture, calendars were based on 360 days in a year; the ancient Chinese calendar also used twelve months, each consisting of thirty days.[10] The Mayan year also consisted of 360 days, called a *tun*. Five days were later added and were considered unlucky, during which time all activities would cease. Even the Inka divided their year into twelve quilla, each being thirty days. The Inka later added an extra five days at the end of the calendar, and after every four years an extra day was added. Consequently, all of the ancient calendars changed to include the extra five days. For the Inka, the extra days added were believed to be unlucky, similar to the Aztec and Mayan cultures. Many of the cultures also describe a different location where the sun would rise: "Ancient Chinese records mention a time when the sky suddenly began to fall northward and the sun, moon and planets changed their positions after the Earth had been shaken."[11] In ancient Egypt, the Harris Papyrus, the Hermitage Papyrus of Leningrad, and the Ipuwer Papyrus each mention a cataclysm that took place. Within the Denderah zodiac, the constellation of Leo shows the location being over the vernal equinox, which is now occupied by Aries.

The architecture of several ruined cities is attributed to the knowledge of a previously undiscovered civilization. The legendary construction of the mysterious city of Nan Madol, dating back to roughly the 12th century CE on the island of Pohnpei in Micronesia, possibly holds clues as to ancient knowledge that might have existed. According to legend, the massive structures of Nan Madol were erected by a magician who flew in the massive stone logs from an unknown location. Many archaeologists refute the legend as fantasy; however, they did not ignore the fact the stones used in the construction of Nan Madol were not from the surrounding region. Archaeologists also fail to explain the movement of these large stones, while many theorize that they were carried over on rafts. Every attempt to prove this theory ends in failure. Other ruins are found near Eastern Island in an isolated section of the Pacific Ocean on Malden Island. The island remains uninhabited, but there is evidence that people previously occupied the island. Ruins provide evidence of temples and other structures, potential remnants of another group of forgotten people from Polynesia.

Unearthed artifacts have also been attributed to ancient civilizations that possessed advanced intelligence. One of these artifacts was found in a tomb in Colombia dating back 1,400 BCE. It is presumed to be a statue of a flying fish; however, when analyzed by zoologist Ivan Sanders, he determined it was not an identifiable animal. He stated that the statue resembled a jet fighter plane with delta wings and other mechanical features, such as ailerons, tail rudder, and rectangular engine casing, complete with a cockpit.[12] In 1961, rock collectors in the Coso Mountains in California came across an interesting stone geode. Analysis reveals that it had a metal core wire surrounded by some odd encasing in what is now petrified wood. A silver chalice was discovered in 1851 during rocking blasting operations in Dorchester, Massachusetts. The time it would take for the rock to form around the chalice suggests that it took thousands, if not millions of years. In 1844, stone cutters working in a quarry near River Tweed in Scotland, discovered a gold thread within a rock eight feet below ground. When the Spanish first invaded the Andes they came across a mine. Inside, they noticed the use of iron nails in the large passageways of the mine, though it is documented that the indigenous people of the Americas did not use steel or iron.[13]

On Table Mountain, in Tuolumne County, California, Miners dug into a huge plateau with hopes of discovering gold and other mineral resources. Instead of finding gold they stumbled across a mortar and pestle 180 feet below the surface. Investigators determined that the mortar and pestle dated back between 33 and 55 million years. Every possible explanation to debunk these artifacts was inconclusive; in other words, there is no reasonable explanation for these artifacts been there. Among other artifacts found at the site were those of human skeletal remains.[14]

In a book published by Christopher Hardaker in 2007, entitled *The First American; the Suppressed Story of the People who Discovered the New World*, respected archaeologists declare that there is a great injustice occurring within the field of archaeology. In Vaslsequillo, Mexico, archaeologists uncovered some of the oldest spearheads in the world. Harvard University officials worked closely with geologists from the United States Geological Survey. The researchers estimated the spearheads to be around 12,000 years old. Archaeologists then estimated that the remains could be 40,000 years old; however, after USGS geologists and researchers collaborated, they dated the remains to be 250,000 years old. Among the things recovered was a mastodon bone with carvings of animals that existed prior to the Pleistocene era. Because many of the dates from the site are considered to be 'too ridiculously old' they were put aside. Afterwards, the site was blocked off to prevent any further investigation. Questions remain as to why this evidence is being ignored and also the length of time that humans have existed in the Americas.

The forward to Christopher Hardaker's book was written by Charles W. Naeser, a geochemist, of the United States Geological Survey, who stated the following:

> As a scientist I am embarrassed that it has taken over 30 years for archaeologists and geologists to revisit the bone and artifact deposits of Valsequillo Reservoir. In the late 1960s and early 1970s, data were presented that suggested Early Man had been in the New World much earlier than anyone had previously thought. Rather than further investigate the discoveries, which is what should have been done, they were buried under the sands of time, in the hope that they would be forgotten...So, now we have at least five independent geological age estimates that all indicate an old, pre-Clovis age for the Valsequillo site...we have the choice of accepting the results of five independent geological techniques as correct, and concluding that the artifacts are greater than 200,000 years old or, alternatively, arguing

that, for the very same reasons, there is something sig-
nificantly wrong with each of the geological age estimates.[15]

Many archaeologists claim to have been 'black listed' for stating the facts, no matter how contrary they might be to the popular conception of history. A lot of anomalous evidence builds
up and is quickly dismissed by those involved. It is possible
that the academic field of science has become a power structure
similar to the Roman Catholic Church. Accusations have ren-
dered the institution as impenetrable. Scientists spend years
building their reputation, only to be condemned. Political
agenda has intertwined with academia which leads to the question: who is controlling who?

Other Evidence

There are many anomalous remains throughout the
world, and though I do not contest them as being actual remains of the Lemurian or Atlantean civilization, I suggest that
they may have influenced other cultures around the world. An
example is the use of artificial cranial deformation used in
many of the ancient cultures. In many Egyptian depictions of
royal families, members would be portrayed as having elongated skulls. In several instances the actual process of artificial
cranial deformation would be undertaken, which consists of
placing boards or pads along the frontal side of an infant's
head, which would be tightly bound by rope. Over time, the
ropes would be bounded tighter and tighter causing the infants
head to slowly become elongated into the desired shape. This
practice dates back to 45,000 BCE in Iraq and can be found
throughout the Americas, as far down as Patagonia. Among
the Maya, artificial cranial deformation was practiced only by
the elites and the royal family. Newer cases of this process
have also been found in Siberia and among the Tiahuanaco ci-

vilization in South America. No other practice is as geographically widespread as artificial cranial deformation. Research suggests that the practice was a form of acknowledging those with artificial cranial deformation within a specific group, lineage, or affiliation. It indicated high status in a culture and was only allowed by a few. For example, Siddhartha Gautama, otherwise known as Buddha, is often depicted as having an elongated skull. Further indications might suggest that the distinctions, based upon archaeological evidence, might have been used in honor of the ancients. I theorize that it was a sign of higher status; however, it was in honor of their predecessors. In many instances, the royal families were seen as descendants of Gods, suggesting that racial mixing between cultures occurred in the distant past. And as homage to those distant ancestors, they would elongate the skulls in honor of their heritage and to display that they were descendants of these 'gods.' In several accounts involving the ancient people, they have been described as being tall and having irregularly sized craniums.

Many believe that the search for these previously undiscovered advanced civilizations is absurd, but the search still continues. Previous investigations were funded directly by illegitimate governments who sought to establish themselves as descendants of these lost civilizations, such as Adolf Hitler's obsession with the story of Atlantis. The Third Reich conducted several investigations to prove the existence of Atlantis, in order to prove their self-declared superiority. By tracing back the Aryan lineages to Atlantis they could once and for all rewrite the history books in their image. In the 1930's, Mustafa Kemal Atatürk, the first president of Turkey, maintained a strong belief in the story of Lemuria and directly funded research in that field. Atatürk believed that there was evidence tying the ancient Turkic civilization to that of Lemuria and hopefully claiming connection to other great civilizations

A Mayan frieze depicting volcanic eruptions, flood, temple
collapsing and victim drowning as a man rows away in his raft.
Frieze was discovered by German archaeologist Teobert Maler
(1842- 1917) in Tikal's North Acropolis at the Great Plaza.
It was dismantled and sent to the Berlin Museum, in Germany,
however, it was later destroyed in the bombings during
World War II.

around the world such as the Aztec and Indus Valley Civilization. The motives behind these governmentally funded cases are examples of why academics refute the existence of advanced ancient civilizations. In many regards, the research must follow unbiased and unmotivated scientific procedures and must be conducted in an objective fashion. As humans, we all posses' cognitive biases; the common belief in science is that we must remove all subjectivity from our rational reasoning to reach undisputable facts.

People believe that a common practice among many of the ancient civilizations was that of cremation, which may explain the lack of physical evidence. It is well known that in many Native American groups, members of the tribe would burn a person's possessions after one's death. This is not to say that all groups around the world engaged in the same practice. There is plenty of anomalous physical evidence to back up an alternative historical and anthropological view. Mummies found around the world severe as an interesting feature toward our historical accumulation of knowledge. Not only do the bone structures remain, but the preservation of the physical characteristics of an individual are still intact. Individual case studies show an interesting correlation between certain physical traits which might trace back to the ancients.

It was long believed that the indigenous Guanches living in the Canary Islands, off the coast of northern Africa, were descendants of Atlantis. Mummified remains of these indigenous people have been located in the islands and they are found to have red and blonde hair. Archaeological evidence suggests the islands were occupied between 1,000 BCE and 100 BCE. Genetic testing has been inconclusive; however, some tests show that the majority of the genetic lineages can be traced back to Euro-Asian and African-Middle Eastern ancestry. Waves of migration from different cultural groups account for the genetic evidence found, more importantly the Spanish ge-

netics found among the people. The Spanish occupied the territory and shortly thereafter the Guanches became extinct.

Other mummies having similar characteristics can be
found throughout the world. Egyptian mummies have been
found to have red, brown, and blonde hair. Queen Tiye,
Ramses II, Queen Hatshetrut, and many other mummified remains feature "Caucasian-like" characteristics. This is a highly
controversial subject with both Eurocentric and Afrocentric
claims. The actual concept of race does not exist, and genetically speaking, all humans are related.

Mummified evidence tracing back 3,000 years can also
be found in the Gobi and Taklamakan Deserts in China. The
region itself used to consist of very fertile lands until desertification over took the land. Because of the desertification
process that took place, mummified remains have been uncovered throughout central China. All the mummies share similar characteristics: tall, and having red, brown, and blonde hair,
as well as other "Caucasion-like" features. Scientific and eth-
nic claims propose that these people occupied much of the East
until the Chinese conquered the land much later. These ancient
people are believed to have had a strong influence on the Chinese culture. Other mummies found in the nearby Tarim Basin
continue to perplex investigators. Professor Victor H. Mair,
from the University of Pennsylvania, stated that the earliest
mummies in the Tarim Basin were exclusively Caucasoid, or
Europoid: "The new finds are also forcing a reexamination of
old Chinese books that describe historical or legendary figures
of great height, with deep-set blue or green eyes, long noses,
full beards, and red or blond hair. Scholars have traditionally
scoffed at these accounts, but it now seems that they may be
accurate," says Mair.[16] The perfectly intact remains of many of
the mummies still baffle scientists. The genetic evidence
points to DNA found in western Eurasia, in the area south of
Russia. While other research conducted by National Geographic in 2007 suggests that they originated from multiple

origins such as Europe, Mesopotamia, India, and another unde-
termined location. The existence of this group may also explain the Roman account of Pliny the Elder, who described tall
and blonde haired individuals in the same area.[17]

Mummies also fitting the same physical characteristics
of being "Caucasian" have been found in South America.
Within the advanced culture of the Chachapoya in Peru the
people were described as tall, white, and with light colored
hair. In the Amazon, several mummies were unearthed 82 feet
below the surface, in a burial vault that had once been used as a
place of worship. The archaeological site was accidentally
stumbled upon by a local farmer in the area. The name Chachapoya itself is translated as "Warriors of the Clouds," whose
name is given to them by their conquerors, the Inka.[18] Several
Chachapoya communities have been located recently, including a vast city containing buildings and structures. Some of the
structures were thought to be over a thousand years old. The
Chachapoya were thought to have been wiped out by the
spread of disease upon the arrival of the Spanish in Peru, in
1535. The Chachapoya women were a highly prized posses-
sion among the Inka, as they were tall and fair skinned.[19]
Countless other mummies have been discovered around Peru,
some being the result of sacrifice, while others were the result
of natural or sometimes war-related deaths, but none were as
unusual as the Chachapoya mummies that were discovered.

A Smithsonian Cover-up?

In investigating several historical occurrences of very
tall and white inhabitants there was an interesting article published online several years ago by Ross Hamilton entitled *Holocaust of Giants: The Great Smithsonian Cover-up*. At first
glance the article seemed rather outrageous and fictitious.
Upon reviewing the article a second time, the information
seemed more compelling and valid. The article is now well

circulated among conspiracy theorists and websites. By further investigating the citations given, the re-written accounts given by Hamilton are accurate. Various accounts recorded by arc-haeologists, newspapers, researchers, and other governmental agencies are rather amazing.

The Smithsonian Institute is one of the largest museum complexes in the world storing high prized collections. Similar to a scene out of the ending of the first Indiana Jones movie, many believe that the Smithsonian Institute withholds its most precious artifacts from the public. Without regards to Native American culture, the Smithsonian Institute undertook many excavations on Native American land and confiscated many of the remains. Many of the grave sites were desecrated by arc-haeological digging in the name of science. With the passing of NAGPRA law (Native American Graves Protection and Re-patriation Act) it was demanded that the remains be returned to each of the tribes. But, of course, with so many skeletal re-mains, the Smithsonian lost track as to the origins for each of its skeletal remains. The Smithsonian later promised to return 18,650 Native American skeletal remains for reburial.

As previously mentioned, Native Americans knew about other visitors who once occupied various regions in the Americas. Archaeological evidence supports theories of the creation of the mysterious mounds found throughout the United States; however, other people argue that the Mound Builders predate the Native Americans, and in fact, many of the Native American groups do not know who built some of these massive mounds. It is well documented that there were several mound building cultures in existence during the time of Spanish explo-ration. The archaeological evidence does support the fact that Native Americans did build the massive mounds (e.g. the Ho-pewell culture). But, it is possible some were built by others.

The Smithsonian undertook several excavations at vari-ous mounds and uncovered interesting skeletal remains and artifacts. The following are actual documented cases of what investigators uncovered at various locations:

Grave *a*, a stone sepulcher, 2½ feet wide, 8 feet long, and 2 feet deep, was formed by placing steatite slabs on edge at the sides and ends, and others across the top. The bottom consisted simply of earth hardened by fire. It contained the remains of a single skeleton, lying on its back, with the head east. The frame was heavy and about seven feet long. The head rested on a thin copper plate ornamented with impressed figures...[20]

Underneath the layer of shells the earth was very dark and appeared to be mixed with vegetable mold to the depth of 1 foot. At the bottom of this, resting on the original surface of the ground, was a very large skeleton lying horizontally at full length. Although very soft, the bones were sufficiently distinct to allow of careful measurement before attempting to remove them. The length from the base of the skull to the bones of the toes was found to be 7 feet 3 inches. It is probable, therefore, that this individual when living was fully 7½ feet high. At the head lay some small pieces of mica and a green substance, probably the oxide of copper, though no ornament or article of copper was discovered.[21]

No. 5, the largest of the group was carefully examined. Two feet below the surface, near the apex, was a skeleton, doubtless an intrusive Indian burial... Near the original surface, 10 or 12 feet from the center, on the lower side, lying at full length on its back, was one of the largest skeletons discovered by the Bureau agents, the length as proved by actual measurement being between 7 and 8 feet. It was clearly traceable, but crumbled to pieces immediately after removal from the hard earth in which it was encased....[22]

The other, situated on the point of a commanding bluff, was also conical in form, 50 feet in diameter and about 8 feet high. The outer layer consisted in sandy soil, 2 feet thick, filled with slightly decayed skeletons, probably Indians of intrusive burials. The earth of the main portion of this mound was a very fine yellowish sand which shoveled like ashes and was everywhere, to a depth of 2 to 4 feet, as full of human skeletons as could be stowed away in it, even to two and three tiers. Among these were a number of bones not together as skeletons, but mingled in confusion and probably from scaffolds or other localities. Excepting one, which was rather more than 7 feet long, these skeletons appeared to be of medium size and many of them much decayed...[23]

No. 11 is now 35 by 40 feet at the base and 4 feet high. In the center, 3 feet below the surface, was a vault 8 feet long and 3 feet wide. In the bottom of this, among the decayed fragments of bark wrappings, lay a skeleton fully seven feet long, extended at full length on the back, head west. Lying in a circle above the hips were fifty-two perforated shell disks about an inch in diameter and one-eighth of an inch thick.[24]

At a depth of 14 feet, a rather large human skeleton was found, which was in a partially upright position with the back against a hard clay wall...All the bones were badly decayed, except those of the left wrist, which had been preserved by two heavy copper bracelets...Nineteen feet from the top the bottom of this debris was reached, where, in the remains of a bark coffin, a skeleton measuring 7½ feet in length and 19 inches across the shoulders, was discovered. It lay on the bottom of the vault stretched horizontally on the back, head east, arms by the sides... Each wrist was encircled by six heavy copper bracelets...Upon the breast was a copper gorget...length, 3½ inches; greatest width 3¾ inches...[25] Three feet above...the skeleton of a large, strongly built man lay extended at full length with the face up, the head toward the east...The skull was obtained almost entire. Under it were thirteen water-worn quartz pebbles. The femur measured 18½ inches...[26]

Found within various burial sites were skeletons over seven feet tall. Well-known Native American activist, author, historian, and professor, Vine Deloria has stated that after talking with several elders, some of them reported seeing other Indians who were "more than average height" and much "larger and taller" than themselves.[27] Several articles describing the amazing finds by the Smithsonian were even printed in several newspapers and research journals:

An old Indian mound has been opened on the farm of Harrison Robinson, four miles East of Jackson, Ohio, and two skeletons of extraordinary size and a great quantity of trinkets have been removed. Some years ago a party of relic hunters, supposed to have been sent out in the interest of the Archeological society visited the Robinson farm, and after a few days search removed a great collection of stone hatchets, beads and bracelets, which were packed and shipped to an Eastern institute, and until this recent accidental discovery it was supposed that everything had been removed by the relic hunters. It is thought by many that more relics are to be found and preparations are being made for a through investigation. [28]

A large Indian mound near the town of Gastersville, [Gastonville?—Ed.] Pa., has recently been opened and examined by a committee of scientists sent out from the Smithsonian Institute. At some depth from the surface a kind of vault was found in which was discovered the skeleton of a giant measuring seven feet two inches. His hair was coarse and jet black, and hung to the waist, the brow being ornamented with a copper crown. The skeleton was remarkably well preserved...On the stones which covered the vault were carved inscriptions, and these when deciphered, will doubtless lift the veil that now shrouds the history of the race of people that at one time inhabited this part of the American continent. The relics have been carefully packed and forwarded to the Smithsonian Institute, and they are said to be the most interesting collection ever found in the United States.[29]

A large quantity of human bones was discovered in a fissure in the limestone near the United States Coast Guard lighthouse. A crude tomb of black stone slabs, of a formation not known on the island, was found many years ago beneath the roots of a huge stump. Eight skeletons were found, one measuring over seven feet in height.[30]

Further inquiries reveal that the government knew of the evidence being gathered by the Smithsonian Institute and took a deeper interest into the investigations being conducted. In 1868, the Surgeon General demanded that the United States Army gather as Native American remains, including skeletons, weapons, and artifacts to be evaluated on "effects of modern bullets and other weaponry on human bodies."[31] The following is an article published in 1872 by the Army Medical Museum in Washington:

The objects here collected which have not been given,
or acquired by exchange, have been purchased for the
use of the museum by order of the surgeon-general...
There is a skeleton of a giant, who, in life, measured
seven feet, prepared by Auzoux and mounted by
Blanchêne's method, which, if I may use that term, is
really a beauty. It is as white and clean as new fallen
snow, and the brass joints and screws which keep it together are bright, and of the latest style and finish...[32]

Other historical accounts have also been found detailing the
removal of skeletal remains, and in some instances the Smithsonian Institute flat out denied the existence of its skeletons:

He further told me of the killing of a big Indian at
Buckchitawa, about the time of the settlement at Ma-
rietta. The Indians had a white prisoner whom they
forced to decoy boats to the shore. A small boat was
descending the river containing white people, when this
prisoner was placed under the bank to tell those in the
boat that he had escaped captivity, and to come to the
shore and take him in. The Indians were concealed, but
the big Indian stuck his head out from behind a large
tree, when it was pierced by a bullet from the gun of the
steersman of the boat. The Indians cried out Wetzel,
Wetzel, and fled. This was the last ever seen of the
prisoner. The Indians returned next day and buried the
big Indian, who, he said, was twenty inches taller than
he was, and he was a tall man. When Chester Bishop
was digging a cellar for Asahel Booth, at Clarington,
many years ago, he came across a skeleton, the bones of
which were removed carefully by Dr. Richard Kirkpa-
trick, and from his measurement the height of the man
when living would have been 8 feet and 5 inches. It is

probable that these were the bones of the big Indian of whom the Indian at Jackson's told me.[33]

Concealing evidence that conflicts with accepted theory is common scientific skullduggery. For years the Smithsonian Institution has been accused of hiding in storage vaults things it doesn't like. In 1968 two Neanderthal-like skulls with low foreheads and large brows were found in Minnesota. As for dating, University of Minnesota scientists said they were reluctant to destroy any of the material, although carbon-14 testing only requires the burning of one gram of bone. They were sent to the Smithsonian. Later Dr. Lawrence Angel, curator of physical anthropology at the institution, said he had no record of the skulls there, although he was sure they were not lost. We have a right to wonder whether some professional scientists mightn't find a really early date for the bones distressing.[34]

The Smithsonian Institute is the storehouse of the Unites States. There have been many hoaxes regarding giants in the United States, such as the petrified Cardiff Giant discovered in Arizona. Many within the archaeological field have even been caught planting fake evidence or changing the results to make their theories appear true. The accounts given previously were undertaken by Cyrus Thomas, who was hired to undertake the Division of Mound Exploration under the Bureau of American Ethnology. The U.S. House or Representatives passed a federal bill funding Cyrus Thomas's research directly. The final outcome consisted of seven hundred pages documenting what the investigations had uncovered. The accusations were forced upon Thomas's research calling it empirical, as opposed to research previously done by Ephraim Squier and Edwin Davis who only investigated 200 mound sites in Ohio, rather than 2,000 undertaken by Thomas. Thomas collected over 40,000 artifacts which directly became a part of the Smithsonian Institute collections.[35]

It was proven that Cyrus Thomas's research was biased. Thomas claimed that Native American cultures were "too primitive" to build these magnificent mounds. This has been proven false: Hernando de Soto's explorations directly stated the existence of "civilized" people in existence in various areas and actually witnessed the building of mounds.[36] Archaeological researchers conclude that Thomas misinterpreted many of the sites and artifacts because of his biased personal beliefs. Thomas is accused of falsifying many of the findings in order to justify the existence of an ancient race. His biases seemed to have been the leading cause for the dismissal of his research.

---

[1] Muck, Otto Heinrich *The Secret of Atlantis*, p. 144

[2] Berliz, Charles *Atlantis: The Eighth Continent*, p. 158-159

[3] Ibid., p. 103

[4] Ibid., p. 104

[5] Ibid., p. 82-88

[6] Hancock, Graham *Underworld: The Mysterious Origins of Civilization*, pp.597-607

[7] Ibid.

[8] Hemming , John *The Conquest of the Incas*, pp.124-5

[9] Ibid.

[10] Hope, Murry *Practical Atlantean Magic,* p, 79

[11] Ibid., p. 80

[12] Berliz, Charles *Atlantis: The Eighth Continent*, p. 132

[13] Ibid., p. 143

[14] Cremo, Michael A. & Thompson, Richard L. *The Hidden History of the Human Race*, pp. 94-101

[15] Hardaker, Christopher *The First American; The Suppressed Story of the People who Discovered the New World*, pp. 9-11

[16] Mair, Victor H. *Mummies of the Tarim Basin*. Archaeology, 48.2 (March/April, 1995), pp. 28-35

[17] Pliny (the Elder) *The natural history of Pliny* Chapter 24 (22)--Taprobane

[18] London Evening Standard *Moment 600 years ago that terror came to Mummies of the Amazon* January 10, 2007

[19] McDermott, Jeremy Telegraph.co.uk *Lost city of 'cloud people' found in Peru* December 3, 2008

[20] Cyrus, Thomas *Report on the mound explorations of the Bureau of ethnology*: U.S. Bureau of American Ethnology. *Twelfth annual report, 1890-91, Annual report of the Bureau of American Ethnology to the secretary of the Smithsonian Institution -- v. 12*. (1894) (Cyrus Thomas' investigations of Etowah), p. 302

[21] Ibid. (explorations in Roane County, Tennessee), pp. 361-2

[22] Ibid. (mounds at Dunleith, Illinois), p. 113

[23] Ibid. (Pike County, Illinois), p. 117

[24] Ibid. (Kanawha County, West Virginia), pp. 418-9

[25] Ibid. (Kanawha County, West Virginia), pp. 426-7

[26] Ibid. (Union County, Mississippi), p. 273

[27] Deloria, Vine *Red Earth, White Lies*, p. 156

[28] *The Adair County News* (Kentucky), January 5, 1897

[29] Peet, Stephen Denison *The American antiquarian and oriental journal, Volumes 7-8*, (1885) Volume 7, p. 52

[30] Thorndale, Theresa *Sketches and Stories of the Lake Erie Islands* Sandusky, Ohio (1898), p. 11

[31] Hamilton, Ross *Holocaust of Giants: The Great Smithsonian Cover-up*

[32] Bagger, Louis *"The Army Medical Museum in Washington"* Appletons' Journal: A Magazine Of General Literature Volume 9, Issue 206 (1873)

[33] *Hardesty's History of Monroe County, Ohio*

[34] Gaddis, Vincent H. *American Indian Myths and Mysteries* (1977), p. 12

[35] Feder, Kenneth L. *Frauds, Myths, and Mysteries: Science and Pseudoscience in Archaeology*, pp. 170-182

[36] Ibid.

Chapter Nine
The Academic Debate

WITHIN the realm of academia, the debate regarding the legends of Lemuria and Atlantis should be clear: there is no proof; therefore, it never existed. The advancements made within scientific academia however tell a different story. Archaeological discoveries allude to a new historical variation that many are at a loss to explain. For example, if archaeologists were investigating a site and discovered something exceeding the historical records, in other words was "too ridiculously old," it would be put aside and forgotten. But what if collectively, there is enough of the same anomalous data that could shed light onto a different perspective? It would be difficult to say for sure what becomes of these pieces of evidence that do not make it into the records. Artifacts often end up uncatalogued in the basement of a university's collection, lost within piles of boxes.

Many believe that archaeological research in a specific location takes place over a long period of time so that nothing can be missed. This true in that archaeologists have all the time needed to conduct proper investigations given that the investigations are taken place in a national park or other restricted areas of land. Many times, archaeologists working in the field work within various Cultural Resource Management (or CRM) groups and do not have the luxury of time. The purpose of CRM groups is to quickly research and investigate a given location for a client, in order to collect anything of historical importance. For instance, a private company is planning to build a set of structures within a given set of acres of land. Upon digging, some workers uncover skeletal remains alongside pottery shards. The private company then puts a halt on all further work in the area, resulting in a great loss of money for the company, and hires a CRM group to investigate. A team of archaeologists are called in to find anything important, and are limited to a strict deadline, usually ranging from two to four weeks. In many instances, the archaeologists are working in front of a bulldozer if the deadlines are even more limited. If skeletal remains are found, another set of procedures must be adhered to because of the complexity of NAGPRA (Native American Graves Protection and Repatriation Act) laws. The team usually picks out a few locations to dig and investigate, while avoiding the rest. Because of time constraints, they have to limit their digs to a few locations to see if anything is found. After the investigation is complete, the bulldozers come in and destroy what remains. This is not limited to private companies, but governmental agencies also use similar tactics. If the state is building or expanding on a freeway, again the same measures are taken and anything that is not retrieved is destroyed.

When the archaeologists conduct their investigations they usually work with an academic frame of mind. If they know a group of indigenous lived within a given area during a certain time period, they correspondingly dig within those layers of the soil. I have heard several stories of archaeologists finding more than they were looking for. I recall a private discussion with a university archaeology professor, telling me a story from his past. He had been working within a CRM team located in Nevada where they were called in to investigate an area for possible Native American remains. The team would dig until they hit a rock-hard layer of volcanic ash. According to historical records, they knew that the volcano had erupted before Native Americans inhabited the land. As a result, they understood that nothing could exist prior to the time of the ancient volcanic eruption. As their deadline was coming to an end, one of the archaeologists decided to randomly start breaking through the hard layers of volcanic rock. It was an arduous task, but eventually he broke through the layer. What he found amazed all the other archaeologists working nearby: he had discovered the ruins of an ancient dwelling or civilization where none was suppose to exist. By that time, their deadline was up, and everything was covered and abandoned.

DNA & Skeletal Analysis

Some of the most amazing discoveries are made by ordinary people when least expected. Some of these findings completely change the way we look at human history as we know it. On July 28th, 1996, two men attempted to get a closer look at a boat race on the Columbia River in Kennewick, Washington. They noticed something unusual protruding from the eroded river bank and quickly notified the authorities. At first glance, archaeologist James Chatters assumed it was a European settler who had died during the 1800's. Radiocarbon tests determined that the body was over nine thousand years old.[1] The man had a projectile point embedded in his hip, several months prior to his death. He had apparently died in his mid 40's from an infection. What was very odd about the individual was that he did not resemble modern day Native Americans; in fact, the skeletal remains looked like that of a "Caucasian." A media frenzy ensued, referring to the skeletal remains as Kennewick Man. Various Native American tribes, including

the Nez, Perce, and Yakama tribes claimed relation and owner-
ship to the skeletal remains, abiding to NAGPRA law. Federal
hearings took place to determine which of the five tribes claiming relations should be granted the remains. The federal judge
stated that further investigations over the remains should take
place before scientists could accurately determine the tribal
descendants.

The case of Kennewick Man marks the first time that
these "Caucasian" remains were fully publicized; however, it
was not the first or nor last time ancient "Caucasian" remains
have been found in the United States. In 1959, archaeologists
uncovered skeletal remains of a "Caucasian" man dating back
over 10,000 BCE on Santa Rosa Island, off the coast of California. There were clear indications of stone tools in the area
dating back between 12,500 and 29,700 BP (Before Present). [2]
Another case is that of Spirit Cave mummy found in Nevada,
in 1940, dating back 9,415 +/-25 years BP.[3] Similar to Kennewick Man, the tribal affiliation of the Spirit Cave mummy
could not be determined. An investigation by the Nevada Bureau of Land Management to determine tribal descendants concluded the following:

> While it is difficult to associate ethnicity or language
> with archaeological materials, the BLM's review of the
> available evidence indicates sufficient discontinuity
> such that it is unlikely that the tribes occupying the Spi-
> rit Cave area in historic times are from same culture as
> the people who buried their dead in Spirit Cave in the
> early Holocene or that they are the direct descendants
> of that group.

> Therefore, BLM's review of the available evidence in-
> dicates that the culture history of the western Great Ba-
> sin shows a pattern of changes in cultural adaptations
> that does not support cultural continuity over the last

10,000 years. The level of discontinuity is sufficient to warrant the conclusion that the remains from Spirit Cave cannot be reasonably affiliated with any modern tribe or individual.[4]

The biological data concluded that "there is no available biological information which clearly supports cultural continuity with contemporary North American Indians."[5] The evidence clearly shows that the mummy was not related to modern day Native Americas. "Analysis showed the Spirit Cave cranium closest to 'Norse' and 'Ainu.' It should be noted that the probability for Norse was 0.00084, with Ainu an even lower probability… though they are distinctive from recent American Indian samples, it is also clear that the recent samples most closely resembling these two specimens are Polynesians and Australians, both populations distinguished by their relatively narrow faces, longer crania, and more projecting faces."[6] Other remains found in Nevada have raised questions as to the tribal affiliation compared to modern day Native Americans. Wizard's Beach Man has an 84.45% craniofacial phenotype similar to modern day Native Americans; it also has a 76% probability of being related to typical Polynesians. The rest of the ancient skeletons found in Nevada maintain 88.5% similarity to modern day Australasians (from Australia and Melanesia).[7] Similar findings are located North and South America and even as far north as Alaska.[8] Likewise, some skeletal remains are said to be taller than average, and some mummified remains are said to also possess red hair.

The search for the oldest skeleton in the Americas still continues. Interestingly enough, other claims presenting "the oldest" skeletons are also seen as "Caucasian." In December, 2004, in Mexico City, a skull dating back over 13,000 years ago was discovered and named "Peñon Woman III." It was the oldest skull found in the Americas, and again, the similar characteristics of the Ainu people were noticeable, bringing up the theory that perhaps they traveled via the coast.[9] In another article by National Geographic from 2008, researchers recovered other "Caucasian-like" remains, this time underwater in a cave off the coast of Yucatán Peninsula. The skeletal remains were dubbed "Eve of of Naharo," and radiocarbon dating estimated it to be 13,600 years old. Three other skeletons found nearby have been radiocarbon dated as being from between 11,000 to 14,000 years ago. Sea levels were 200 feet lower around the area at the time of their existence which was once a wide open prairie. Dramatic melting of the polar ice caps roughly 8,000 to 9,000 years ago caused the sea levels to rise and flood the caves. Other interesting findings within the caves show the existence of elephants and giant sloths.[10]

Anthropological testing best suggests relation to the indigenous Ainu found in Japan. Historically, the Ainu can be traced back to the Jōmon period in prehistoric Japanese history, dating as far back as 14,000 BCE. The Ainu are not "Caucasian," but are tall, hairy, and light-skinned. Initially, researchers thought that a group of people from northern Asia migrated across the Bering Strait during the Ice Age in pursuit of large animals. Researchers now hypothesize that waves of migration occurred not only through the ice-free corridors but also through coastal route migrations. As mentioned previously, recent mitochondrial DNA researchers revealed that 95% of all modern Native American populations can be traced back to six women who lived approximately 18,000 to 21,000 years ago. And what made the results more interesting was that the DNA evidence suggests they did not originate from Asia as previously thought; their DNA signatures aren't found in Asia. The DNA concludes that they lived in Beringia, the now underwater land bridge that once existed between Alaska and eastern Serbia. [11] [12]

Various anthropologists believe that at one point in time there might have been waves of migration alongside the coastal regions of the Americas. The Coastal Migration Theory is supported by evidence discovered around the Pacific, and the technological and cultural similarities between the Western Americas to those around the Pacific, spanning from Japan down into Australia. Rare isolated pockets of unique mtDNA have been found from North America to South America. The mtDNA of the Chumash Native Americans, which are found in southern California, can be found in isolated prehistoric settlements in Alaska, Mexico, among the Mapuche in southern Chile, and in sites found in Tierra del Fuego/Patagonia.[13] Coincidentally, some of the aforementioned areas are where the early Spanish encountered "white Indians." The level of sophistication of the Chumash raises many ideas regarding their origins. On the Channel Islands which where once inhabited by the Chumash, rare species of flora found nowhere else in the world exist there.[14] A study of the some of the islanders reveals skeletal similarities between European races, similar to other rare Native American populations found around California. [15] Following written accounts in the Americas that make mention of a prehistoric, already existing population of "white people" in existence, the question then arises; are these rare populations (such as the Chumash and Mapuche) a part of those "white people" previously mentioned? Or did the original white predecessors assimilate with the arrival of the Native Americans?

As previously mentioned, Yurok Native American Lucy Thompson stated that there were originally white predecessors occupying the continent who later mixed with the incoming Native Americans populations.[16] Later, the white people "left this land before the world was cover with water."[17] And when they left, they left behind the people who were still three-quarters Indian, which is why some of the Yurok are fair-skinned.[18] Does one simply ignore the 'myths and lore' presented by Thompson? Or does one investigate deeper to reveal the parallels between the stories that have long since been ignored and the actual evidence?

The study of Native American DNA reveals four main haplogroups, those being A, B, C and D.[19] Haplogroups are genetic markers that determine the evolutionary pattern found within the Y-Chromosome in mitochondrial DNA (or mtDNA for short). There is a rare X-haplogroup among Native American populations, which is also one of the ten haplogroups found in Europe (at a rate of 3%) and nowhere in East Asia.[20]

> Among Native Americans, haplogroup X appears to be essentially restricted to northern Amerindian groups, including the Ojibwa (~25%), the Nuu-Chah-Nulth (11%–13%), the Sioux (15%), and the Yakima (5%), although we also observed this haplogroup in the Na-Dene–speaking Navajo (7%).[21]

The study shows the prehistoric nature of the skeletons being tested, leaving out the possibility of post-Columbian European mixing. The results of the study concluded that there was no relation between the native Nuu-Chah-Nulth (near Vancouver in Canada) who have haplogroup X, with any other Native American populations who also have haplogroup X. In other words, the study showed that there was no normal distribution which would occur if migration took place. The study also concluded that the haplogroup X found in Europe was in fact one of the earliest found among the Americas.[22] As the study suggests, could it be that there was already a preexisting group with haplogroup X and after several waves of migration, might be able to account for the haplogroup found among various tribes?

If migration from Europe is suspected, then there should be evidence of migration from Europe through eastern Asia and Siberia. However, the uniqueness found within various studies shows that haplogroup X only appears in isolation among western Eurasians and Native Americans.[23]

These findings leave unanswered the question of the geographic source of Native American X2a in the Old World, although our analysis provides new clues about the time of the arrival of haplogroup X in the Americas. Indeed, if we assume that the two complete Native American X sequences (from one Navajo and one Ojibwa) began to diverge while their common ancestor was already in the Americas, we obtain a coalescence time of 18,000 +/- 6,800 YBP [Years Before Present], implying an arrival time not later than 11,000 YBP.[24]

And yet another study shows that the evidence might actually dismiss the idea of various waves of migration entering the Americas (based on the genetic diversity found among Native Americans). The study determined "the migration of two founding lineages." Furthermore, the lack of a mutation found among people with haplogroup X, show the resemblance between Native American and European populations.[25]

Europeans assigned to haplogroup X lack a mutation at np 16213 in the HVSI that all Native Americans exhibit. However, the larger sample size of individuals assigned to haplogroup X in the present study reveals that a substantial number of Native Americans in multiple geographic regions also lack the np 16213G mutation and therefore have haplotypes identical to those of European and Asian members of haplogroup X.

The present study raises doubt about interpretations of previously reported evidence for the number of migrations to the Americas... Many researchers have interpreted similar estimates among at least four of the five Native American haplogroups as evidence that all haplogroups entered the Americas at the same time.[26]

Reanalyzing the evidence may reveal an already pre-existing ancient population inhabiting the Americas prior to the arrival of Native Americans. Some research concludes that the population with haplogroup X might have been among the first wave of migration into the New World, but Native American ethnographies dismiss that theory. Many Native American populations believe that they originated from this land, being born unto the earth at their present location. Other Native American stories state that they ventured from a distant homeland later entered into the Americas. It is still unclear, genetically speaking, as to what might have actually taken place. The mystery of haplogroup X is still among the most controversial topics in the study of genetics. Implications of those claims can perpetuate ideas of racism, Eurocentrism, and false justifications over claims to land. In support of Native American mythology regarding a pre-existing ancient population, research shows that the original population with haplogroup X occupied the Americas up to 36,000 years ago, making them among the first people to inhabit the Americas: [27]

> Time estimates for the arrival of X in North America are 12,000–36,000 years ago, depending on the number of assumed founders, thus supporting the conclusion that the peoples harboring haplogroup X were among the original founders of Native American populations.[28]

> ...it is possible that this mtDNA was brought to Beringia/America by the eastward migration of an ancestral Caucasian population, of which no trace has so far been found in the mtDNA gene pool of modern Siberian/eastern Asian populations.[29]

And in comparison to Native American stories, Lucy Thompson stated the following:

After we left the beautiful valley of *Cheek-cheek-alth,*
for years we wandered down a European land, always
moving toward the south, having our origin in the far
north. Over this land we wandered having our origin in
the far north. Over this land we wandered like exiles,
we know not how long, as it might have been centuries
until we reached the rolling waves of the ocean. Upon
reaching this salt water we made boats or canoes, and
paddled over the waves until we reached the opposite
shore, having crossed the straits in safety. [30]
When The Indians first made their appearance on the
Klamath River it was already inhabited by a white race
of people known among us as the *Wa-gas.* These white
people were found to inhabit the whole continent, and
were a highly moral and civilized race. [And] after a
time there were intermarriages between the two races,
but these were never promiscuous.[31]

Hypotheses

The Solutrean hypothesis speculates that early Europeans may have once crossed the Atlantic Ocean, bringing with
them their technology. This accounts for the technology that
predates the Clovis people, who are thought to be the first mi-
grants into the New World. Dennis Stanford, an anthropologist
at the Smithsonian Institute, was among the first to support this
theory. The early migrations, in the Solutrean hypothesis, suggest that early Europeans in the southwestern area around
France and Spain traveled in boats to the New World during
the ending of the last Ice Age. The unique hypothesis is based
on rare Solutrean projectile points found predating the unique
Clovis points. This evidence is also supported by the rarity of
haplogroup X, as well as the skeletal evidence found (e.g.
Kennewick Man).[32]

There has since been an argument against the Solturean hypothesis as found in an article entitled *Ice Age Atlantis? Exploring the Solutrean-Clovis 'connection.'* [33] The article states that researchers Dennis Stanford, along with Bruce Bradley, jump to many conclusions, making false claims with 'imaginative evidence' to support their arguments. Bradley and Stanford later wrote a rebuttal against the article stating that the researchers were unfounded in their arguments and wrong in their interpretations. The evidence argued on both sides is very detailed and scientific. But the final word on the issue was made by Bradley and Stanford:

> The bottom line is that our technological analyses distinguish two strong clusters, nonbifacial Solutrean Upper Palaeolithic/Beringian (including Alaska) and Solutrean/pre-Clovis/fluted point. This is certainly not conclusive evidence of a connection between Solutrean and pre-Clovis/Clovis, but it does clearly indicate that there are strong similarities, which is not the case with Beringian and pre-Clovis/Clovis. What it comes down to is that all technologies present in pre-Clovis/Clovis are found in Solutrean (except fluting) while most but not all Solutrean technologies are represented in pre-Clovis/Clovis. The same cannot be said for the Siberian/Beringian materials. We ask again: would we have any doubt of the origin of pre-Clovis/Clovis if Solutrean technologies were found in Beringia at the LGM [Last Glacial Maximum]? [34]

The various hypotheses given by scholars allude to a pre-conceived notion as the main motivation behind their research. Perhaps, a paradigm shift needs to occur before future analysis can be considered. Many researchers once believed that the oceans were the true borders of the world, preventing people from moving across them. In recent times, however, the scientific community has accepted many proposed theories regarding the movement of sea-ferrying people. Throughout Polynesia and the Norwegian seas, the evidence created a paradigm shift. Though it was a gradual process of filtering through the false assumptions and pre-conceived beliefs that people once maintained. As today we have new ideas speculating pre-Columbian trans-oceanic contact, a favorite among many pseudoscience proponents, the ideas must invariably be forced to be examined under a different light. Though evidence does support the colonization of the Norse in North America, there is no other evidence to support the idea of other Europeans making their way across the Atlantic Ocean. The Polynesian debate regarding the early establishments in the Americas, on the other hand, is finding more and more support through analysis of various coastal populations (e.g. the Chumash in particular). Proponents of early Polynesian navigators are along the lines of early Coastal Migration theories, and so indeed, it may soon be an established fact. The Mesa Verde site in Chile was the leading reason why previous Clovis-first theories were disproved; however, a new academic paper might prove the theory to be true.

The main argument against the Solturean hypothesis is new research based on mtDNA. Results show that there was in fact one single pre-Clovis migration with a coastal route (including haplogroup X). "Our results strongly support the hypothesis that haplogroup X, together with the other four main mtDNA haplogroups, was part of the gene pool of a single Native American founding population; therefore they do not support models that propose haplogroup-independent migrations, such as the migration from Europe, posed by the Solutrean hypothesis."[35] The original pre-Clovis people came over Beringia and expanded along the Pacific coastline. The results of the research showed the following:

Under our model, three periods that may define a date
for the peopling of the Americas can be delineated: (1)
the colonization of Beringia (because about half of it
was "America" at that time) by the founding population; (2) the movement out of Beringia—characterized
by the fast colonization of the continental Pacific coastal plain—south of the ice sheets; and (3) the more recent and more extensive colonization of inland continental masses. Furthermore, the probability of coalescence of mtDNA lineages within a population and the
chance of finding ancient archeological evidence go in
opposite directions.[36]

In this 2008 study, the evidence shows the existence of
a wave of migration into the New World. As with any other
evidence, it may quickly be disputed and bring into light yet
another theory. And so, the hunt for evidence supporting Pre-
Siberian human migrations still continues. Some archaeologists proclaim that researchers are just pushing the migration of
the Clovis people further and further back to account for much
of the evidence. And the topic itself will remain a much heated
debate on both sides, accounting for both evidence and the lack
of evidence. The mystery of haplogroup X as well, is still not
at an end, in due time certainly new evidence will emerge
shedding new perspectives.

Case for the White Indians

Investigations reveal many accounts of "white Indians"
in existence throughout the Americas. Scholars have translated
original documents according to their own pre-conceived notions: "white" has often been translated as "lighter-skinned," in
many cases. The justification for doing so is that the Spaniards
were ignorant, regarding their views on other people. Everything not black, through their eyes, was considered white,

which was incorrect. Regardless, there might have been several instances where white was substituted for lighter-skinned; however, in most of the cases, they were accurately portraying their encounters. Some descriptions mention these white Indians as having beards, while in other descriptions the indigenous state that the other tribes of whites were as white as the Spanish.

Documented accounts of white indigenous in the Americas have been researched as far recently as the 1920's, but most of the cases have proven false. Several academic news outlets published the ongoing research, including *Science News-Letter*, later known as *Science News*. There was a large amount of scientific controversy at the time regarding white Indians found in Darien jungles of Panama, originally discovered by an expedition led by Richard O. Marsh. At first they believed that they might have been a mixed race (between indigenous and European), and later they presumed that they might be a new race. Their skin was described as being similar to that of the northern white Europeans with a rosy tint, while their hair was described as golden.[37] Early investigations provided descriptive examples: "These children have golden hair, hazel or hazel-blue eyes and pink gums."[38]

After the publications became known, various research scientists took interest of the white Indians of Panama. A team of scientists decided to further investigate including Dr. Ales Hrdlicka, anthropologist of the Smithsonian Institution, Dr. Charles B. Davenport of the Station for Experimental Evolution, and Dr. C. W. Stiles of the U. S. Public Health Service. Further investigations revealed that the earliest sighting of these natives could be traced back to 1679 to Alexandre Exquemelin, a buccaneer for both English and French ships. Exquemelin landed on the islands of Zambles, located west of the River Darien, where he notes that several of the Indians were 'fairer than the fairest of Europe' with "hair as light as flax."[39] After several investigations, anthropologists believed that they may in fact be a new white race, while other anthropologists believed that they were albinos. Later, scientific research established that in fact it was albinism that existed at a very high rate among the Kuna tribe from Panama, a result of inbreeding. However, the Albino children are seen as Moon Children, high leaders among the community.[40]

Investigations regarding the so-called "white" Native Americans mentioned so frequently before are non-existent today. If tribes of "white" indigenous do exist, they will most likely exist in the unknown regions of the Amazon. After the colonization of the New World, disease and war ran rampant and decimated a majority of the indigenous populations. Though some of the predominant genes are attributed to "Caucasian-like" features that once existed, such as with the case of Kennewick man, phenotypically are no longer predominant, yet alone existent. That is why it is difficult to determine the descendants of these ancient remains. I remain skeptical that any of the 'white Indians' had survived the conquering of various regions by the incoming Europeans. The 'white Indians' lived after the attacks of so many indigenous tribes and prior civilizations. Even if the mysterious 'white Indians' survived all the brutality that took place, they would not be any match for the Europeans. The relocation of tribes, along with the various factors of assimilation and warfare, constituted a great genocide in the Americas, leaving no room for cultural preservation.

[1] Swedlund, Alan & Anderson, Duane *Gordon Creek Woman Meets Kennewick Man: New Interpretations and Protocols Regarding the Peopling of the Americas.* American Antiquity. Vol. 64, No. 4 (Oct., 1999), pp. 569-576

[2] Orr, Phil C. *Arlington Springs Man.* Science Magazine. New Series, Vol. 135, No. 3499 (Jan., 1962), p. 219

[3] Barker, Pat Ph.D., Ellis, Cynthia M.A., and Damadio, Stephanie Ph.D. July 2006. *Determination of Cultural Affiliation of Ancient Human remains from Spirit Cave, Nevada* Bureau of Land Management Report Summary (Nevada State Office), p. 1

[4] Ibid., p. 6

[5] Ibid., p. 7

[6] Barker, Pat Ph.D., Ellis, Cynthia M.A., and Damadio, Stephanie Ph.D. July 2006. *Determination of Cultural Affiliation of Ancient Human remains from Spirit Cave, Nevada* Bureau of Land Management Full Report (Nevada State Office), p. 39

[7] Powell, Joseph Frederick *The first Americans: race, evolution, and the origin of Native Americans*, p. 200

[8] List of similar skeletons found in North America: Kennewick Man ~9,500 BP (Washington), Prospect Man ~6,800 BP(Oregon), Arlington Springs Man ~10,000 to 13,000 BP (California), Anzick Burials ~10,800 BP (Montana), Buhl Woman ~10,800 BP (Idaho), Spirit Cave Man~9,400 BP (Nevada), Wizard Beach Man ~9,200 to 9,500 BP (Nevada), Grimes Point Burial Shelter ~9,740 BP (Nevada), Whitewater Draw ~8,000 to 10,000 BP (Arizona), Wilson-Leonard ~ 9,000 to 11,000 BP (Texas), Pelican Rapids Woman ~7,800 BP (Minnesota), Browns Valley Man ~8,900 BP (Minnesota) , Hour Glass Cave ~7,700 to 7,900 BP (Colorado), Nebraska Remains, Gordon Creek ~9,7000 BP (Colorado), and Horn Shelter ~9,600 BP (Texas); taken from the organization 'Friends of America's Past' website page, "Evidence of the Past: A Map and Status of Ancient Remains" <http://www.friendsofpast.org/earliest-americans/map.html>

[9] Legon, Jeordan *Scientist: Oldest American skull found* CNN.com News

[10] Barclay, Eliza *Oldest Skeleton in Americas Found in Underwater Cave?* National Geographic News September 3, 2008

[11] Ritter, Malcolm *Native American DNA Links to Six "Founding Mothers"* National Geographic News Associated Press March 13, 2008

[12] Achilli, A.; et al. *The Phylogeny of the Four Pan-American MtDNA Haplogroups: Implications for Evolutionary and Disease Studies* PLoS One. 2008 Mar 12;3(3):e1764. "The phylogenies of haplogroups A2, B2, C1, and D1 reveal a large number of sub-haplogroups but suggest that the ancestral Beringian population(s) contributed only six (successful) founder haplotypes to these haplogroups. The derived clades are overall starlike with coa-

lescence times ranging from 18,000 to 21,000 years." This study does not in any way imply that all Native Americans populations can be traced back to only six women; rather, a majority of Native American populations, genetically speaking, may be associated to a founding population. The main criticisms for this study maintain that it does not account for Haplogroup X, and uses a very small sample size to account for a whole population.

[13] Raab, L. Mark, Cassidy, Jim, and Yatsko, Andrew *California Maritime Archaeology: A San Clemente Island Perspective*, pp. 237-8

[14] Faber, Phyllis M. *California's Wild Gardens: A Guide to Favorite Botanical* Sites, p. 152

[15] Heizer, R.F. and Whipple, M.A. *The California Indians*, pp. 100-1

[16] Thompson, Lucy *To the American Indian: Reminiscences of a Yurok Woman*, p. 81

[17] Ibid., p. 182

[18] Ibid., p. 84

[19] Smith DG, Malhi RS, Eshleman J, Lorenz JG, Kaestle FA. *Distribution of mtDNA haplogroup X among Native North Americans American Journal of Physical Anthropology Volume 110 Issue 3,* pp. 271 - 284

[20] Ibid.

[21] Brown MD, Hosseini SH, Torroni A, Bandelt HJ, Allen JC, Schurr TG, Scozzari R, Cruciani F, Wallace DC *mtDNA Haplogroup X An Ancient Link between EuropeWestern Asia and North America?* American Journal of Human Genetics 1998 Dec;63(6):1852-61

[22] Smith DG, Malhi RS, Eshleman J, Lorenz JG, Kaestle FA. *Distribution of mtDNA haplogroup X among Native North Americans American Journal of Physical Anthropology Volume 110 Issue 3,* pp. 271 - 284

[23] Reidla, Maere; et al. *Origin and Diffusion of mtDNA Haplogroup X* American Journal of Human Genetics 2003 November; 73(5): 1178–1190.

[24] Ibid.

[25] Malhi, RS; et al. *The Structure of Diversity within New World Mitochondrial DNA Haplogroups: Implications for the Prehistory of North America* American Journal of Human Genetics 2002 Apr;70 (4):905-19.

[26] Ibid.

[27] Smith DG, Malhi RS, Eshleman J, Lorenz JG, Kaestle FA. *Distribution of mtDNA haplogroup X among Native North Americans American Journal of Physical Anthropology Volume 110 Issue 3,* pp. 271 - 284

[28] Ibid.

[29] Ibid.

[30] Thompson, Lucy *To the American Indian: Reminiscences of a Yurok Woman*, p. 76

[31] Ibid., p.81

[32] Oppenheimer, Stephen *The Real Eve: Modern Man's Journey Out of Africa*, pp. 317-8

[33] Straus, Lawrence Guy, Meltzer, David, Goebel, Ted. Ice *Age Atlantis? Exploring the Solutrean-Clovis 'connection'* World Archaeology, Volume 37, Number 4, December 2005 , pp. 507-532(26)

[34] Bradley, Bruce and Stanford, Dennis *The Solutrean-Clovis connection: reply to Straus, Meltzer and Goebel* World Archaeology, Volume 38, Issue 4 December 2006 , pp. 704 - 714

[35] Fagundes, Nelson J. R.; et al. *Mitochondrial Population Genomics Supports a Single Pre-Clovis Origin with a Coastal Route for the Peopling of the Americas* The American Journal of Human Genetics, Volume 82, Issue 3, 583-592, 28 February 2008

[36] Ibid.

[37] Shrubsall, F. C., Haddon, A. C. and Buxton, L. H. Dudley *The "White Indians" of Panama*
 Royal Anthropological Institute of Great Britain and Ireland Man, Vol. 24, (Nov., 1924), pp. 162-164

[38] H. L. Fairchild *White Indians of Darien* Science, New Series, Vol. 60, No. 1550, (Sep. 12, 1924), pp. 235-237

[39] *White Indians Seen in Panama in 1679* The Science News-Letter, Vol. 9, No. 274, (Jul. 10, 1926), pp. 9

[40] Louis, Regis St. and Doggett, Scott *Panama*, p. 273

Chapter Ten
Unveiling a New Mystery

L EGENDS regarding the ancient lands of Lemuria and Atlantis endure to this day. With so many books being written on the topic of Atlantis, it is no wonder why so many people continue searching for the elusive land. From video games to movies, the concepts reflect the idea and at the very least invoke the curiosity that remains within the minds of people. Romanticized ideas of finding a long lost city, or coming across the last forgotten tribe hidden in the Amazon still persist. Despite harsh criticisms that idealists face, the trend will continue and many enthusiasts will remain in the pursuit of the lost kingdoms. Only time will tell if these investigative endeavors will result in discoveries. The exact locations for these lost paradises are disputable. And being divided on the issues, reluctantly, many open themselves up to further skepticism and inquisitional attacks. Unorganized investigations lead many researchers into making giant unfounded speculations, causing more harm to the integrity of the field. Many researchers still continue on their investigations, including many notable academics, and hopefully these theories will one day change from mythology to fact.

Human ignorance will continue to cause destruction in our society. Cyclical movements throughout history have demonstrated the amount of destruction that can be inflicted upon others. The great library of Alexandria, containing millions of books, was attacked several times until finally being destroyed in the seventh century by invading forces. During the Middle Ages, many books were destroyed by Christians who believed that books served as pleasure to the mind and not for the salvation of the soul. Many of the ancient manuscripts were also destroyed during that period because of a shortage of writing materials. As already mentioned, the Spanish conquest destroyed many of the ancient Mayan and Aztec writings, under the order of Bishop de Landa. Countless codices were destroyed and only a few survived, which leads one to imagine what other pieces of knowledge could have existed, relating to the ancients of Lemuria and Atlantis. During the reign of Adolf Hitler, tens of thousands of books were burned in Germany because they did not meet the standards imposed by Nazi ideology. Fragmented bits throughout history come into existence at different times and shed light into ancient civilizations existing prior to our Westernized conception. It is still categorized as mythology because no archaeological or geographical evidence exists. Regardless, the imagination still strives for the answers regarding these pre-deluge civilizations. And in the end it all becomes part of a collective quest to seek out the unknown.

The Legends Continue...

An interesting case from 1670 involves Jesuit Missionary Frey Juan Lucero, who worked within the mission of Santiago de la Laguna in Peru. He mentions having several encounters with mysterious white Indians during his travels on the Huallaga River, which is a headwater tributary for the Marañón and Amazon Rivers. He referred to the white Indians as *Curveros*, and said that they had a King-leader who descended from the Inka Tupac Amaru, and who during the conquest fled into the jungles east of Cuzco with 40,000 Peruvian Inkas. Frey Lucero associated these white Indians with *El Gran Payti-ti (Paytiti* meaning Jaguar*)*, who were ruled by a "Jaguar-king" in a "white house" by the great lake. Presumably, these are the descendants of the pre-Inkan white race of people who lived on Lake Titicaca and who were later exterminated by the Inka. *Paytiti* (also spelled *Paititi*) is a great legendary tale of Inka gold which may still remain within a hidden city in the jungle (brought over secretly during the conquest as a last refuge). Frey Lucero claimed to have seen some of the mysterious Inka gold, which consisted of plates, *half-moons*, and earrings, all made of gold. [1] A more recent encounter of these mysterious Indians took place in 1932, as reported by a German missionary. According to him, they were timid and shy. They approached him at the edge of a lake deep in the forest and afterwards ended up bartering with one another. [2]

Mysterious tales of *Paititi* still persist, from the earliest expeditions by Spanish explorers, to Percy Fawcett, to current expeditions seeking the fabled lost city. Many of the expeditions being led into the jungles of South America never make it out alive, almost as if being swallowed up by the earth. Tales of similar expeditions date back to the earliest of Spanish settlers, who likewise went in search of *Paititi*. Don Alonso Sole-to Pernia and his family settled in San Larenzo, in what is now Beni, Bolivia. Several captured indigenous people told Don Pernia of *Paititi*, and how their forefathers journeyed into in the lost city until they fled from the white people with shiny silver metal and armor. Don Pernia rounded up a group of people and led an expedition into the jungles. They came across a fort containing odd symbols. They took over several forts with the aid of Indian captives. Later, they discovered an empty pueblo, presuming that the inhabitants had fled upon their arrival. The streets were unusually clean and in the village plaza they found a building containing thirteen beautiful sculptures resembling monks or priests. In another village, they found an intricate statue resembling the crucifixion of Jesus on a nearby alter. Because of dwindling supplies, they had no other option but to head back home. Don Pernia was pressured into returning to the villages. Several Indians told him that they knew exactly where the city was within the jungle. Again they ventured back, this time to a mountaintop overlooking a valley. They were astonished at what they found: a great city surrounding a lake. Because there were only six of them, they could not risk taking the city, so they retreated and ended their search for *Paititi*. [3] [4]

Other tales detail complex tunnel systems spanning from ancient Inka temples across many miles into the deep jungles. There is a story of a man in the 1800's emerging from an ancient Inka tunnel during mass in the church of Santo Domingo in Cuzco. The treasure seeker disappeared into the tunnels a week prior to the incident. During mass, in a church that was converted from the old Inkan Temple of the Sun, a priest and the congregation started hearing loud noises coming from underneath the floor. The priest demanded that the stone floor be removed; the man emerged clenching gold bars in each hand. Legends have always told of men going into the deep tunnels, which lead into a complex labyrinth maze, only to come out insane or not come out at all. In the early 1920's, the Peruvian government decided to investigate these tunnels first hand. A team from the University of Lima conducted the scientific investigations with a well experienced speleologist. The team embarked on a journey towards the Pacific Ocean in the east and took detailed measurements along the way. Communication between the explorers in the tunnels and those still at the entrance became completely cut off. For twelve days nobody heard anything from the team until a solitary man reappeared. Starving and exhausted, he spoke of the labyrinths and deadly obstacles that lay within the tunnels. The police later went back and dynamited the entrance to the tunnel, completely sealing it shut.[5] The main entrance to these tunnel systems are said to begin in Sacsayhuamán, right outside the city of Cuzco.

Several tunnels have been discovered as far west as Lima and as far south as Chile. Spanning thousands of miles, there have been many rumors regarding these tunnels as being interconnected. In 1884, a Catholic priest was called to give the last rites to a dying Quechua man. Before the man died he whispered into the ears of the priest a story regarding a labyrinth and ancient tunnels dating back to the Inka emperors. Under confession, the priest would not be able to share the story for fear of facing the penalty of death. As the priest was traveling to Lima, he encountered an Italian man who hypnotized him into revealing the story. "I will reveal to thee what no White man, be he Spaniard, or American, or English, knows," the Quechua man told the priest. The man told of how the queen ordered the closure of the tunnels when Atahualpa was being held by Pizarro. Another similar tale is that of Father Pedro del Sancho, during the early parts of the conquest in Peru, who mentions the story in his written account. A dying Indian revealed the story to the priest during his last confession: "…my informant was a subject of the Inca Emperor. He was held in high esteem by those in power at Cuzco. He had been a chieftain of his tribe and made a yearly pilgrimage to Cuzco to worship his idolistic gods. It was a custom of the Inkas to conquer a tribe or nation and take their idols to Cuzco. Those who wished to worship their ancient idols were forced to travel to the Inkan capital. They brought gifts to their heathen idols. They were also expected to pay homage to the Inkan emperor during these journeys…these treasures were placed in ancient tunnels that were in the land when the Inkas arrived. Also placed in these subterranean repositories were artifacts and statues deemed sacred to the Inkas. When the hoard had been placed in the tunnels, there was a ceremony conducted by the high priest. Following these rites, the entrance to the tunnels was sealed in such a manner that one could walk within a few feet and never be aware of the entrance...My informant said that the entrance lay in his land, the territory which he ruled. It was under his direction and by his subjects that the openings were sealed. All who were in attendance were sworn to silence under penalty of death. Although I requested more information on the exact location of the entrance, my informant refused to divulge more that what has been written down here."[6] As far back as the1830's, the Peruvian government expressed interest in the search for these tunnels, they sent several teams of investigators to find them; however, they were unsuccessful.

Similar stories of interconnected cavern systems have been closely associated with the Hollow Earth theory. The Hollow Earth myths can be dated back as far as ancient Greece, where legendary underworld tales take place such as those between Hades and Persephone. In recent hypothesizes, the Hollow Earth theory suggests that the interior of the earth may be hollow instead of completely solid, similar to the skin of an orange peel. Tales regarding legendary cities, such as Agartha, or even Telos in Mount Shasta, have been associated with ancient advanced civilizations that still reside within the interior of the earth. By all accounts, these tales are completely refutable, if not completely fictional; however, it has nonetheless had an effect on the imaginations of so many.

Many of these early stories regarding Lemuria and Atlantis later influenced several books. Theosophical literature written by Madame Helena Blavatsky, Rudolf Steiner, and Scott-Elliot seemed to be at the forefront of the pseudomythical portrayals. The Theosophical Society believed in various epochs of mankind consisting of various root races emerging from Lemuria and Atlantis. They were highly based off the earlier stories of Atlantis and Mu, and elaborated extensively upon through "psychic interpretations." These later published books influenced other artists, moviemakers, and fiction and pulp writers as well, such as H.P. Lovecraft and Taylor Caldwell. H.P. Lovecraft, for example, used a lot of the Scott-Elliot's ideas in order to make his horror stories realistic and convincing. This is most evident in Lovecraft's work regarding the *Cthulhu Mythos*, based around fictional elaborations of ancient beings, referring them to as the 'Great Old Ones.' In a letter to Clark Ashton Smith, H.P. Lovecraft admits the sources for his inspiration:

> . . . I've also been digesting something of vast interest as background or source material—which has belatedly introduced me to a cycle of myth with which I have reason to believe you are particularly familiar—i.e., the Atlantis-Lemuria tales, as developed by modern occultists & the[o]sophical charlatans. Really, some of these hints about the lost "City of the Golden Gates" & the shapeless monsters of archaic Lemuria are ineffably pregnant with fantastic suggestion; & I only wish I could get hold of more of the stuff. What I have read is *The Story of Atlantis & the Lost Lemuria,* by W. Scott Elliott. [7]

Reading many of the books compelled me to investigate; there had to have been clues left behind regarding these ancient people. I started my research with local accounts associated with these ancients. Like many have mentioned previously, maybe these ancients arrived in the Americas after the destruction of their own civilization, or maybe California was once a part of the ancient continent itself. Going back to the book by Wishar S. Cervé (Dr. Harvey Spencer Lewis), I researched the accounts of strange lights in the San Francisco Bay Area. These lights were so bright that they were visible from several locations in the Bay Area. I pinpointed the location as described in the book and newspaper articles: Mission Peak, in Fremont, stands over 2,000 feet tall, and from the top one has a clear view all the way to San Francisco. The location itself was a grove. I was surprised to learn that a trail ran through it called the 'Grove Trail.' The trail was the only location that matched the description. From this vantage point, the lights would have been visible all around the bay. The small unmaintained path leads alongside a fenced off area enclosing the dark grove itself. Before entering the grove, there is a park ranger's house situated at the end of a stream. The stream leads straight to a natural spring that is used to supply the ranger's house with running water. Hiking around the vicinity I came across a stone wall, too short in height to keep out the grazing cows and appearing to not serve any purpose. Thinking it was just a geological anomaly, I carefully research the wall and found out that the wall itself spanned from that area and as far north as Marin Country in the North Bay Area, roughly seventy miles away.

The wall itself must span at least 100 miles in distance going up from San Jose to Berkley before ending up in Point Reyes. Some of the basalt stones, that weigh a ton or more, are closely-fitted, ranging from only a foot tall to over five feet in height. Most of the wall has been destroyed by vandals and road-builders. Anthropology professors from the University of Berkeley, as well as others, completely dismiss any further inquiry into the walls. Early scholar and ethnologist Henry C. Meyers stated that the walls were "undoubtedly erected centuries ago" and "neither man nor men of the present day could possibly put the large stones of these walls in place without appliances of some kind."[8] Some researchers believed that the walls might have been built by Ohlone Native Americans or early European settlers. Former president of the Mission Peak Heritage Foundation, Dr. Robert F. Fisher, looked into the wall and agreed with other researchers that the wall may have a prehistoric origin based on old mission records kept by the early Spanish missionaries dating back to 1797. "These walls are just enigmas...they predate the Indians. They predate the Spaniards. It doesn't fit with any of the later history." Malcolm Margolin, author of *The Ohlone Way* (1978), says "it was not typical of the Ohlone to go off and move heavy stones around...it sure beats the heck out of me what those walls are doing up there."[9]

Long time researcher Russell Swanson has always been puzzled by the walls. Swanson has long since investigated the walls and has taken notes over course of many years. He has found the walls extensions near Mount Diablo, and as far as Point Reyes where it breaks off into 400 straight sections, and the two ends stop at the cliff facing the Pacific Ocean. The walls seem to serve no purpose: there are no relics, no astronomical alignments, no significant land barrier or any other meaningful purpose. Swanson stated the following regarding the walls:

> In the past twelve years, I have visited over forty miles of these stone structures. To call them walls is something of a misnomer. Some do go in a straight line, others twist like a demented snake up a steep hillside, others come in a spiral two hundred feet wide and circle into a boulder with a six-inch knob carved on the top of it. Some are massive, over six feet tall and run for miles.[10]

Other mysterious walls have also been found from Texas and Mississippi to Mexico, northern Cuba and Florida, while another wall adjacent to Venezuela, over thirty feet in height, stretches into the sea.[11] Many of the walls have been debunked by archaeologists and geologists alike as natural structures; however, some of the walls continue to perplex scientists.

Recently, another Basalt rock wall was found, but this time it was found in the ocean near Taiwan. A biodiversity professor by the name of Jeng Ming-hsiou uncovered the massive wall structure while conducting research in the Taiwan Strait (Pescadores archipelago). The wall stretches over 650 feet in length and 32 feet in height, resembling thousands of pillars packed together. "It was completely unexpected," he said. The basalt wall in Taiwan resembles other basalt walls found on the coast of Ireland (dubbed the Giant's Causeway), and the Wairere Boulders found in New Zealand. The basalt wall structures are primarily found on land and are rarely discovered underwater. The assumptions made by scientists are that the walls were created by a volcanic eruption over 1,800 years ago; however, that has not stopped the media from comparing the wall to that of a man made city wall. [12]

Strange petroglyphs found around the world have also been attributed as evidence to the lost civilizations of Lemuria and Atlantis. In the Americas, researchers have found strange petroglyphs that are not of native origin. Archaeological researchers cannot carbon date rocks, so no actual dating can be taken. In an old Life magazine there is an interesting article regarding an ancient lost race and the paintings they left behind. In 1962, author Eric Stanley Gardner investigated writings found inside unexplored caves on the peninsula of Baja California, Mexico. In the harsh terrain, it is believed that these people existed at a period in time where food stability could have been sustained. Some of the paintings reflect men ranging from five feet to eleven feet in height, as well as localized fauna that once existed. According to Dr. Clement Meighan (who later led an expedition with Gardner), chairman of the department of anthropology and sociology, said this was "one of the most important and dramatic archaeological discoveries made in the Western Hemisphere in recent times."[13] Gardner conducted the investigations to discover evidence regarding the legends surrounding a lost race in Mexico, a race

Ancient Pueblo Native American petroglyphs
in Albuquerque, New Mexico

whose height averaged seven feet, and "whose bones were found from time to time in burial caves."[14] The native Indians in that area were known as Pericúes, and had been extinct for over 200 years, shortly after the first missions were established. Other strange writings have been found on the California-Oregon border in the Klamath Basin. It has long been believed that the hieroglyphic writings may also be pre-Native American in origin:

> Those who have attempted to interpret the hundreds of feet of these characters on the stones in various sections surrounding the lake have discovered that there is a un-iformity to the writing. They have not been able to evolve an alphabet or a code which will reveal the messages written there, which were intended to inform future generations regarding the nature of the colony surrounding this lake and the story of their catastrophe and struggles for life...
>
> For instance, part of the lake valley was known to the Modoc Indians who lived there in later generations as the *Valley of Knowledge* because there was every evidence that this place had been the seat of learning for some ancient tribes of people. These American Indians called this valley of knowledge *Walla-Was-Skeeny*. The Indians said that this meant "*Valley of Knowledge*," but it was found that these words were not like any other words in their language or dialect.
>
> Then it was discovered that these Indians had inherited this name, or had received it from the descendants of the early tribes who were still living there when the Indians came...[15]

Many of the paintings and petroglyphic writings that have been found have been believed to be the result of shamanic trances. While in ritualistic trance, or for other sacred purposes, the people would venture to the isolated region to visibly express their deep visions, however, this being one interpretation, the true origins of the writings will still remain a mystery.

Searching for the Submerged Lands

The true location of Atlantis has been a carefully researched topic among many scholars. The evidence regarding Atlantis is still very controversial and hopefully one day researchers will pinpoint the exact location. Until then, one can only hope that the scientific community might one day explore possibilities regarding this lost civilization. In the public sphere, the search for Atlantis continues: with the newest in technological advancements anyone can join the search, even from their own home. In the beginning of 2009, internet articles began circulating regarding the discovery of a possible Atlantis sighting via Google Earth. The Google Earth program consists of detailed layouts of the entire earth. Two scientists, David Sandwell of Scripps Oceanography and Walter Smith of the National Oceanic and Atmospheric Administration, were hired by Google to create the oceanic floor map imagery. The coordinates are 31 15'15.53N, 24 15'30.53W, and the image resembles a grid spanning 103 miles in width and about 78 miles in length. The grid itself is thought to resemble roadways, each 'block' spanning roughly eight miles in diameter. According to Google, the lines were nothing more than ship tracks left from gathering bathymetric data of the ocean floor. In other words, the ships sonar echolocation (used to measure the ocean floor) left impressions resembling a grid underneath the water.[16] What made this anomaly even more coincidental was that less than two hundred miles to the east were the exact the coordinates given by the *S.S. Jesmond's* Captain David Robson. In the coordinates provided by the captain, there appears to be a large underwater mass resembling a mountainous region.

The lost civilization of Lemuria presents a different matter altogether. The locations suggested through many mythological tales place the location in the Pacific Ocean, the Indian Ocean, and the Arctic Ocean. Anthropology and Geography professors scoff at any notion regarding the ancient land of Lemuria. In my investigations, I have discussed at great lengths with professors regarding the pro and con arguments toward the possibility of a continent once existing. Though some were quite open to the possibility, others quickly dismissed my questions and refused to hear me out. While studying as an undergraduate, under an Astronomical Physics professor, we discussed Lemuria. I was enticed to take one of his Physical Earth Science courses where we had the opportunity to discuss the subject further. Later, as it turns out, he already had an interest in Lemuria. Going through several of the books on Lemuria, he stated that there probably was not any oceanic evidence to support it. In general, there might be some bits and pieces; however, there was not enough evidence to support the idea of a massive continent existing at any point in time. Dating of the ocean floor may provide evidence that Lemuria once existed in the Pacific Ocean.

If Lemuria existed in the Pacific Ocean, then it would lay within the borders of the Ring of Fire, which accounts for 75 percent of the world's active volcanoes. The Pacific Plate is sliding underneath the North American Plate, which is called subduction. This action forces magma to be pushed to the surface, thus creating volcanoes. In some areas, such as Lassen Peak and Cape Mendocino in California, which are approximately the same latitude on the coast, they do not have subduction zones. Instead of the regular west to east movement in the subduction zones, the main movement is from south to north along the San Andreas Fault below the cape in California. If Lemuria was to have existed, presumably at one point rubbing next to California as Cervé suggests, then the evidence might lay within the subduction zones that include Mount

Shasta. Over millions of years, the sea floor sediments have been forced eastward against the western continent. The ancient seafloor remnants did not sink under the continental plate, but because it is lighter it rose above to become parts of Northern California and the Northwest. With that in mind, it takes about ten million years for the sea floor to move around 320 miles to the east at a rate of two inches per year. [17]

In some of the maps depicting Lemuria, the continent spans a great distance containing California up along the Pacific Plate and downwards toward Australia (e.g. based on the Rosicrucian and Lemurian Fellowship's maps of Lemuria). In other maps the continent resembles more of an island smack in the middle of the Pacific Ocean (e.g. Col. James Churchward's map). It would make sense if a great cataclysm took place within the Ring of Fire (due to extreme volcanic activity). Perhaps even the Hawaiian Islands resemble the islands of the Azores, with such rich soil and its lush vegetation. However, in the case of the Tamil nationalists, the map of Lemuria, otherwise known as *Kumari Kandam* to the Tamil, is placed as a landmass adjacent to India extending outward into the Indian Ocean. The 'continent,' according to Tamil maps, was connected between Madagascar and Australia. Scientific inquires made into this landmass, once existing in the Indian Ocean, have proven to be nonexistent. Though the belief is still strongly held among the people in India and Sri Lanka that the remnants of their great ancestors lay somewhere underneath the waves of the Indian Ocean

The location of the lost continent of Lemuria might perhaps be found within the Native American legends regarding their ancestral homeland. The ancestral cradle of civilization for the Aztecs is referred to as Aztlán. Many of the Chicano movements perpetuated these ideas to determine and support their own political agendas. It is said that Aztlán lay in the far north, so at first it was assumed that the homeland may lay within the ancient Anasazi sites found within the four corners territory (in New Mexico, Arizona, Colorado and Utah).[18] In 1652, after most of the pueblos were conquered around the New Mexico region, a Spanish chronicler mentioned a more specific location for Aztlán. According to Fray Antonio Tello, in his *Crónica miscelánea*, the Aztec homeland lay "between the north and the west." Many within the Chicano movements picked up this idea (along with other early written accounts) and determined that it was actually the Los Angeles area that was the ancient homeland of the Aztecs; however, Fray Tello took it a step further by stating that the journey of the Aztecs to central Mexico started further away than previously thought. The Aztecs "passed the strait of Anián, and that the province of Aztatlán [Aztlán] lies on the other side of the strait."[19] The strait of Anián was long believed by Spanish explorers to be an unknown passage linking Europe directly to the Orient and lay toward the far north of the Americas. Fray Tello then admitted that this legend may have been based on pure speculation alone and that "even now...no one knows exactly where the province of Aztatlán [Aztlán] is, nor have any of our Spaniards seen it; we only know we have heard of it and that it lies toward the north."[20] It was the intermixing of legendary tales such as the Spanish's Seven Cities of Gold (or *Cíbola* and *Quivira*) with the Aztec's Seven Caves of Chicomoztoc on Aztlán that eluded the Spanish conquistadors for so long. Ultimately, the strait of Anián was never found and the passage was forgotten. Could the strait of Anián refer to the Bering Strait to the far north and to the west? How could the Aztecs have known of the Bering Strait several thousands of miles away? Was it perhaps a distant memory from when the original Native American populations migrated over? And if so, could the location of Lemuria finally be determined?

In northern California, Yurok Native American Lucy Thompson recalls the secret story of their ancestral homeland. Being the last of those initiated within the Talth priest/priestess society, she was taught sacred traditions that were unknown within the general Yurok society. Thompson states that from the land of *Cheek-cheek-alth*, the first Native American came to be and traveled "down [into] a European land, always moving toward the south, having our origin in the far north…we wandered like exiles, we know not for how long, as it might have been centuries until we reached the rolling waves of the ocean. Upon reaching this salt water we made boats or canoes, and paddled over the waves until we reached the opposite shore, having crossed the straits in safety."[21] Upon reaching this continent it was here that they first encountered the mystical race of ancient white people, the *Wa-gas*, who also had "their origin in [the] same land of *Cheek-cheek-alth*."[22] Two distinct Native American cultures, thousands of miles away from each other, recall the crossing between the Bering Strait. The mythical homeland of these ancient people must be located somewhere beyond the Strait and above in the Arctic region. How could the people of Lemuria have existed in such freezing temperatures? Could there have also been different periods and a continuation of various inhabitants occupying this lost land? As it was often referred to as the 'cradle of civilization,' perhaps other cultures might have likewise originated from there. Speculative and scientifically refutable, it will remain unclear as to the explanation given by Lucy Thompson regarding *Cheek-cheek-alth*.

Above Siberia and Northern Europe lays a frozen land of snow and ice. In this area of the Arctic region, it is well known that the most common of industries are based on natural resources (such as coal and oil). Fossil fuels, such as coal, originate from ancient trees and plants which decay and become pressurized by the ongoing building of sedimentary layers. On Spitsbergen, one of the largest islands on the Svalbard archipelago in the Arctic Ocean, they have found vast amounts of petrified tropical fruits, proving that the Arctic region was once a lush tropical paradise. The dating of this lush forest can be traced back to the Middle Eocene, roughly 45 million years ago, with high humidity and a completely ice-free environment.[23] There is no archaeological evidence to support any humans existing at that time. The first human-like hominids, according to evolutionary scientists, would not appear until 42 million years later in Africa.

The account of ancient Lemuria would certainly match up to the various descriptions, especially those made by Wishar S. Cervé, who mentions Lemuria as having gigantic flora and fauna within a tropical-like environment. It is likely, however, that the cradle of civilization is rooted in Africa, as many scientists declare; but maybe it was in an unknown land now submerged in the depths of the oceans. With roughly seventy percent of the earth consisting of water, it is no wonder scientists do not fully know what lays inside the oceans. We know more about other terrestrial planets in our solar system than we know our own.

The Ancients among Us

Several accounts refer to the existence of present day ancients living among us, more specifically the Lemurians. They are not immortal beings, but their ancestry has remained intact in deep isolation from the changing world. Lucy Thompson claims that these ancient mystics left and took with them other racially mixed individuals, vowing to one day return. This is similar to various other cultural groups that also mention an individual with mystical knowledge leaving, vowing to one day return. Could it be that these beings still remain alive somewhere to this day? And if this is true, where are they now?

In southern California, as well as on the Channel Islands, we find the remnants of a sophisticated coastal Native American population known as the Chumash. The earliest account of the Chumash comes from Cabrillo, who in 1542 described them as a uniquely light skinned people. After the mission system was established, the Chumash population declined, and by the 1900's, there were only 200 Chumash left. Wishar S. Cervé, in 1931, said that one of the supposed colonies of these ancient Lemurians once existed on the islands off the coast of Santa Barbara in California, where the Chumash were once located. Furthermore, the Chumash were among the descendants of these people already occupying the various territories. "If ever the proper expeditionary work and research efforts are made in the soil of the islands off the coast of Santa Barbara and in the deep soil…there will be rich contributions made to the history of humans and the history of this great state."[24] It would not be until 28 years later when, on Santa Rosa Island, they uncovered the remains of the oldest skeleton found in North America. As previously mentioned, almost all of the mtDNA in the Americas can be traced back to five founding lineages; however, the Chumash is not one of those.

Researchers several years ago were trying to determine the correlation between the Chumash and skeletons found in On Your Knees Cave in Alaska to determine if the earliest migrations of Native Americans consisted of a coastal route (rather than an inland route). Of the 47 samples taken, only four matched the descendants of the Chumash in California. The conclusion made was that the Chumash were among the earliest of settlers in the Americas along a Coastal route down to the tip of South America.[25] The genetic isolation among the Chumash shows that Coastal Migration was possible. But again, as Lucy Thompson suggests, racial mixing may have occurred among the earliest Native American settlers and the ancient people already inhabiting the Americas. Though there is no evidence supporting haplogroup X, it can still be found among other tribes, as well as those who share a common genetic ancestry with the Chumash (e.g. the Nuu-Chah-Nulth). It is unfortunate that the skeletal remains found on Santa Rosa Island cannot be genetically tested, but surely it would support early Native American migrations via a coastal route. And even so, might prove intermixing, due to other skeletal remains found on the Channel Islands that resemble features common among some distinct European races.[26][27]

To this day, various New Age groups and cults take pilgrimages to Mount Shasta in California due to the belief that the ancient people who descended from Lemuria still reside within the mountain. Some of these groups include the "I Am" religious movement (that claims that ascended masters live within Mount Shasta like Saint Germain), and the controversial Lemurian Fellowship founded by Dr. Robert D. Stelle, who claimed to maintain Lemurian teachings from several masters. Richard Kieninger, for example, later broke away from the Lemurian Fellowship and claimed to have prophetic doomsday visions. He later founded small communities of like-minded individuals in preparation for the 'New Age.' After Kieninger was involved in some scandals, including the assaults on a few women, he was exiled from Illinois and moved to Texas to continue his group until his death in 2002. Other people claim that reptilian beings are the ones actually living within Mount Shasta, while others believe that the Lemurians are working with aliens in order to prepare for the end of the world. In light of all the negative publicity surrounding these flocks of people heading to Mount Shasta for spiritual enlightenment, the truth of the situation might actually be contrary to their held beliefs. In 1936, there was an interesting article published that clearly mentioned the Lemurian inhabitants around the vicinity actually abandoning their Mount Shasta home.

After the book *Lemuria: the Lost Continent of the Pacific* was released by the Rosicrucian Order in San Jose, California, in 1931, word quickly spread regarding these ancient inhabitants living within the Mount Shasta region. People from all around traveled to Mount Shasta, and people would throw small explosive devices into the caverns, take loaded guns into the woods, and disperse at anything that moved. A few people did manage to stubble into the entranceways that led into the subterranean dwellings and would destroy the things inside. Various fraudulent people decided to capitalize on the opportunity and so they made promises to the public that they would lead them to unimaginable riches or at least remarkable experiences in exchange for their financial support. Groups of these people base camped around Mount Shasta for several years, oftentimes even during the winter months all with disappointed outcomes. Writers, lecturers, and others also capitalized on Mount Shasta claiming to have remarkable visions or other worldly experiences. This was all due to the book and articles for which the Rosicrucian Order originally published regarding these ancient inhabitants.

Dr. Harvey Spencer Lewis, Imperator of the Rosicrucian Order AMORC, stated in a private article to Rosicrucian members that the people living within Mount Shasta were packing up and leaving. According to Dr. Lewis he had met four times with strange visitors within a fifteen year period, first of which being in 1919 while in San Francisco. Their first meeting in San Francisco was established in a very secretive manner. During their first meeting they spent several hours with him and left him with several papers, photographs, drawings, and contacts to get a hold of in California (as well as other parts of the United States and the Orient). Based on the information collected from them, he published the book on Lemuria in 1931. In their last meeting, a group of people arrived in San Jose during the first week of August in 1936, where they talked about the unwanted publicity taking place since the book was published. Beginning on October 13th 1935 these people began to slowly relocate during the winter and rainy season when the presence of curious investigators was at its lowest. The article states that it would have been impossible for these mystics to travel by automobiles or by train without attracting a great deal of attention because of their strange appearance and attire. These people were in close contact with several secretive people in the surrounding Shasta region who helped them relocate. The following was described by Dr. Lewis in the article:

> Heavy pieces of furniture and large caskets of iron, strange boxes, were moved in wooden crates that were prepared to look like ordinary express shipments, and these were taken to various points near Mt. Shasta for shipment by railroad and motor trucks without creating any excitement or interest on the part of those who handled the large crates. They were delivered to two or three different points near the old mystical location where the reestablishment of their activities was to take place and then gradually brought to the location by trucks or private automobiles. Other articles of a more portable nature were taken in trucks direct or in what appeared to be private automobiles...
>
> ...these persons were taken by private automobile owned by a few friends, to an open area just north of Shasta and there placed in a strange dirigible which rose into the air at night and proceeded southward taking twelve to fifteen of the persons on each trip and making a number of trips back and forth to Mexico, bring and taking various objects and persons to the old colony previously referred to.[28]

During one of these trips, a thunderstorm ravaged the landscape and lightning illuminated the sky, revealing the strange craft in the air. Local people reported the craft to the military stations along the border. Several newspapers reported on this incident and with the report of hundreds of eye witnesses it was hard to ignore. Neither the army nor navy could give a clear explanation as to what the object was. The account states that other colonies of these inhabitants lay within isolated regions of California, Baja California, and Mexico; the larger colony existing in the foothills of an extinct volcano not far from the

United States border in Mexico.[29] In Mount Shasta, there are
only a few individuals willing to take on the responsibility of
maintaining and protecting the possessions left behind, but
"will carry on no mystical activities and will refrain from being
seen or contacted in any way by any who may approach that
district."[30]

Dr. Harvey Spencer Lewis mentioned that in a future
article, he would reveal many more details regarding the
strange visitors and their future plans. He ended the article
with a piece of advice regarding many of the fraudulent people
to come, though he underestimated one thing, it still has not
ended:

> One thing is certain, however, and that is that all the
> stories we have been reading in newspapers, magazines,
> and especially the literature of various travelling teach-
> ers and lectures regarding their connections with the
> Mt. Shasta colony of mystics and their ability to take
> their students to Mr. Shasta for mystical initiation have
> been absolutely untrue and unsound, and by this move
> of the colony from the old location to a new secret
> place which will not be revealed, thousands of foolish
> followers of such matters will have a sad awakening.
> We have predicted this from time to time and have tried
> to warn our members not to give credence to such
> claims as have been offered in the past year or two.
> Many were misled, however, and we are glad that this
> will not be continued for long.[31]

Sadly, Dr. Lewis passed away three years later at the age of 56
before anything more could be written.

Lucy Thompson described the only thing that remained
from the *Wa-gas*, or ancient 'white people,' were ancient stone
houses called *Oc-lo-melth*.[32] One of these stone houses was located less than two hundred yards from where the White

Deerskin Dance was held (present day Johnsons, California- on the Yurok Reservation).[33] In one of these ancient houses, that the *Wa-gas* constructed before the Indians came, was where Lucy's mother was born and remained within her family for many generations after "the *Wa-gas* left this land before the world was covered in water."[34] Many of these ancient houses exist in various villages along the Klamath River from the Pacific Ocean to Trinidad. Most of these houses are left in ruins to sink into the soil. Lucy said that many rattlesnakes protect the houses from unwanted visitors and many have been bitten upon coming too close to the house while the family was away; however, the family never feared the rattlesnakes because they would quickly disperse as soon as the family would enter the house. Lucy's mother owned the house while Lucy wrote her book (originally published in 1916), though she did not live in it for over fifteen years prior. The closing statement by Lucy on the *Wa-gas*, was truly a sad reality for whatever remained of these ancient people to lay forgotten and undiscovered for the generations to come:

> For the past twenty years she [(Lucy's mother)] has been breaking up and pounding to pieces the stone bowls, trays and all the ancient implements that were left by the *Wa-gas*. She is endeavoring to destroy all these sacred reminiscences of the prehistoric days that they may never be ruthlessly handled and curiously gazed upon by the present white race. The stone trough that the deer fed out of is so large and heavy that she cannot break it into pieces, but is letting it sink into the ground; and it is being covered with rubbish, together with its strange charm and fascinating history, where my pen has failed to impress, this deep sentiment, therefore its wonder tradition has faded with the closing of this chapter where a new era has dawned. My mother gave my husband two of the small stone bowls as relics

of the days that are gone forever, and he keeps them as cherished memories.[35]

Mount Shasta in Northern California and
inside a collapsed cave nearby.

[1] Wilkins, Harold T. *Mysteries of Ancient South America*, p. 48

[2] Ibid.

[3] Wilkins, Harold T. *Secret Cities of Old South America*, pp. 243-53

[4] Childress, David Hatcher *Lost Cities and Mysteries of South America*, pp. 117-9

[5] Mills, Charles A. *Lost Treasures and Wonders*, p. 28

[6] Childress, David Hatcher *Lost Cities and Mysteries of South America*, p. 65-66

[7] Letter to Clark Ashton Smith from H.P. Lovecraft (June 17, 1926): *Selected Letters*, Vol. II, p. 58.

[8] Burress, Charles *Unraveling the Old Mystery of East Bay Walls*, San Francisco Chronicle, December 31, 1984

[9] Ibid.

[10] Swanson, Russell; *The Berkeley Walls and Other Enigmas*, Bay Area Rock Art News, 15:7, June 1997

[11] Andrews, Shirley *Lemuria and Atlantis: Studying the Past to Survive the Future*, p. 202

[12] Jennings, Ralph *Basalt Rock Wall found in Ocean near Taiwan*, Reuters News, January 5, 2009

[13] Garnder, Erle Stanley *A Legendary Treasure left by a Long-lost Tribe* Life magazine (July 20, 1962), pp. 56-64

[14] Ibid.

[15] Cervé, Wishar S. *Lemuria: the Lost Continent of the Pacific*, pp. 171-172

[16] Paul, Ian *Google's Atlantis Discovery Explained*, PC World News Blog, February 24, 2009

[17] Fradkin, Philip L. *The Seven States of California: A Natural and Human History*, pp. 119-120

[18] Anaya, Rudolfo A. and Lomelí, Francisco A. *Aztlán: Essays on the Chicano Homeland*, p. 61

[19] Ibid., p. 62

[20] Ibid., pp. 62-3

[21] Thompson, Lucy *To the American Indian: Reminiscences of a Yurok Woman*, p. 76

[22] Ibid., p. 83

[23] Jahren, A. Hope *The Arctic Forest of the Middle Eocene* Annual Review of Earth and Planetary Sciences, Vol. 35: 509-540 (May 2007)

[24] Cervé, Wishar S. *Lemuria: the Lost Continent of the Pacific*, p. 157

[25] Lovgren, Stefan First *Americans Arrived Recently, Settled Pacific Coast, DNA Study Says* National Geographic News, February 2, 2007

[26] Heizer, R.F. and Whipple, M.A. *The California Indians*, pp. 100-1

[27] Goodman Ph.D., Jeffrey *American Genesis: The American Indian and the origins of modern man* pp. 175-6, 178-80

[28] Lewis, Dr. Harvey S. *A New Lemurian Mystery: A surprising story about the mystics of Mt. Shasta* The Rosicrucian Digest, September 1936

[29] In another account, the mention is made that perhaps another colony may be in existence in the Vancouver, British Columbia vicinity within the isolated forests in Canada.

[30] Ibid.

[31] Ibid.

[32] Thompson, Lucy *To the American Indian: Reminiscences of a Yurok*, p. 181

[33] Using old maps I located the rough location of this house, though I do not feel appropriate to disclose its location due to it being on private property on the Yurok Reservation (which abides to Tribal sovereignty restrictions).

[34] Thompson, Lucy *To the American Indian: Reminiscences of a Yurok*, pp.181-4

[35] Ibid., p.184

Chapter Eleven
The Eternal Return

THE research presented in this book does not aim to prove the existence of Lemuria and Atlantis. An imaginative spark of curiosity and awe was hopefully stimulated, perhaps leading to further investigations and supportive evidence. The allegorical perspectives behind Lemuria and Atlantis provide a foundation on which to analyze our future social progressions. With such uncertainty in the future, parallels can be made between our current state of affairs and past generations; regardless if one chooses to believe that these lands of Lemuria and Atlantis once existed. What are important are the lessons that can be taken away from these stories. These common stories found throughout the world should be taken as a valuable lesson in which to reflect upon our own current condition.

Many concepts of time reflect a cyclical motion that repeats until a dramatic change occurs moving us into a different cycle altogether. In biological terms, Stephen Jay Gould offers an evolutionary model that reflects dramatic changes that occur naturally, known as *punctuated equilibrium*, which states that evolutionary changes happen quickly and change very little until evolving again. This theory only focuses on biological development; however, a similar parallel may also be drawn toward human civilizations. Great empires come into existence: progressions are slowly made over time, but quickly evolve into something else, unless dissipating from existence. The evolutionary role of civilizations remain within a cyclical movement, and in due time, technological advancement will be made. After a civilization has exceeded its maximum sustainability, it ultimately collapses. The strides in progression usually produce better systematic civilizations than those that existed previously. Evolutionary progress tends to move forward, but sometimes the opposite takes place, retrograding back to a 'primitive' state. The famous Albert Einstein quote alludes to such a possibility: "How will World War III be fought? I do not know; but I do know how World War IV will be - with sticks and stones."

America: The New Atlantis

Our age of gold will pass and some day the Golden Age will come again. A future greatness is right now casting its long shadow across the face of Nature. With each passing generation the responsibilities of the American people will increase. More and more we shall be looked to as a source of courage, strength, and hope.

And it will be in this way that we shall fulfill the destiny for which our nation was created by dreamers of long ago. From the Blessed Isles of the West must come the fulfillment of the promise of the ages. [1]

The distant memory of Lemuria and Atlantis serve as a reminder, even if mythological in origin, that we must reflect upon our own current state. If we are to understand that it has always been heightened civilizations at the forefront of progression that were the ones to fall. Then we must look upon our society today as part of a common global civilization eventually reaching its limit. And at the heart of this great empire is America' the leader of globalization and western imperialism. Dating back to the earliest of writings regarding the New World, there was always a parallel reference to America being the New Atlantis. In Sir Francis Bacon's *Nova Atlantis* (*New Atlantis*), written in 1623, he dreamed that in America the bounds of human wisdom would exceed anything imaginable at the time. It was almost a destiny for the people in America to become revolutionary leaders in philosophical and scientific movements. Other writers believed America was destined to become a utopia where everything was possible, where new advancements were to be made, and all people would fulfill their highest ideals. Among the founding fathers, the secret ideals of the Rosicrucians and Freemasons alike were to be at the forefront of this new country. Ideas of equality, liberty, and justice for all were based on moral imperatives for generations to come.

> Poseid arose to an altitude which the wildest dreams of science have not predicted for the modern world; arose, flourished and decayed, in the fullness of cyclical times. And America is Poseid come again, reincarnated, and shall see its scientific people repeat, but on a higher plane, the attainments of Atla. As the centuries pass it shall see the successive enfleshment of those souls which in Atla made that land proud, prouder, and proudest. But it shall do more, for America hath developed that soul-element which, when her people were Poseidi, was first faintly traced. So, through repeating, it shall do more- it shall have all Atla's marvels wedded to the glourious soul foreseen for mankind...It shall flourish so, and then, in the fullness of its time, decay. [2]

Undoubtedly, our society has reached a point where the continuation of certain values, once held with such high regard, are being replaced by other qualities. We have entered into the *Age of Unreason*: a slow social depletion that has inadvertently focused its attention to irrational ideas. These fragmented ideas break off into a wide variety of newer creations, such as half-truths, and overall logical fallacies which become normalized within society. Slowly, a new social progression emerges, taking a detour, if not a complete recession to its former state. The emergence into a dark Orwellian reality may be closer than we might think. Realities created within dystopian novels, such as Orwell's *Nineteen Eighty-Four*, Huxley's *Brave New World*, or even Bradbury's *Fahrenheit 451*, may not be farfetched.

False concepts and notions become conditioned and reinforced into cognitive collective ideology (e.g. *groupthink*). Contradictory ideas also become accepted, representing a hypocrisy between two contradictory ideas, such as with Orwell's *doublethink* (or in psychological terms called *cognitive dissonance*). For example, we think of the Unites States as an equal and fair place where anyone can achieve anything he/she desires; however, how can we *compete* in an equal race, if everybody starts at different places on the track? If we are all equal, why must some people work harder than others to achieve the same things? That is the conceptual view of equality in America, and most people neglect to question this hypocrisy. We start living within this false contradictory reality, and we go to stores where we think we have the freedom to choose from a wide variety of brand name clothing. Yet the clothing itself is put in place by fashion trends provided by networking companies who instill a false sense of freedom of choice, but inadvertently we are choosing the same style products but from different companies.

A transformative process of commodities gradually takes place. The transition moves from once vital necessity to sustainability (or subsistence), and now into unnecessary commodities (or unwarranted materialism). The ideal of youthfulness (to be careless and ignorant) is a highly marketable industry. Consumerism, and society overall, shifts its focus toward anti-intellectualism and careless lifestyles. Those who do not fit in within the new scheme become more reclusive and pushed into further isolation. The transition into a false sense of 'independence' (or ego-motivation) within society has become ever increasing. Even as technology continues to advance, the very technology that brings people together also begins to isolate them. Over time, slowly people begin to live impersonal lives, rejecting face-to-face human interaction, and focus more on individuality.

The institutions themselves started incorporating these new ideas and started reinforcing a perpetual motion of the status quo. The shift has moved toward the questioning of our own personal beliefs. By all means, there is nothing wrong with believing in what one chooses, nor is there anything wrong with changing ones view; however, the level at which the constructed institutional role has irrationalized certain beliefs as fictitious or even absurd, reflects poorly upon the society. Another division takes place, but this time a division of beliefs. Indoctrination within academic institutions serves to alienate those with different beliefs as not meeting their standards. *Scientific atheism* is reflective upon our foundation within the academic world and its progression from the "old ways of thinking." It stands invariably at the forefront of rational thinking, becoming representative of 'true progressive science (or academia),' while completely dismissing our intrinsic human nature with such concepts as empathy, subjectivity, and introspectivity.

Arguments over trivial discrepancies are the primary focus in what education is leaning towards. Theory after theory, no regard toward the true human condition or even the natural mysteries around us is respected. "We find in all of the writings and records of the ancients that, even thousands of years after Lemuria had attained its greatness in scientific learning and spiritual development, the people had not fallen into the error of creating theoretical explanations and establishing hypothetical conditions to explain the phenomena of life. Our scientific schools today are filled with this sort of mental food, and it constitutes one of the great errors of our education."[3] In the time leading up to Atlantis's final demise, we find the depletion of the human condition through institutions, which led to its own downfall. Though the people of Atlantis achieved great technological success, they eventually turned towards other interests. We learn about clues alluding to the eventual fading of values and corruption at the highest levels in Atlantis. A similar correlation may be drawn upon this current time and then we may begin to understand these cyclical movements of great civilizations which ultimately lead to their own demise.

Apocalyptic Prophecy

In recent times there has been a strong fascination regarding prophecies about the end of times. This fanaticism regarding the apocalyptic end of days is reminiscent of groups of people who claim to know the actual date of the end of the world. Anything is possible at any given time, and yet we are the only beings with the freewill to progressively alter our futures; destiny itself being a false and altered concept. There being no single destination for anyone, the paths laid out are chosen based on individual decisions through circumstantial events. In our current human condition, the world strives toward two main objectives: one involving the collective progression to exist as efficient inhabitants on earth, to prevent wasteful consumption and to furthermore ecologically help sustain the environment for generations to come; the second objective is maintained by many individuals who believe we should prepare for the end. The amount of optimism involving the first objective is regarded as impossible and will never happen. But it does not stop millions of people working to sustain the environment. Many negatively capitalize on these ideas by creating *greenwashed* products and other supposed charitable productions. On the other hand, we find ideas regarding the preparation for the apocalypse and the coming of the messiah. In psychological terms, we can associate this form of thinking as a *self-fulfilling prophecy*, whereby a person will bring about his or her held beliefs and actually create the reality. Collectively, the implications of a *self-fulfilling prophecy* can cause severe dissonance within entire populations. Decisions will be made accordingly, and people will plan according to their beliefs. In fundamental Christianity, the belief seems more apparent and more frightening as time continues. "We will be saved!" or "The end of times is upon us! Repent now!" these collective informalities self-perpetuate ignorance and intolerance, causing a social rift between those who believe, and those who do not.

Rather than helping the situation, many misinformed New Age groups also perpetuate the ideas of the end of time regarding 2012, or the end of a great cycle. Unwritten testimony of past civilizations seem to be exaggerated and lacking the creditability within many of these groups. Again, we find several examples of *cognitive dissonance* whereby many of these people are environmentally conscious; however, they believe that the end of the world is inevitable.

There are other possibilities involving global events that could lead to severe crisis. With the rise in Carbon dioxide in the air leading to the rise in temperature, or even rising sea levels or frozen methane gas underneath the oceans melting, those are real possibilities that many scientists support while being ignored by the majority. One example is of the projected global water shortages by the year 2025, as published by several governmental agencies, including the U.S. Department of the

Interior. The statistics state that fresh water is slowly dissipating, leading to a worldwide drought. Without water, all life forms will face a critical turning point. These are realistic scenarios that people should take into account before wasting water. If our collective reasoning focuses on the objective of being ecologically assertive, then the solutions will fall into place on their own. But, if we continue to fix problems with temporary solutions, we are doomed to exist in a non-sustainable world for the generations to come.

If a cataclysmic event is likely to occur, then the proper steps will be taken by the few who understand the gravity of the situation. They will be the ones to survive the cataclysmic changes in the world, as long as they pay attention to the signs of an impending disaster. The survivors of Lemuria and Atlantis succeeded in staying alive by relocating prior to great cataclysms. As the preoccupations of violence and problems exceeded the majority, a minority who were not blinded by what was going on understood the signs and took the initiative to lead others to safety. While based on mythological or interpretive notions, the fact remains that these are valuable lessons that are passed down for a reason. In many of the stories regarding the destruction of the Americas due to a massive flood, the few who survived did so by following the signs found in nature. In the instances prior to the cataclysm, many animals were seen fleeing to higher ground and onto the tops of mountains and hills; only a few realized that they should follow the animals. They are the ones who later survived. Many animals were seen fleeing to higher ground during the tsunamis that took place in Indonesia in 2004. Several reports mention strange animal behavior over an hour prior to the tsunami hitting the coastline. Many of the elephants started to behave erratically, and some of the owners, upon unleashing the elephants, started fleeing to higher ground. They followed the elephants and survived to tell their amazing stories.

Several predictions have been made regarding an apocalyptic future. Various researchers pull 'evidence' from ancient American cultures such as the Mayan, Aztec, Hopi, and Inka. I do not doubt the sophistication of their prophecies and ancient astronomical systems of dating; however, many interpretations have been based on more recent ideas put forward by several pseudo-researchers. Cyclical movements throughout time have been observed for countless eras, and I do not doubt that to some degree these ancient cultures are based on cosmological beliefs around cyclical movements in time. As we can predict the changes through the four seasons today, we neglect to focus on a small part of these cycles in nature. There are larger cyclical movements, including some which we do not see. The rates of molecular decay to even large biological organisms maintain a pattern from creation to decay (and with smaller cycles in between). This natural process can be observed, and with anything else, presumably some of these ancient cultures observed a larger cyclical motion for the progressions of civilizations. What will happen is not written; it has only been assumed. The reason is perhaps, again, because of human freewill being the ultimate determinant of one's fate, or collectively as a human race. For this reason alone, it is impossible to make predictions of future events because of the changing balance. Progressional movements might determine a critical time when something is more likely to happen, but the overall determination is based on countless factors.

While in Peru I learned about *Taripay Pacha*, which was not a prophecy in the sense of what was going to happen; instead, it proposed a critical time when people will reflect upon their actions and take action. These actions will ultimately determine the final outcome for whatever is to take place. *Taripay Pacha* means the 'time of judgment,' but is used to refer to a period in time from 1993 to 2012 (according to several sources), whereby we will meet ourselves again. Humanity, during this age, will be able to evolve consciously into a higher state of being, and hopefully, ascend to a new golden age. It does not state what will happen if this does not take place, nor does it specify what will happen if it does; it leaves it open as an interpretive and power-inducing idea. Retrospection based on this idea might influence decisions within one's life in managing freewill accordingly to what feels right. Instead of going to gurus, leaders, psychics, the responsibility rests solely within each individual. Everyone possesses great potential and the responsibility to better ourselves and to help others change the current situations plaguing our world. Many tend to blame others for the world's current problems and place the responsibility solely on others rather than themselves.

World Stability

In 1963, a famous book was published by Hannah Arendt, entitled *Eichmann in Jerusalem: a Report on the Banality of Evil*. Hannah Arendt was a German-born Jewish philosopher who fled Europe during the Nazi occupation. The analysis made by Arendt was on the trials of Adolf Eichmann, a Nazi during World War II, who was in charge of the logistics regarding the deportation of Jews to the concentration camps. Arendt aims to determine what would cause a person to do such horrible things, or even be a part of it. Her conclusion leads her to use the term *the Banality of Evil*, meaning that the evil deeds done throughout history are not done by maniacs or sociopaths, but rather by ordinary people. Eichmann maintained such a minimal position, but was part of an elaborate overall scheme to exterminate people. Eichmann never hated anybody, and would simply reply that he was "doing his job" and following orders. Those who do not question the normalized routines of daily life are more likely to participate in such horrible events. Evil deeds are undertaken by ordinary men and women who do not question their actions.

Three months after the start of the Eichmann trial, a psychological experiment was devised to measure the willingness of ordinary people to obey orders from an authoritative figure. The Milgram experiment involved one participant administering electric shocks to another participant inside a closed room. What the person administering the shocks did not know was that the person inside the room was an actor. As the level voltage in shocks increased when the participant answered a question incorrectly, the recipient would cry out in agony from inside the room and demand the test be stopped. But by the strict instructions of the scientist, the person administering the shocks was not allowed to stop. The test aimed to determine when a person would disobey the orders and completely stop. It was predicted that only three percent of participants would actually continue the administration of shocks until the very end, results however showed surprisingly that sixty-five percent of participants obeyed and continued until ordered to stop.

In 1971, another psychological experiment was conducted in the basement of the Psychology department at Stanford University by Professor Philip Zimbardo. Twenty-four undergraduate students were divided into two groups: a few would take on the role of guards and the rest would be prisoners. The basement was converted into a prison with cells and the study was to measure the same results given by the Milgram experiment. The prisoners were randomly picked up by police and placed inside the mock prison. The guards had full attire and batons, while the prisoners wore prison uniforms. The experiment lasted only six days after which it was shut down. The situation got out of hand very quickly, and the roles took on a life of their own. Prisoners were beaten, ridiculed, and endured severe emotional trauma as the guards abused their power. Even Zimbardo himself took on the role of prison warden. The roles became internalized, while the guards abused their power, the prisoners just blindly accepted the punishments. And throughout the whole experiment nobody realized that they were just willing participants and could stop at any time.

The Milgram and Stanford Prison experiment serve as important lessons. In 1946, Viktor Frankl wrote *Man's Search for Meaning*, detailing his experiences inside concentration camps during World War II. In his book he states that "we who lived in concentration camps can remember the men who walked through the huts comforting others, giving away their last piece of bread. They may have been few in number, but they offer sufficient proof that everything can be taken from a man but one thing: the last of the human freedoms-to choose one's attitude in any given set of circumstances, to choose one's own way."[4] Despite all the atrocities that persist to this day, the responsibility falls solely on individuals to determine the final outcome. While in Peru I learned about the highest law that exists throughout the Andres: Sacred Reciprocity.

Sacred reciprocity, or *Ayni* in Quechua, is a belief of the indigenous people that states that what you will give, you shall so receive. The interpretation is not limited to only to material objects, but also living natural energy from *Pachamama* (Mother Earth). Everything in the community is based on this idea of sacred reciprocity: it is what binds the community together though a continuous cycle of giving and receiving. Between man and nature the interconnection of sacred reciprocity is held with high regard.

A controversial book was published in 1902 entitled *Mutual Aid: a Factor of Evolution*, written by Peter Kropotkin. The book is a response to Charles Darwin's theory of natural selection, whereby Kropotkin lists many examples from various species on how cooperation and mutual aid are needed for the survival of their species. "It is well known that there always are a number of bees which prefer a life of robbery to the laborious life of a worker; and that both periods of scarcity and periods of an unusually rich supply of food lead to an increase of the robbing class…We thus see that anti-social instincts continue to exist amidst the bees as well; but natural selection continually eliminate[s] them."[5] Kropotkin uses examples from various tribes and civilizations who conduct themselves according to cooperation and mutual aid, instead of competition. There are many problems with Darwin's ideas, and ideas such as survival of the fittest and competition are among our traits as a society. From our economy to our education, our society conducts itself according to these false notions. How long can we survive if our society bases itself on these ideas?

We identify our current society as being ahead in everything, though we cannot fully maintain and take care of our own people. We pride ourselves on our progress, and yet we still wage warfare and divide ourselves according to our beliefs. Stephen Jay Gould offered the term *Non-overlapping magisterial*, which suggests that religion and science are compatible with one another, as opposed to the dominant idea that religion beliefs cannot be compatible with science. His views were bashed by the scientific community and pushed his reputation into the fringes of controversy. The ideas of Atheism and Darwinism seem to be more closely associated with one another within academics. Ironically, the Roman Catholic Church has faded out favor with the majority population and replaced by academic institutions as the new dogmatic authority.

Will the infinite reality of time continue on its progression through the universe? Or will we finally reach the *eternal return*? Civilizations such as the Minoan or Roman city of Pompeii, and Sodom and Gomorrah were destroyed by cataclysms. The mythological dramas of Lemuria and Atlantis as described by Plato and countless others serve as ethical and moral lessons for future generations. Lessons that warn us that with great achievements in technology, we must develop equal or greater moral value, for with each new invention comes equal responsibility. In the world that we live in today, we have become desensitized to common human experiences and interactions. However, the true human condition remains unchanged after generations. Emotions, thoughts, reactions, and reason exist innately within each individual. The popularity of these stories regarding great civilizations that once existed will continue to be explored. As our own society advances, we may begin to lose touch with the simplicity of our creative and natural imaginations. Few people who hold on to these imaginative stories and relate to our current circumstances understand the correlations. It has occurred before and it will always happen again unless our society breaks free from this self-induced amnesia. It will always be the few imaginative minds and dreamers who will understand the conditions plaguing the minds of others. Distraught by what they see, they become reclusive in their thoughts. The awakening of the imagination can lead to new paths for our society to explore. Civilizations rise and perish, and the mythical lands of Lemuria and Atlantis were no different; but it will always be our collective passions and creative spirit that will remain forever.

> ...with us perishes the true name of God to my people. With it has perished from the earth our true Indian laws, our sublime religion, our deeds of chivalry, as rich as the civilized world has ever beheld; as our glorious manhood and womanhood. Immoral, corrupt, tottering, downtrodden and debauched by a superior race, we have perished in that winter night of the transition period. At a simple blow our laws were torn asunder; loathsome diseases we had never known crushed out the life and beauty of our physical bodies and demented our spiritual minds with lowly passions. Poisonous spirituous drink has set the brain on fire, degrading man and womanhood. Thus as a race we have perished, and this great land, the richest the world has ever known, the land of our forefathers for so many thousands of

years. Now another race is struggling on where our reign has ended. Already our great rulers are at rest, and forever; laurelled with the glories of the primeval ages that have passed away in silence. As a nation, like the ancient Egyptians, we have grown old and passed away; we have seen a great civilization endowed with a splendor of its own, rising of the debris of the eternal years.[6]

---

[1] Hall, Manly P. *The Secret Destiny of America*, p. 46

[2] Phylos *A Dweller on Two Planets*, p. 429

[3] Cervé, Wishar S. *Lemuria The Lost Continent of the Pacific*, p. 85

[4] Frankl, Viktor Emil *Man's search for meaning*, p. 75

[5] Kropotkin, Peter *Mutual Aid: a Factor of Evolution*, p. 19

[6] Thompson, Lucy *To the American Indian: Reminiscences of a Yurok Woman*, p. 74

Bibliography

Achilli, A.; et al. . "The Phylogeny of the Four Pan-American MtDNA Haplogroups: Implications for Evolutionary and Disease Studies." *PLoS ONE* 3 (2008): e1764.

Anaya, Rudolfo A. , and Francisco A. Lomelí. *Aztlán: Essays on the Chicano Homeland.* 1989 ed. Albuquerque: University of New Mexico Press, 1991.

-. "Ancient Sources for the Atlantis Story ." *Rosicrucian Digest* 84.2 (2006): 11-12.

Andrews, Shirley. *Atlantis: Insights from a Lost Civilization.* Seventh Printing, 2005 ed. St.Paul: Llewellyn Publications, 2002.

Andrews, Shirley. *Lemuria & Atlantis: Studying the Past to Survive the Future.* St. Paul: Llewellyn Publications, 2004.

Arieti, James A.. *The Scientific & the Divine: Conflict and Reconciliation from Ancient Greece to the Present.* Lanham: Rowman & Littlefield Publishers, Inc., 2003.

Bagger, Louis. "The Army Medical Museum in Washington." *Appletons' Journal: A Magazine Of General Literature* 9.206 (1873): -.

Baldwin, John D. *Pre-historic nations;: Or, Inquiries concerning some of the great peoples and civilizatins of antiquity, and their probable relation to a still older civilization ... of the Ethiopians or Cushites of Arabia.* New York: Harper & Brothers, 1896.

Barclay, Eliza. "Oldest Skeleton in Americas Found in Underwater Cave?." *National Geographic News.* N.p., 3 Sept. 2008. <http://news.nationalgeographic.com/news/2008/09/08 0903-oldest-skeletons.html>.

Barker, Pat, Cynthia Ellis, and Stephanie Damadio. "Determination of Cultural Affiliation of Ancient Human remains from Spirit Cave, Nevada." *Bureau of Land*

Management Report Summary (Nevada State Office) - (2006): -.

Beebe, Rose Marie , and Robert M Senkewicz. *Lands of Promise and Despair: Chronicles of Early California, 1535-1846 (California Legacy Book) (California Legacy Book)*. San Francisco: California Historical Society Press. Berkeley: Heyday Books, 2001.

Berlitz, Charles. *Atlantis: the Eighth Continent* . New York City: Putnam, 1984.

Bierlein, J.F.. *Parallel Myths*. Chicago: Ballantine Books, 1994.

Blavatsky, H. P.. *The Secret Doctrine: the Synthesis of Science, Religion, and Philosophy: Index to Volumes 1 and 2*. Paris: Adamant Media Corporation, 2006.

Bradley, Bruce, and Dennis Stanford. "The Solutrean-Clovis connection: reply to Straus, Meltzer and Goebel ." *World Archaeology* 38.4 (2006): 704 - 714.

Braghine, Colonel A.. *The Shadow of Atlantis*. kempton: Adventures Unlimited Press, 1997.

Brown, et al.. "mtDNA Haplogroup X An Ancient Link between EuropeWestern Asia and North America? ." *American Journal of Human Genetics* 63.6 (1998): 1852-61.

Buckley, Thomas. *Standing Ground: Yurok Indian Spirituality, 1850-1990*. Berkeley: University of California Press, 2002.

Burress, Charles. "Unraveling the Old Mystery of East Bay Walls." *San Francisco Chronicle* 31 Dec. 1984: -.

Campbell, Joseph, and Bill Moyers. *The Power of Myth*. New York: Anchor, 1988.

Campbell, Joseph and Toms, Michael. *An Open Life: Joseph Campbell in Conversation with Michael Toms*. New York: New Dimensions Foundation, 1989.

Castleden, Rodne. *Atlantis Destroyed*. New York: Routledge, 2001.

Cerve, Wishar S.. *Lemuria: The Lost Continent of the Pacific*. 1931. Re San Jose: Grand Lodge of the English Language Jurisdication, AMORC, Inc., 1997.

Chaisson, Eric J. *Epic of Evolution: Seven Ages of the Cosmos*. Columbia: Columbia University Press, 2005.

Childress, David Hatcher. *Lost Cities and Amcient Mysteries of South America*. 1989. Re kempton: Adventures Unlimited Press, 1999.

Childress, David Hatcher. *Lost Cities of Ancient Lemuria and the Pacific (The Lost City Series)*. 2002 ed. kempton: Adventures Unlimited Press, 1988.

Choi, Charles Q.. "Human Ancestors Walked Upright, Study Claims | LiveScience." *LiveScience | Science, Technology, Health & Environmental News*. N.p., n.d. <http://www.livescience.com/strangenews/071009-upright-early.html>.

Churchward, Col. James. *The Lost Continent of Mu*. 1931. Re Binghamton: Vail-Ballou Press, Inc., 1944.

Cortes, Hernan. *Letters from Mexico*. 1971. Re New Haven: Yale University Press, 2001.

Crane, WM. H. . "Memoirs of Townships.-Vermillion ." *Firelands Historical Society* I-II (1858): 38-9.

Cremo, Michael A., and Richard L. Thompson. *The Hidden History of the Human Race (The Condensed Edition of Forbidden Archeology)*. Badger: Govardhan Publishing, 1994.

Cyrus, Thomas. "Report on the mound explorations of the Bureau of ethnology: Twelfth annual report, 1890-91, Annual report of the Bureau of American Ethnology to the secretary of the Smithsonian Institution ." *U.S. Bureau of American Ethnology* 12 (1894): 113-427.

Deloria, Vine. *Red Earth, White Lies: Native Americans and the Myth of Scientific Fact*. New York: Scribner, 1995.

Donnelly, Ignatius. *Atlantis: The Antediluvian World*. 1882. Re New York: Harper & Brothers, Franklin Square, 1941.

Eichorn, Arthur Francis. *The Mt. Shasta story; Being a concise history of the famous California mountain*. Second Printing 1971 ed. Boston: Mount Shasta Herald, 1957.

Einstein, Albert. *The World As I See It*. New York: Filiquarian Publishing, Llc., 2007.

"Evidence of the Past: A Map and Status of Ancient Remains." *Friends of America's Past*. N.p., n.d. Web. <http://www.friendsofpast.org/earliest-americans/map.html>.

"Expedition Reports Nine-Foot Skeletons ." *Hot Citizen* 5 Aug. 1947: -.

Faber, Phyllis M.. *California's Wild Gardens: A Guide to Favorite Botanical Sites*. 1997. Re Berkeley: University of California Press, 2005.

Fagundes, Nelson J. R.; et al. . "Mitochondrial Population Genomics Supports a Single Pre-Clovis Origin with a Coastal Route for the Peopling of the Americas." *The American Journal of Human Genetics* 82.3 (2008): 583-592.

Fairchild , H. L. . "White Indians of Darien." *Science, New Series* 60.1550 (1924): 235-237.

Feder, Kenneth L.. *Frauds, Myths, and Mysteries: Science and Pseudoscience in Archaeology and Index*. New York City: McGraw-Hill Humanities/Social Sciences/Languages, 2008.

Filler, Aaron G.. *The Upright Ape: A New Origin of the Species*. Franklin Lakes: New Page Books, 2007.

Forde, Daryll . *African Worlds: Studies in the Cosmological ideas and Social Values of African Peoples*. London: Oxford University Press, 1954.

Fradkin, Philip L.. *The Seven States of California: A Natural and Human History*. 1995 ed. Berkeley: University of California Press, 1997.

Frank, Emilie A.. *Mt. Shasta: California's Mystic Mountain*. Nashville: Photografix Publishing, 1998.

Frankl, Viktor E.. *Man's Search for Meaning*. 1946. Re Boston: Beacon Press, 2000.

Gaddis, Vincent H.. *American Indian Myths & Mysteries*. New York: Signet Books, 1978.

Gamboa, Pedro Sarmiento de. *History of the Incas*. Cambridge: Cambridge University Press, 1897.

Garnder, Erle Stanley . "A Legendary Treasure left by a Long-lost Tribe ." *LIFE Magazine* 20 July 1962: 56-64.

Goodman, Jeffrey. *American genesis: The American Indian and the origins of modern man*. New York: Summit Books, 1981.

Grann, David. *The Lost City of Z: A Tale of Deadly Obsession in the Amazon*. New York: Doubleday, 2009.

Griaule, Marcel. *Conversations with Ogotemmeli: An Introduction to Dogon Religious Ideas (Galaxy Books)*. New York: Oxford University Press, USA, 1975.

Hall, Manly P.. *The Secret Teachings of All Ages*. 1928. Re boston: Wilder Publications, 2007.

Hamilton, Ross. "A Holocaust of Giants." *Ancient Mysteries & Forbidden Archeology - Xpeditions Magazine*. N.p., n.d. <http://www.xpeditionsmagazine.com/magazine/articl es/giants/holocaust.html>.

Hancock, Graham. *Underworld: The Mysterious Origins of Civilization*. New York: Three Rivers Press, 2003.

Hardaker, Christopher. *The First American: The Suppressed Story of the People Who Discovered the New World*. Franklin Lakes: New Page Books, 2007.

Hemming, John. *The Conquest of the Incas*. Orlando: Harvest/Hbj Book, 2003.

Holberg, Jay B.. *Sirius: Brightest Diamond in the Night Sky (Springer Praxis Books / Popular Astronomy)*. New York: Springer, 2007.

Hope, Murry. *Practical Atlantean Magic: A Study of the Science, Mysticism and Theurgy of Ancient Atlantis*.

Great Britain: Aquarian Pr, 1992.

Jacobsen, Thorkild. *The Treasures Of Darkness: A History Of Mesopotamian Religion.*. New Haven: Yale University Press, New Haven, 1976.

Jahren, A. Hope . "The Arctic Forest of the Middle Eocene ." *Annual Review of Earth and Planetary Sciences* 35 (2007): 509-540 .

Jennings, Ralph. "Basalt Rock Wall found in Ocean near Taiwan." *Reuters News.* N.p., 5 Jan. 2009. <www.reuters.com/article/scienceNews/idUSTRE504 0GV20090105>.

Judson, Katharine Berry. *Myths and Legends of California and the Old Southwest.* Chicago: A.C. McGlurg & Co., 1912.

Katchongva, Dan. *Hopi: a Message for All People.* Los Angeles: Committee for Traditional Indian Land and Life, 1972.

Keeling, Richard. *Cry for Luck: Sacred Song and Speech Among the Yurok, Hupa, and Karok Indians of Northwestern California.* Berkeley: University of California Press, 1993.

Kroeber, A. L.. *Yurok Myths.* Berkeley: University of California Press, 1978.

Kropotkin, Peter. *Mutual Aid: A Factor of Evolution (Forgotten Books).* 1902. Re asdbjsadjkas: Forgotten Books, 2008.

Lamb, David. *The Search for Extra Terrestrial Intelligence: A Philosophical Inquiry.* New York: Routledge, 2001.

Lanser, Edward. "A People of Mystery." *The Los Angeles Times* 22 May 1932: -.

Leeming, David. *A Dictionary of Asian Mythology.* New York: Oxford University Press, USA, 2001.

Legon, Jeordan. "Scientist: Oldest American skull found." *CNN.com.* N.p., 4 Dec. 2002. <http://archives.cnn.com/2002/TECH/science/12/03/ol

dest.skull/index.html>.

Lewis, Dr. Harvey Spencer . "The New Lemurian Mystery." *The Rosicrucian Digest* Sep. 1936: -.

Louis, Regis St., and Scott Doggett. *Panama*. Oakland: Lonely Planet Publications, 2004.

Lovecraft, H. P.. *Selected Letters, Volume II: 1925-1929*. Sauk City: Arkham House Publishers, 1968.

Lovgren, Stefan . "First Americans Arrived Recently, Settled Pacific Coast, DNA Study Says." *National Geographic News*. N.p., 2 Feb. 2007. <http://news.nationalgeographic.com/news/2007/02/07 0202-human-migration.html>.

de León, Pedro de Cieza de. *The Second Part of the Chronicle of Peru. Translated and edited, with notes and an introduction, by Clements R. Markham*. Elibron Classics ed. London: The Hakluyt Society, 1883.

de León, Pedro De Cieza De. *The Second Part of the Chronicle of Peru*. Paris: Adamant Media Corporation, 2001.

de León, Pedro de Cieza de. *The Travels of Pedro de Cieza de León, A.D. 1532-50, Contained in the First Part of His Chronicle of Peru*. Paris: Adamant Media Corporation, 2001.

Macaulay, G. C.. *The History of Herodotus*. New York: Kessinger Publishing, 2004.

Mair, Victor H.. "Mummies of the Tarim Basin." *Archaeology* 48.2 (1995): 28-35.

Malhi, RS, and et al.. "Structure of Diversity within New World Mitochondrial DNA Haplogroups: Implications for the Prehistory of North America." *American Journal of Human Genetics* 70.4 (2002): 905-19.

Martin, Paul S. . *Pleistocene Extinctions*. New Haven: Yale University Press, 1967.

McDermott, Jeremy. "Lost city of 'cloud people' found in Peru ." *Telegraph.co.uk*. N.p., 3 Dec. 2008. <http://www.telegraph.co.uk/news/worldnews/southa

merica/peru/3545998/Lost-city-of-cloud-people-found-in-Peru.html>.

Mcclintock, James H.. *Mormon Settlement in Arizona: A Record of Peaceful Conquest of the Desert*. Charleston, SC: Bibliobazaar, 2007.

Mills, Charles A.. *Lost Treasures and Wonders*. Moorestown: Apple Cheeks Press, 1996.

"Moment 600 years ago that terror came to Mummies of the Amazon." *London Evening Standard*. N.p., 10 Jan. 2007. <http://www.thisislondon.co.uk/news/article-23381234-moment-600-years-ago-that-terror-came-to-mummies-of-the-amazon.do>.

Mooney, James. *Myths Of The Cherokee And Sacred Formulas Of The Cherokees*. 1891 ed. New York: Kessinger Publishing, Llc, 2007.

Muck, Otto. *The Secret of Atlantis*. New York: HarperCollins Publishers Ltd, 1979.

Nequatewa, Edmund. *Truth of a Hopi: Stories Relating to the Origin, Myths and Clan*. Boston: Wilder Publications, 2008.

Oga-Make . "Tribal Memories of the Flyings Saucers ." *FATE Magazine* Sep. 1949: -.

Om, Gupta. *Encyclopaedia of India, Pakistan and Bangladesh*. New Delhi: Gyan Books, 2006.

Oppenheimer, Stephen. *The Real Eve: Modern Man's Journey Out Of Africa*. New York: Carroll & Graf Publishers, 2004.

Orr, Phil C. . "Arlington Springs Man. ." *Science Magazine* 135.3499 (1962): 219.

Page, Raymond Ian. *Norse Myths*. Austin: The Bath Press, 1990.

Paul, Ian. "Google's Atlantis Discovery Explained." *PC World News*. N.p., 24 Feb. 2009. <www.pcworld.com/article/160088/googles_atlantis_discovery_explained.html>.

Peet, Stephen Denison . "-." *The American Antiquarian and Oriental Journal* 7 (1885): 52.

Percy, Smith S.. *Hawaiki: The Original Home of the Maori; With A Sketch of Polynesian History*. Melbourne: Whitcomb & Tombs, 1910.

Peterson, Scott. *Native American Prophecies*. New York: Paragon House Publishers, 1990.

Pigafetta, Antonio. *Magellan's Voyage : A Narrative Account of the First Circumnavigation*. 1969. Re New York: Dover Publications, 1994.

Plato. *Timaeus and Critias*. New York: Digireads, 2009.

Pliny (the Elder) , John Bostock, H. T. Riley, and H. G. Bohn. *Natural History of Pliny Vol. 2*. London: Questia Media America, Inc., 1855.

Plongeon, Augustus Le. *Maya/Atlantis: Queen Moo and the Egyptian Sphinx*. 1942. Re New York: Kessinger Publishing, 1997.

Powell, Joseph F.. *The First Americans: Race, Evolution and the Origin of Native Americans*. New York: Cambridge University Press, 2005.

Prescott, W.H.. *History of the Conquest of Peru*. London: Phoenix Press, 2002.

Raab, L. Mark, Jim Cassidy, and Andrew Yatsko. *California Maritime Archaeology: A San Clemente Island Perspective*. Walnut Creek, CA: AltaMira Press, 2009.

Ramaswamy, Sumathi. "History at Land's End: Lemuria in Tamil Spatial Fables." *The Journal of Asian Studies* 59.3 (2000): 575-602.

Ramaswamy, Vijaya. *Historical Dictionary of the Tamils (Historical Dictionaries of Peoples and Cultures)*. Lanham, Maryland: The Scarecrow Press, Inc., 2007.

Reidla, Maere, and et al.. "Origin and Diffusion of mtDNA Haplogroup X." *American Journal of Human Genetics* 73.5 (2003): 1178â€"1190.

Reymond, E.A.E.. *Mythical Origin of the Egyptian Temple.*

Manchester and New York: Manchester University Press, 1969.

Ritter, Malcolm. "Native American DNA Links to Six "Founding Mothers."" *Daily Nature and Science News and Headlines, National Geographic News*. Associated Press, n.d. <http://news.nationalgeographic.com/news/2008/03/08 0313-AP-native-amer.html>.

Ritter, Malcolm. "Native American DNA Links to Six "Founding Mothers."" *National Geographic News*. N.p., 13 Mar. 2008. <http://news.nationalgeographic.com/news/2008/03/08 0313-AP-native-amer.html>.

Schultz, Richard. "Essene Lineage in California: Carmelites and Rosicrucians at Carmel in 1602 ." *Rosicrucian Digest* 86.2 (2007): 12-20.

Scott-Elliot, W.. *The Story of Atlantis and The Lost Lemuria*. Wheation, Il: The Theosophical Publishing House, 1930.

Scranton, Laird. *The Science of the Dogon: Decoding the African Mystery Tradition*. New York: Inner Traditions, 2006.

Selvius . "Descendants of Lemuria:A Description of an Ancient Cult in California ." *The Mystic Triangle* Aug (1925): -.

Selvius, Frater. "Descendants of Lemuria: A Discription of an Ancient Cult in California." *The Rosicrucian Digest* May (1931): -.

Sharp, William. *From the hills of dream; threnodies. songs and later poems* . London: W. Heinemann, 1907.

Shrubsall, F. C., A.C. Haddon, and L.H. Buxton. "The "White Indians" of Panama ." *Royal Anthropological Institute of Great Britain and Ireland Man* 24 (1924): 162-164.

Smith, Bernard. *European Vision and the South Pacific, Second Edition*. New Haven: Yale University Press,

1985.

Smith, DG, RS Malhi , J Eshleman, JG Lorenz, and FA Kaestle. "Distribution of mtDNA haplogroup X among Native North Americans." *American Journal of Physical Anthropology* 110.3 (1999): 271 - 284.

Spence, Lewis. *The Occult Sciences in Atlantis*. Spi Rep ed. Tampa: Mokelumne Hill Press, 1976.

Spence, Lewis. *The Problem of Lemuria: The Sunken Continent of the Pacific*. Plymouth: Rider & Co, 1933.

Squire, Charles. *Celtic Myth and Legend: Poetry & Romance* . .: Forgotten Books, 2007.

Steele, Paul Richard , and Catherine J. Allen. *Handbook of Inca Mythology* . Santa Barbara, CA: ABC-CLIO, 2004.

Straus, Lawrence Guy, David Meltzer, and Ted Goebel. "Ice Age Atlantis? Exploring the Solutrean-Clovis connection." *World Archaeology* 37.4 (2005): 507-532(26).

Swanson, Russell. "The Berkeley Walls and Other Enigmas." *Bay Area Rock Art News* 15 July 1997: -.

Swedlund, Alan, and Duane Anderson. "Creek Woman Meets Kennewick Man: New Interpretations and Protocols Regarding the Peopling of the Americas." *American Antiquity* 64.4 (1999): 569-576.

Temple, Robert. "The prehistory of panspermia: astrophysical or metaphysical." *International Journal of Astrobiology* 6.2 (2007): 169-180.

Temple, Robert. *The Sirius Mystery: New Scientific Evidence of Alien Contact 5,000 Years Ago*. Dallas, TX: Destiny Books, 1998.

Thibetan, Phylos the. *A Dweller on Two Planets or, the Dividing of the Way*. Los Angeles: Borden Pub. Co., 1952.

Thompson, Lucy. *To the American Indian: Reminiscences of a Yurok Woman*. San Francisco: California Historical Society Press. Berkeley: Heyday Books, 1991.

Thorndale, Theresa. *Sketches and Stories of the Lake Erie Isl-*

and. Sandusky: I. F. Mack & Brothers, 1898.

Tigay, Jeffrey H.. *The Evolution of the Gilgamesh Epic.* 1982. Re Wauconda: Bolchazy-Carducci Publishers, 2002.

"Trace of Giants Found in Desert." *San Diego Union* 4 Aug. 1947: -.

Valdés, Gonzalo. Fernández de Oviedo y. *HISTORIA GENER-AL Y NATURAL DE LAS INDIAS. Islas y Tierra-Firme del Mar* . *Prologo de J. Natalicio Gonzalez. Notas de Jose Amador de los Rios. Tomos I-XIV.* Asuncion, Buenos Aires: Editorial Guarania, 1947.

Walton, Bruce. *Mount Shasta, Home of the Ancients.* New York: Health Research, 1985.

Waters, Frank. *The Book of the Hopi.* Boston: Penguin (Non-Classics), 1977.

Weiss, Richard S.. *Recipes for Immortality: Healing, Religion, and Community in South India.* New York: Oxford University Press, USA, 2009.

Whipple, R.F. &, and M.A. Heizer. *The California Indians A Source Book.* Berkeley: University of California Press, 1971.

-. "White Indians Seen in Panama in 1679 ." *The Science News-Letter* 9.274 (1926): 9.

Wilkins, Harold T.. *Mysteries of Ancient South America* . 1947. Re kempton: Adventures Unlimited, 1996.

Wilkins, Harold T.. *Secret Cities of Old South America.* 1952. Re kempton: Adventures Unlimited Press, 1998.

Williams, Mark R.. *In Search Of Lemuria.* San Mateo: Golden Era Books, 2001.

Willis, Roy. *World Mythology.* new york: Owl Books, 1996.

Wilson, Terry P.. *Hopi: Native American Wisdom Series: Following the Path of Peace (Native American Wisdom).* San Francisco: Chronicle Books, 1994.

Wright , James. "The Discovery of Fossil Vertebrates in North America." *Journal of Paleontology* 17.17 (1943): 36.

Zitman, Willem H.. *Egypt: "Image of Heaven": The Planis-phere And the Lost Cradle*. kempton: Adventures Un-limited Press, 2006.

Merriam Webster's Collegiate Encyclopedia. Springfield: Merriam-Webster, 2000.

van Beek, Walter E. A. "Dogon Restudied: A Field Evaluation of the Work of Marcel Griaule." *Current Anthropology* 32.2 (1991): 139-167.

Made in the USA
Lexington, KY
16 September 2012